A live and immediate ~~snapshot~~ of the COVID-19 pandemic, *On Necrocapitalism* stands as an important document of an indelible year. "M.I. Asma" insists on the rigor and energy of a non-universalist "we" that refuses to return to business—literally—as usual.

Anjuli Fatima Raza Kolb, Associate Professor of English at the University of Toronto and author of *Epidemic Empire: Colonialism, Contagion, and Terror, 1817–2020*

Is the pandemic really unprecedented? Not according to these authors, who demonstrate that the events of the last two years are wholly predictable within the logic and imprisoned imaginary of capitalism itself. Part manifesto, part chronicle, part theoretical rumination, *On Necrocapitalism* recasts debates about defunding police, essential workers, dystopian codification, and reformist temptations, providing necessary revivification of communist horizons that de-exceptionalize crisis and dispense with pragmatism. An inspiring read.

Jasbir K. Puar, Professor of Women's, Gender and Sexuality Studies at Rutgers University and author of *The Right to Maim: Debility, Capacity, Disability* and *Terrorist Assemblages: Homonationalism in Queer Times*

Framing the ongoing present—and deadly non-futurity(ies)—of the COVID-19 pandemic within the historical framework of "necrocapitalism," this dynamic, multivocal project is a radical testimonial against the thick normality of targeted peoples' casualties, suffering, and immiseration. Unapologetically, joyfully, and simultaneously theoretical, narrative, and polemical in presentation, the authors defend as they illuminate the possibilities of a communism for the present as well as the endangered future. What might it mean to apprehend the outpouring of humanist concern, charity and philanthropy, emergency funding, and outraged demands for care under the terms of pandemic as evidence of necrocapitalism's advancement, rather than signs of its collapse or momentary dysfunction? I urge readers to bask in the writers' incisive, explosive, and utterly necessary dismantling of liberal ideology as an extension of racial capitalist, white nationalist domestic and global warfare—that is, of liberal discourse as fundamentally complementary to the spectrum of contemporary right-wing reaction, not antagonistic to it.

Dylan Rodríguez, Professor of Media and Cultural Studies at the University of California Riverside, former President of the American Studies Association, and author of *White Reconstruction: Domestic Warfare and the Logics of Genocide*

On Necrocapitalism
a plague journal

On Necrocapitalism: A Plague Journal
by M.I. Asma (J. Moufawad-Paul, Devin Zane Shaw,
Mateo Andante, Johannah May Black, Alyson Escalante,
D.W. Fairlane)

ISBN 978-1-989701-14-0

Published in 2021 by Kersplebedeb

To order copies of the book:

Kersplebedeb
CP 63560, CCCP Van Horne
Montreal, Quebec
Canada
H3W 3H8

info@kersplebedeb.com
www.kersplebedeb.com
www.leftwingbooks.net

On Necrocapitalism
a plague journal

M.I. Asma
J. Moufawad-Paul
Devin Zane Shaw
Mateo Andante
Johannah May Black
Alyson Escalante
D.W. Fairlane

KER
SPL
EBE
DEB
2021

CONTENTS

PREFACE

THE PRESENT VOLUME COLLECTS, WITH SOME REVISIONS, the entries from the blog *On Necrocapitalism*, written by M.I. Asma, the collective designation for six authors representing a variety of revolutionary anticapitalist theoretical persuasions: J. Moufawad-Paul, Devin Zane Shaw, Mateo Andante, Johannah May Black, Alyson Escalante, and D.W. Fairlane.

We set out to produce a serial theoretical-philosophical project focused on class struggle in the midst of the COVID-19 pandemic. We wrote up a prologue, and then the rest followed a process like that of a collaborative chain novel—though, of course, we could not know where events would take us. One of us would write an entry, and the next contributor would be entirely free to take the discussion in whichever direction they saw fit.

The results, we believe, present a cohesive perspective. Nonetheless, some challenges arose while collecting the entries in book form. We have aimed to preserve what we consider one of the unique aspects of this "plague journal"—its provisional and contemporary attempt to provide class analysis and philosophical criticism to events as they unfolded. Nonetheless, in some cases we have revised the tense of some passages, since the events they discuss have now moved from the future to the past (the most notable instances concern conjectures about the impacts of the US presidential elections on broader social struggles).

We have also updated or deleted obsolete information where it does not affect the analyses. Despite these changes, we believe that our observations, as they developed sometimes even week-to-week, present a valuable, critical record of one year of the pandemic.

"*Let us not, however, flatter ourselves overmuch on account of our human conquest over nature. For each such conquest takes its revenge on us.*" Friedrich Engels

"*The crisis consists precisely in the fact that the old is dying and the new cannot be born, in this interregnum a great variety of morbid symptoms appear.*" Antonio Gramsci

PROLOGUE

A VIRUS IS HAUNTING THE GLOBE, ONE OF PANDEMIC proportions, whose threat has necessitated unprecedented measures to forestall death and violence worse than the present crisis. But the cruelty, violence, and depredations that have accompanied the COVID-19 pandemic aren't merely detritus in the wake of its spread; they characterize the necrocapitalism of this conjuncture.

From its beginning to its current senile form, capitalism has presided over a massive graveyard. The slavery and genocide that marked its bloody emergence, the workhouses filled with bodies laboring to death and streets glutted with the starving poor, these have persisted through the present, combining with exterminatory wars and environmental devastation. And then, beyond that, two world wars: the first a squabble between imperialist nations, which forced their poor to fight in trenches for the interests of the rich; the second caused by the most reactionary form capitalism can take, fascism. There have been many others since then, all waged upon the oppressed nations in the global periphery in the interest of capitalist hegemony and accumulation. Half of Korea burned to the ground; Vietnam was invaded and brutalized in an attempt to prevent its national self-determination; multiple overt and covert wars, too many to detail here, where regimes were overthrown, dictators friendly to capitalism installed, and all resistance murdered and disappeared—assassinated,

mass-murdered, hunted down like dogs, starved and tortured, thrown out of helicopters, and written out of official
history; for others among the colonized and dispossessed,
some combination of apartheid, forced assimilation, death
squads, famine, and disease were and are a direct result
of both military and economic intervention. Meanwhile,
the prisons in the most powerful capitalist countries have
grown to absurd proportions. It is entirely laughable to call
a nation-state such as the US "the land of the free" when
it houses 22 percent of the world's prisoners; it is absurd
to call the Global North the home of democratic values
when its prisons disproportionately house Black, brown,
and Indigenous peoples targeted by wars on drugs, terror,
or the poor—and this before we even factor in the bloody
legislation that enables the dehumanization and detention
of the migrant proletariat. Indeed, the identification of
the US (and other such nation-states) with freedom was
always ludicrous, considering that its legacy of colonialism and slavery has meant that it has been a "prison house
of nations" since its inception.

This bloody and ongoing legacy is not an aberration
of capitalism; it is not proof that "capitalism is broken,"
but, rather, it is evidence that it is functioning very well.
Capitalism's core logic, which in layperson's terms is simply about making the rich richer at the expense of the labor
of the poor, always points towards what Robert Biel has
termed "exterminism"; the politics it eventually generates
is like what Achille Mbembe has called "necropolitics." Or
maybe Sayek Valencia's notion of "gore capitalism" is an
apt description. Mark Steven's *Splatter Capital* analyzed
capitalism according to violent horror films and adequately

summed up the exterminist necropolitics of this system: "capitalism is both literally and figuratively the protracted splattering of human bodies."[1] Necrocapitalism, a term coined by S.B. Banerjee, is an appropriate name.[2]

Which is why all of the depredations and violence revealed by the COVID-19 pandemic, all of the contradictions of capitalism laid bare, should not be surprising. "Corona is a black light," comedian Megan Amram tweeted, "and America is a cum-stained hotel room." But not just America—though as the most powerful capitalist country with the least level of social welfare it best represents this analogy—because every capitalist state's necrotic underbelly is being exposed. Subsidies for the corporations and banks and paltry welfare cheques for only some of the poor hit hard by the crisis; entire populations exposed to death and disease; refugees and immigrants subjected to harsher deportation measures. Quarantine laws subordinated to capitalist logic. New security measures, the preface for possible states of emergency continuing after the crisis has run its course, are brought into being: pigs now patrol every street and in larger numbers, like they were in a Mad Max movie—or, more appropriately, like filibusters and scalp-hunters policing colonial frontiers; the settler garrison manifesting on every block. And when the pandemic ends it is reasonable to expect, in these various capitalist nation-states, that the new austerity and security measures will remain, that the poor and marginalized will be expected to pay for the crisis for years to come, while the people on top will continue to get rich. And this is to say nothing of the global peripheries, which will bear the larger death toll of the crisis, which may not even be given the vaccine if and when it arrives because they cannot afford to buy it from the biomedical corporations that will surely patent the cure when it is discovered—just as they cannot afford already existing vaccines for other diseases, which result in yearly pandemics that could be easily cured.

We are living in a necrocapitalism that has always been necrotic but is again wallowing in its exterminism. Or, more accurately, this wallowing is being exposed at the very heart of its "civilization." The question is how many of us will accept this exposure, laugh it off, and keep living right through it because its nightmare has become normative. Already, in the midst of the pandemic, some "leftists" are singing the praises of the government when it enacts emergency measures, acting as if some version of a "responsive state," as opposed to the laissez-faire "restrained state" (to use Martha Fineman's terms), is evidence of socialism. It is rather shocking to witness activists who once militated against closed borders, who advocated for migrant and refugee justice, laud their governments for border closures—closures that most immediately affected migrants and refugees—in the interest of community "safety." What will we be primed to accept as the new normal when this emergency has run its course? And what factions of the broad left will be lured into a post-pandemic patriotism that, dressing up reactionary notions in progressive looking costumes, will focus on rebuilding national unity while accepting that some populations deserve to live and thrive more than others? All crises, as Lenin once wrote, "make manifest what has been hidden; they cast aside all that is relative, superficial, and trivial; they sweep away the political litter."[3] And this crisis not only revealed the "hidden" contradictions of capitalism; it also revealed the contradictions in the left itself—contradictions that will take on new life in the post-pandemic reality.

We intend to examine the current historical conjuncture as a moment of necrocapitalism. The term necrocapitalism should not be understood as an absolute break with capitalism hitherto. Proclamations of new phases are always accompanied by proclamations of new revolutionary theories that condemn to the historical dustbin what our revolutionary history has earned by its hard work and sacrifices. Not surprisingly, such proclamations tend to collaborate with the capitalist imaginary by promoting a willful historical amnesia. What is often asserted as singularly new and unique is in fact a novel rearticulation of intrinsic morbid properties of the mode of production and its imperialist world system. Hence, globalization was once treated as an entirely new phase when in fact it was merely a newer articulation of the same old imperialism: newer technologies, newer institutions, newer deployments and alliances of imperial power, but the same fundamental processes and relations functioned beneath the epiphenomena of novelty.

Clearly it is not the case that capitalism has distinct stages beyond its imperialist apotheosis since, as a mode of production, it preserves its underlying meaning as it historically rearticulates itself; it was always cancerous, murderous, and imperialist. But this complaint misses the point: capitalism does mutate through periods of class struggle; the bourgeoisie tinkers with its ideology. We can thus talk of conjunctural mutations and the way in which capitalism, through these mutations, imagines and codes its reality, encouraging everyone incorporated into this reality to think according to its imagination.

This project is wagered as a disruption of this necrotic capitalist imaginary. That is, based on the truth that capitalism is the most murderous economic system that has ever existed, the following entries seek to disrupt its imaginary by engaging with the discursive mechanics in which this necropolitical and exterminist order has normativized its mass murder. We seek a rigorous critique of the present, a present that increasingly appears to have bypassed the antinomy of "socialism or barbarism" popularized by Rosa Luxemburg, where instead we merely end up modelling, like the potential impacts of COVID-19, choices between competing barbarisms. Thus our critique seeks to:

1. Provide an alternative to theories of the COVID-19 crisis that obfuscate its material conditions—theories of biopolitics, necropolitics, and sovereignty that focus on *power* but not *capitalism*. Although it is the case that these theories can and have contributed useful insights for thinking this crisis, and we have no problem in drawing on some of them if they are useful, by themselves they have been partial conceptions of reality. Rather than focusing solely on this crisis, we need to also examine it in light of the broader processes of necrocapitalism.

2. Think the general outline of a communist alternative, one which refuses all forms of nostalgia for liberalism, social democracy, and the New Deal, one which seeks not merely the end of the present crisis but all forms of oppression, dispossession, and capital accumulation which throw us into one mortal crisis after another. Such a thinking is not intended to replace the ways in which

a communist alternative can and should be thought by anti-capitalist movements. Rather, we seek to emphasize what these movements are trying to accomplish so that we do not lose sight of the goal of a radical political critique of capitalism that is always foreclosed by the capitalist imaginary: making communism.

NOTES TO PROLOGUE

1. Steven, *Splatter Capital*, 45.

2. Those familiar with Banerjee's use of the term will discover that our usage, while adjacent, is not identical. Moreover, after starting this project, we discovered that "necrocapitalism" is a neologism that has been coined multiple times with apparently no awareness of the other uses with each coining. Kwame Holmes coined it again in his essay "Necrocapitalism, Or, The Value of Black Death" (2017) to conceptualize the ways in which the US white middle class's economic anxiety over property values was reliant on Black death. Midway through our project Mark LeVine re-coined the term—again without any awareness of these other two uses or even our ongoing serial—in "From Neoliberalism to Necrocapitalism in 20 Years" (2020) to argue precisely what we were warning against, a new "phase" of capitalism. What these coinings and recoinings perhaps reveal, though, is a visceral recognition that capitalism means death.

3. Lenin, *Lessons of the Crisis*, 87.

A: NECROSIS

April 23 2020–May 29 2020

CHAPTER ONE

DIAGNOSIS AND DEPARTURE

ON APRIL 5, THE VICTIMS OF COMMUNISM MEMORial Foundation (a reactionary and fascist-adjacent organization that continues to propagate Cold War lies about communist "genocide") proclaimed that every COVID-19 death could be added to their already manufactured communist death toll.[1] Following the lead of Donald Trump, Boris Johnson, and other racist politicians who insisted on calling the coronavirus the "Chinese Virus" or the "Wuhan Virus," Victims of Communism claimed that everyone who died during the pandemic was also a victim of communism because China is to blame for the pandemic. Leaving aside the fact that China has been on the capitalist road since the 1970s, and leaving aside the fact that China did try to contain the virus and has since provided the DNA mapping of it to the rest of the world, this announcement on the part of Victims of Communism demonstrates how reactionary thought has always generated the numbers of its death tolls: by an absurd ideological interpretation of statistics. If blaming communism for the depredations of the pandemic seems ludicrous—especially since the majority of deaths are the result of shitty medical systems, privatized biomedical research, and politicians who publicly lied about the pandemic while dumping their stock and secretly telling their rich friends to protect themselves—keep in mind that what communism has always been blamed for, and what all revolutions have been charged with, were equally ludicrous. But people are already repeating these lies and, as absurd as the claims of Victims of Communism are, it is possible that they will become part of hard right conspiracy thinking in the decades following the pandemic. Most importantly, though, this discourse provides insight into how a truly necrotic capitalist imaginary functions.

Capitalism's hegemony is such that it has produced an ideology wherein its murderous logic is concealed, excused, and shrugged aside. A doctrine of excuses and dismissals is part of this ideological defense: capitalism is called "the best of the worst," democracy and capitalism are conflated, and in the grossest deformation of reality the greatest revolutionary challenges to capitalist business as usual are depicted as even more monstrous than capitalism. In an insidious reversal, and in an attempt to defend capitalism against moral challenges, the history of communism has been misrepresented as more murderous than capitalism. The Cold War produced dubious think tanks that fabricated massive death tolls in the Soviet Union and the Chinese Revolution, and this legacy, despite the fact that many academics have demonstrated the falsity of this accounting, haunts the present so as to thwart any attempt to surmount the state of affairs: memoirs of communist victims, subjectivist accounts, reminders that nobody should dare think beyond the capitalist end of history. The fact that the origin of these accounts is located in the US propaganda machine right at the time it was maintaining Jim Crow, trying to pretend that it had not courted fascism before World War II, and was seeking an ideological solution to maintain its myth of being a free country matters less than its ideological effect: it established a narrative about the moral right of capitalism to persist; all challenges to its murderous order were classified, by simultaneously obscuring evidence of its own charnel logic, as *worse* than business as usual. With a stunning sleight of hand, this ideology temporarily succeeded in deleting fascism from capitalism's rap sheet with the "horseshoe theory" whereby fascism and communism—despite the fact that the latter had always fought the former and, in fact, was mainly responsible for Nazi Germany's historical defeat— were depicted as equal extremes.

But now even the "horseshoe theory" is too far "left" according to the moribund imaginary that has possessed most liberals. Communism is worse than fascism; it's even violent for daring to suggest that harming Nazis is a good thing! An imaginary death toll of communist victims is intended to be much larger than victims of fascism so as to let fascists off the hook. To redeem them, even, as potential glorious leaders during and after the pandemic. The recent statement by Victims of Communism regarding COVID-19 plugs itself into this kind of thinking.

This discourse of communist atrocity should not be surprising. Largely it expresses the legitimate horror experienced by the powerful at the mere possibility of revolutionary violence. Both real and imagined excesses of revolution occupy the nightmares of the ruling class; revolutionary reversal is perceived as monstrous. We find the same horror in ruling class narratives surrounding the Terror of the French Revolution. As Rebecca Comay writes: "we must recall that the Terror was persistently troped as cannibalistic: print after grisly print depicts the guillotine as a flesh-eating monster. In *Dantons Tod* George Büchner will compare the revolution to Chronos devouring his own children."[2] The notion that revolutions are monsters that eat their young is thus not original to contemporary capitalism. It is the projection of the fears of the powerful upon the disempowered, transformed into a mantra of capitulation: your revolution will harm you as well, it will fail, there is no point but to accept this state of affairs.

Thus we are given books such as *The Black Book of Communism*, a study produced by pseudo-academic hacks, aimed at justifying capitalism by claiming that its discontents are responsible for a sinister death toll. (Will this bullshit book be updated, we need to ask, in the post-pandemic world, with the coronavirus dead inflating its already inflated statistics?) Despite the reality that the real "black book" is the history of capitalism, and scholars such as Samir Amin have persistently claimed that such a book needs to be written, we are still exhorted to disavow all revolutionary challenges to business as usual. The truth, however, is that the litany of the dead produced by both the emergence and consummation of capitalism is innumerable: we are tasked with itemizing a seemingly infinite graveyard, which began with slavery and colonial genocide, the millions simultaneously worked to death in Western Europe, and every mass murder since then. Chronicling the mass deaths of capitalism is, at this moment, a task that is without end. This very real exterminatory impulse of capitalism, however, is swept under the proverbial rug by a discourse of mass deaths assigned to communism, the sources of which originate in propaganda intended to sanitize capitalism by ascribing its own murderous logic to communism, but which have become a dogma amongst bourgeois historians and pseudo-historians — now figures can be repeated (ranging everywhere from ten million to seventy million, sometimes counting Nazis as "victims," whatever is convenient) as dogma because of the strength of the discourse. And now even the pandemic deaths that result from capitalist management of populations are absurdly being blamed on communism!

Hence, we need to question the entire imaginary that has resulted from this end of history narrative about the triumph of capitalism. "An imaginary," Gabriel Rockhill writes in *Counter-History of the Present*, "is simultaneously theoretical and practical; it is a way of thinking that is also a way of being and acting. Furthermore, it traverses the various dimensions of social existence, including values, norms, affects, and representations. It is the ingrained modus operandi of social agents, which is part of interstitial cultural fabric rather than being imposed only from above or being purely subjective."[3] Similar to Gramsci's notion of hegemony or Deleuze and Guattari's notion of delirium, to speak of a capitalist imaginary is to speak of the way in which ideological norms permeate the way we think, the way we are operationalized to think, the default mode of thinking and imagining the world and our relationship to the world.

Therefore, a particular capitalist imaginary results from this end of history narrative and this imaginary leads to a closure of thought. Such an imaginary is an ideological constellation: everything wagered to declare that capitalism is the only expression possible. The result of accepting this imaginary, that capitalism is the only order of reality, is an erosion of critical thinking. Such an imaginary infects even its dissidents—which is why Mark Fisher, who called this end of history discourse "capitalist realism," could simultaneously critique this discourse *and* accept part of its narrative in his complaints about "Stalinism."[4] The ideological constellation is so powerful that its most invested critics will accept the reality it imagines (an undying hatred of communist revolutions) while simultaneously complaining about its containment of critique. Here we should be reminded of Stefano Harney's and Fred Moten's thoughts in *The Undercommons* regarding the ways in which "critique" of dominant politics is often compromised by these same politics.[5] Thus, it is not altogether strange that Fisher could complain about the ideological boundaries drawn by an "end of history" capitalism while still upholding the ideological narrative of this "capitalist realism" regarding past communist revolutions. The way of thinking produced by a concerted anti-communist ideology is so powerful, commands such a power over the imagination, that one can accept it while also seeing right through it.

Against this closure of thought, and as noted in the prologue, we may have reached the point where we are faced with only a choice of barbarisms. Indeed, we are living under the aegis of a capitalism that imagines itself eternally triumphant. Having defeated its main challengers, claiming the right to redefine their meaning, capitalism has progressed far past the point of Fukuyama's "end of history" or George H.W. Bush's "new world order," to megomaniacally seizing and determining the horizon of thought itself. It is no longer just the end of history; it is history itself, prophetically proclaimed by the ancient world. It is no longer a new world order but appears as a metaphysical principle of reality. Recall, for example, that the writers of the *Avengers* movies could not imagine an existence where the Malthussian logic of overpopulation and available resources could ever be surmounted, not even with magic that could alter reality itself! Even in the realm of pure fantasy, where innumerable characters possess fantastic abilities and where the time-space continuum is subject to subversion, an imagination determined by the limits of capitalism remains dominant. The villain Thanos can bend all of reality *except* for the metaphysics of capitalism.

Inscribing the certainty of its triumph upon every subject and object in the world, decades past the point where it won the Cold War, capitalism no longer needs to justify itself as a moral utopia. It can openly wallow in its authentic dystopia because it has declared itself synonymous with reality. Capitalism is just the way things are, the only reality capable of being real. Everything else is impossible. Again, this is not entirely new; since its beginning capitalism has distorted reality to accord with its logic, to raise itself to the level of metaphysical principle and generate an imaginary that accords with this principle. In the *Grundrisse*, Marx notes that a bourgeois conception of reality "appears as an ideal, whose existence [bourgeois ideologues] project into the past. Not as a historic result but as history's point of departure."[6] Today capitalism has not only decided that it is the historical point of departure; it is also the point of destiny. Its imagination is total: it is the past, present, and future; it is inescapable. We encounter this doctrine in school, at work, and especially in the cultural sphere. The doctrine that capitalism is all of reality is immanent.

Born or reassembled as subjects in this phase of triumphant capitalism, our imagination is overdetermined by the facticity of capitalist totalization. Capitalism in itself is not, to reference Fanon, "a thinking machine" but in fact is a machine that thinks only according to the subjects assembled under the ideological order generated by its persistence and mutations. It thinks because we think it, it persists because we persist with it, and the ruling ideas of the class in command become all the more compelling for the exploited and oppressed masses who are socialized to imagine there is no alternative. Even when some of us fetishize these alternatives we usually do so with melancholy and *ressentiment*. Our desire for a better world is deployed throughout various social networking technologies, captured by old revisionist currents of thought that become lost in a stale celebration of actually existing socialism. The ability to imagine a future beyond the boundaries policed by capitalism is often frustrated by a turn towards a defeated past; the horizon of the possible is foreclosed.

With this claim upon our imagination apparently secure, capitalism enters its most insidious moment, which is mainly a perfection and open celebration of what it always was. Decades ago there was talk about something called "late capitalism" or "the late stage of capitalism"; there was also talk of something called "the cancer stage of capitalism" or "senile capitalism." There have of course been those uncomfortable with these classifications, just as some complain about Lenin's classification of imperialism as "the highest stage of capitalism," although such a classification remains far more concrete than these other notions.

The term "late capitalism" is admittedly vague, and probably should be questioned as a stand-in for other conceptions that can better explain the novel articulation of this conjuncture. But if there is something we can call "late capitalism," it is that period where capitalism has reached its dusk, where its continuation will ensure barbarism because it will undermine human existence in order to persist. This late period of capitalism—*late* as being a later period that has arrived like a warped version of Hegel's owl of Minerva—is indeed cancerous, signifying the dusk of the human species.

NOTES TO CHAPTER 1

1. Marion Smith, "Blame the Chinese Communist Party for the coronavirus crisis" (https://victimsofcommunism. org/blame-chinese-communist-party-coronavirus-crisis). On the Victims of Communism project and its ties to the far right, see Taylor C. Noakes, "Victims of communism memorial received donations honouring fascists, Nazi collaborators, according to website" (https://www.cbc.ca/news/politics/ victims-communism-memorial-fascists-1.6112809).

2. Comay and Ruda, *The Dash*, 80–81.

3. Rockhill, *Counter-History of the Present*, 109.

4. Fisher, *Capitalist Realism*, 20.

5. Harney and Moten, *The Undercommons*, 18–19.

6. Marx, *Grundrisse*, 83.

CHAPTER TWO

FROM ŽIŽEK TO COMMUNIST POSSIBILITY

NECROCAPITALISM NECESSITATES THAT WE CON-
tinue, in the face of the pandemic, a clear-sighted and
principled criticism of our situation. Numerous philosophers have already intervened in the present conjuncture
by outlining the possibilities and dangers of pandemic
measures. Giorgio Agamben, who likens COVID-19 to
"the normal flus that affect us every year," asserts that
pandemic measures have forced societies to sacrifice
many social relationships and convictions in order to
preserve "bare life."[1] Our collective fear of contracting
COVID-19, he claims, undermines our capacity to maintain social solidarity. He writes: "Bare life—and the danger of losing it—is not something that unites people, but
blinds and separates them."[2] Agamben's comments are
refuted by the forms of mutual aid and organizing that
have emerged in the absence of public support. But it is
also mistaken to conflate the revitalization or buttressing of social systems already present in capitalist societies with "Communism." The most vocal self-described
leftist to do so is Slavoj Žižek, whose recent social and
cultural criticism on responses to COVID-19 have been
collected in his recent *Pandemic! Covid-19 Shakes the
World.*

Focusing on Žižek might give the mistaken impression that his work plays a significant role within leftist theory and organizing when it does not. He does, however, carry some credibility in radical academic circles, built upon books such as *The Sublime Object of Ideology* and *Did Somebody Say Totalitarianism?* Therefore, I am interested in criticizing how his repeated insistence that the pandemic necessitates a communist possibility mischaracterizes the possibilities of communism. As I will argue, Žižek conflates increased state power, largely in terms of state command over the distribution of social goods, with communism—and this conflation precludes, as possibility, political revolution, the seizure of the means of production by proletarian struggle.

Indeed, we might read *Pandemic!* as a series of lures that appear radical at first glance but side-step a more principled analysis. The first problem arises almost immediately. At the outset, Žižek adopts the slogan that "we're all in the same boat now" (the title, in fact, of the first chapter) without submitting it to proper criticism. The slogan, or the many variations upon it, is appealing because it designates that the pandemic has ramifications for people across the globe. However, it clearly has different ramifications for different people, as classes, according to their economic standing, not to mention race, gender, and other factors, are largely left to the side of Žižek's analysis. Thus, we should differentiate between what we might call the existential threat and the material threat posed by COVID-19. The virus is an existential threat to all human beings because our individual susceptibility is determined by contingent factors (age, co-morbidities, human finitude) beyond our control. From this perspective, humanity faces a common threat. The idea that we are all in this together does point toward an ethical principle that blunts the ambient social Darwinism of necrocapitalism. As Žižek writes, "our first principle should be not to economize but to assist unconditionally, irrespective of costs, those who need help, to enable survival"—to do otherwise marks the acceptance of what he calls "barbarism with a human face."[3]

To be fair, Žižek identifies how an uncritical adoption of slogan solidarity is problematic. For instance, the claim that we are all facing a common threat is typically understood within the ideological terms of neoliberalism, which overemphasizes personal responsibility and occludes the systemic conditions of personal choice. This is a common failing in conversations about environmental ethics that encourage recycling or foregoing cars for public transit, but which rarely confront how the ecological repercussions of the global system moving resources and commodities around the globe dwarf any particular choice or even any set of specific local group actions. As Andreas Malm argues, because "globally mobile capital will relocate factories to situations where labor power is cheap and disciplined—where the rate of surplus-value promises to be largest—by means of new rounds of massive consumption of fossil energy," any meaningful attempt to combat anthropogenic climate change must combat capitalism itself.[4] In the context of COVID-19, media reports and politicians tend to stigmatize individual behaviours as selfish or narcissistic when people gather in public spaces where social distancing is difficult. The behaviours could, of course, be rooted in selfish exceptionalism or narcissism, but they could also indicate failures of city planning (narrow pedestrian access) or insufficient housing facilities (homes without outdoor access).

And, right after Žižek concludes the first chapter by noting that "we're all in the same boat now," he begins Chapter Two by recognizing that we are not:

> The coronavirus epidemic confronts us with two opposed figures that prevail in our daily lives: those, like medical staff and carers, who are overworked to the point of exhaustion, and those who have nothing to do since they are forcibly or voluntarily confined to their homes.[5]

Here Žižek verges closer to the heart of the problem: there are two pandemics, one experienced by those with the material means and familial supports to self-isolate, and the other, experienced by those who do not. This latter group extends far beyond medical staff and care support, though, to any number of workers who are deemed necessary to maintain supply chains in essential services, such as food production, distribution, and service. And then, the latter group extends beyond traditional concepts of the working class to those who work in the informal economy, refugees, undocumented migrants, the homeless, prisoners, and other groups neglected by public support but targeted by policing. And, in settler-colonial societies, we must recognize the pandemic among settlers and the pandemic among Indigenous communities. Any discussion of the socialist or communist characteristics of pandemic measures must account for the many dispossessed.

As is well-known, in *The Communist Manifesto*, Marx and Engels argue that history is an expression of class struggle, which ends "either in a revolutionary reconstitution of society at large, or in the common ruin of the contending classes." As noted, one purpose of this project is to map the coordinates of a possible radical future beyond the present crisis and to submit existing commentary to rigorous critique. Therefore, it is necessary to demonstrate the paucity of Žižek's vague idea of communism. Here are representative examples of his use of communism:

- "Measures that appear to most of us today as 'Communist' will have to be considered on a global level: coordination of production and distribution will have to take place outside the coordinates of the market."[6]

- "We are not talking about old-style Communism, of course, just about some kind of organization that can control and regulate the economy, as well as limit the sovereignty of nation-states when needed."[7]

- "Coronavirus will also compel us to re-invent Communism based on trust in the people and in science."[8]

Despite the reference to trust in the people, working-class organizing and mutual aid factor little into Žižek's typical description of communist measures. Instead, he tends to appeal to extending the reach of global organizations, such as the World Health Organization,[9] or state power. Hence, in terms of the latter, he suggests that President

Trump's invocation of the Defense Production Act ("to instruct the private sector to ramp up production of emergency medical supplies") is vaguely communist. He then proceeds to portray this Communism necessitated by survival—analogous to "war communism" in the Soviet Union—as a multilayered process of international and national public interventions.

Here, Žižek's desire to invert traditional political categories to produce counterintuitive results precludes a more detailed class analysis. A conservative reader might be horrified at the suggestion that Trump—*Trump!*—is a communist, but they will be mollified by more recent developments, such as Trump's executive order (evoking the Defense Production Act, incidentally) forcing meat processing plants to remain open despite workers testing positive for COVID-19 and presumably, given the long, gruesome history of the meat-processing industry, a systemic lack of worker protections.[10] Of course, it is not difficult to refute Trump by means of Trump. But it does point to basic failures in Žižek's analysis. First, of course, as Lenin argues, the state is an instrument of bourgeois dictatorship—so we cannot expect that the state's measures will extend beyond what is necessary (or perceived to be necessary) to shore up hegemony in a moment of crisis. As Trump's executive order shows, state intervention in production and distribution of food maintains a class character, for it is workers who bear the brunt of the risk in these facilities—so state intervention itself is *not* communism!

On the basis of this error, Žižek then conceptualizes federal and state intervention and militant organizing as working in tandem. Federal direction, he argues, "is just the beginning: many more measures of this sort will be needed, as well as local self-organization of communities if state-run health systems collapse under too much stress."[11] By placing different levels of state intervention and locally-organized mutual aid in a continuum, Žižek also strips their conflicted relationships of their class character. It is worth recalling that in *The Communist Manifesto*, Marx and Engels describe the class struggle in the era of capitalism twice. The first details the development of the bourgeoisie as a class and their ascendency to power. The second traces, in the midst of bourgeois competition, the formation of the proletariat as a political class. And then, of course, it summarizes the theory of Communism as the abolition of private property.

Therefore, we can summarize Žižek's argument by analogy to our brief synopsis of the *Manifesto*. Žižek has traced the development of measures to ensure bourgeois hegemony during the pandemic and conflates them with communism, as if they amount to the abolition of private property. Proletarian struggle rarely enters the picture, but when it does, he frames mutual aid as a fallback "if state-run health systems collapse." A communist theory must disentangle these two social forces. While physical distancing measures make it difficult to mount a street-level mass movement, the ongoing organizing to free prisoners and undocumented migrants or forms of mutual aid to deliver critical supplies to those most exploited and marginalized demonstrates the resiliency of left movements even in this time of crisis. It seems that, despite Žižek's appeal to imagining unprecedented possibilities during the pandemic, the one possibility he never enter-tains is the overthrow of capitalism and the seizure of power by the proletariat. (In this regard, his analysis har-bors an implicit cynicism not far from Agamben's explicit cynicism.) Instead, the state repeatedly intervenes in his account as a *deus ex machina* implementing so-called com-munism. As we should know from the last two centuries of history, the bourgeoisie prefers the common ruin of contending classes over the abolition of private property, and the pandemic will not change that. Once upon a time, in *Revolution at the Gates*, Žižek attempted to outflank his Marxist peers by arguing that the "key 'Leninist' les-son today is: politics without the organizational form of the Party is politics without politics."[12] Today, ironically, with *Pandemic!* he's now the vanguard of "communism without communism."

NOTES TO CHAPTER 2

1. Agamben, "The invention of an epidemic" (https://www.journal-psychoanalysis.eu/coronavirus-and-philosophers/).

2. Agamben, "Clarifications" (https://itself.blog/2020/03/17/giorgio-agamben-clarifications/).

3. Žižek, *Pandemic!*, 60–61.

4. Malm, *Fossil Capital*, 333.

5. Žižek, *Pandemic!*, 20.

6. Ibid., 15–16.

7. Ibid., 34.

8. Ibid., 31.

9. Ibid., 32.

10. Note also that the United Food and Commercial Workers Union points to the failures to implement and enforce CDC guidelines issued in response to the pandemic.

11. Žižek, *Pandemic!*, 64.

12. Žižek, *Revolution at the Gates*, 297.

CHAPTER THREE

BELOW THE SURFACE FROTH

WE ARE CONSTANTLY INVITED TO REFLECT UPON THE allegedly "unprecedented" nature of the pandemic, as though it has already been decided that something new is actually occurring. Here, too, we have to be careful that self-styled radical guides don't lead us astray. One good thing that can be said about Žižek is that he correctly gleans the importance of qualitative leaps from his afore-mentioned reading of Lenin. The problem is that in his writings he also gives the unsettling impression of seem-ing to find them everywhere. This speaks to a dangerous defect and a bitter irony in much self-styled radical theory, one that leads to its mirroring of the crudest ideological banalities of the apologists of capital.

Specifically, theory goes wrong whenever it fetish-izes the surface froth of capital, misreading it as in some way profound and strategically important. Theory often speaks as though because something appears to be new or very interesting, or because it titillates or unsettles, it must in some way be ground-breaking, or its apparent darkness must actually be pregnant with resistant energies. Novelty is only what emerges as new but then doesn't really stick. So it's a fatal error to try to ground a critical position in it; doing so amounts to tailing the latest cultural muta-tions of capital, quasi-journalistically, and only ever lead-ing from behind. This, incidentally, helps to explain why theory chasing after the new for its own sake comes off as so exhausted and exhausting, dated before it even goes to press.

It's by sticking to the unfashionable but perennially solid and cannily adaptable parameters of a communist critique that we have a chance of getting our bearings in the breakneck surface churn of late capitalism in general, and it's no different today in the jaws of the COVID-19 pandemic. To speak of a "qualitative leap" in the communist sense evokes a situation where the genuinely new actually emerges, where we need to question in a principled and disciplined way the very coordinates of the world we've up until now taken for granted, in order to map out a way forward. What we are living through in the pandemic is absolutely not in and of itself such a qualitative leap, though of course it's daily tearing at the ideological veil and real functioning of capitalism and therefore invites a rigorous critique of the present.

Admittedly, the pandemic and its effects may indeed be "unprecedented" in many ways, as we constantly hear in mainstream commentary; certainly, it's a first for me to have to excuse myself from a work meeting to go help a toddler to wipe his ass in the next room. But no amount of this kind of bullshit, whether trivial or life-ruining, justifies our treating the pandemic and its effects as constituting the genuinely new. Rather, we are dealing with an overall predictable cascade of effects running from the mildly exploitative to the openly murderous, all of which are baked into the logic of capital itself. The example of parenting while teleworking is to some extent technologically novel and it comes from a place of privilege, certainly, but it illustrates a core truth of capitalism: the rearing of children is a "free gift of human nature" that capital will always try to exploit to the maximum, pressing literal reproduction into its own reproduction.[1] And the more deadly implications of what is called the "opening back up" of the economy via the starving out of lower-paid frontline workers also shows only what capitalism has always been prepared to do: to continue to grow at the expense of the lives of the very workers who make it possible.

Here the rhetoric of sacrifice does its usual work, masking the depressing familiarity of what is actually happening at the point of service and production and reproduction. There is widespread public recognition of the fact that "essential workers" are now being exposed to disproportionate risks, and this recognition is overall a good thing. But the mainstream reaction has been mostly to heroize them. Heroizing is precisely akin to recasting their needless deaths as "sacrifices," and once again, there is nothing new to see here. As Wendy Brown points out, neoliberalism may be construed in terms of how it recasts the concrete individual as a "sacrificial subject."[2] In particular, Brown emphasizes how the subject bears the consequences of the risks she is forced to assume *qua* living financial portfolio, while Melinda Cooper spins out how the family increasingly supplants public institutions as one of the only remaining safety nets.[3] Together, Brown and Cooper track how neoliberalism perverts the social contract of classical liberalism; it's no longer a question even nominally of what the state owes the subject and vice versa, but rather of what the subject (and by extension, her family) owes to "the economy," abstracted away from the flesh and blood humans (and nonhuman animals) who comprise it. Against the idealistic tendencies in any analysis inspired by Foucault, it must be constantly reiterated that neoliberalism is only a logic of governance beholden to capital. One might therefore fairly re-christen it "necroliberalism"—but then again, we're not about novelty for novelty's sake.

In any case, capitalist bootlickers are already feverishly disseminating the rhetoric of sacrifice. It's worth remembering that they simply do not take life seriously, and they never have. Rather, they long ago learned to toggle back and forth between the sanctity of life and the tragedy of sacrifice as per the ideological demands of the moment. Ben Shapiro offers an obscene but pitiably predictable spectacle here. According to the argument (sic) staked out by 2009 Ben,[4] even something as limited in scope and ambition as the Affordable Care Act was to be feared and despised for how its logic of "rationing care" would necessitate the institution of "death panels" to decide whether Grandma lives or dies in the imagined coming socialist scarcity. But fast forward to 2020 and Ben is no longer a brave Kantian defender of every single human life. Rather, for the good of the capitalist economy he now coolly defends the necessity of baldly utilitarian "actuarial deductions" and the possibility of opening things back up mid-pandemic, when the worst of the infection rates is still likely ahead. It turns out that Grandma can be readily killed off after all—just so long as we frame her death as a sacrifice to the economy. Perhaps if Ben were helped along here, and encouraged to imagine the actuaries involved in such calculations as sitting on "panels," this would cause some flicker of recognition.

The answer to such ghoulishness is not of course simply to show that capitalist apologists want it both ways. They always do, and pointing it out ad nauseum when capitalists actually hold the reins of power risks perpetuating cynicism and defeatism. The first step in any response to this wholly *ordinary* situation—ordinary, that is, by necrocapitalism's own logic—is coordinated mass strikes at the point of service, production, and reproduction, materially and ideologically supported by those of us with the dubious privilege of being held in white-collar quarantine.

NOTES TO CHAPTER 3

1. See Harvey's *Marx, Capital, and the Madness of Economic Reason* (2019).

2. See Brown's *Undoing the Demos: Neoliberalism's Stealth Revolution* (2015).

3. See Cooper's *Family Values: Between Neoliberalism and the New Social Conservatism* (2019).

4. His bullshit will be referred to and dragged, but never cited.

CHAPTER FOUR

BOURGEOIS PHILOSOPHY IN THE TIME OF PANDEMIC

FOR THE PHILOSOPHICALLY INCLINED, FOR THOSE who do philosophy and those who are learning to do philosophy during necrocapitalism, it is natural to wonder what the role of philosophical activity is or ought to be during a pandemic.

Not unlike Žižek's vague notion of communism, deficient in its ability to untangle the social forces relevant to understanding and mounting opposition to capitalism's increasingly speedy descent to the common ruin of contending classes, some ways of answering questions about the role of philosophical activity during the COVID-19 pandemic from establishment philosophers obscure what's needed to bring philosophical clarity to theories about the crisis. This is a dimension of the hegemony that capitalism has on imagination. While the capitalist imaginary limits critical thought and produces unquestioned assent to transparently false claims like those made about the death toll of communism in *The Black Book of Communism*, it also makes philosophical activity into something of no practical use so that it amounts to no more than humanist wishful thinking.

To be clear, the case of Agamben, whose effort to articulate a problem in the world with idealist categories put his analysis on the level of celebrity anti-vaxxers like Jenny McCarthy and Charlie Sheen, is somewhat different from the phenomenon I have in mind. But it only differs because the focus is not the self-liquidating affirmations of COVID-19 truthers, but the claims of philosophers who want to contribute something positive in the face of a very real and grave pandemic.

Popular philosopher Skye Cleary, answering the question "How can philosophy help us in this time of crisis?" in the Unthinkable philosophy column of *The Irish Times*,[1] points to aspects of Simone de Beauvoir's philosophy as a way to cope with the disruption of daily life brought on by measures designed to contain the spread of the virus: if you feel uncertain or anxious, accept it, it is a condition for existence. Yes, you may feel isolated in quarantine, but really, you are not alone because everyone faces the human condition. And with what amounts to wishing really, really hard that humanist values will in the end do more than they've ever done before, Cleary extends a metaphor of Beauvoir: "Beauvoir describes humanity as like stones in an arch: the healthier the stones, the healthier the arch. While our global arch is compromised by pandemics, it is strengthened by being generous, caring for the vulnerable, and supporting one another."[2]

It seems that a turn to philosophical reflection that centers interconnectedness, mutual support, and coming together is appropriate given events happening all over the world and with outstanding inefficiency and graft in the wealthiest countries: with massive shortcomings at all levels of capitalist infrastructure from acquisition and delivery of needed PPE for medics and the general population,

including test shortages and no systematic way of testing and establishing quarantine, to rapid and widespread
unemployment with no support or guarantee of food or
housing, and where prison, jail, and nursing home populations have been overwhelmingly savaged by the virus. In
thinking through how strife, sacrifice, scarcity, and death
are positioned as "novel" and "unprecedented," we've
noted that these are everyday facts of capitalism, highlighted now because of existential and material threats
posed by COVID-19. Yet another everyday fact is this: deep
in necrotic capitalism there is always enough generosity,
caring for the vulnerable, and mutual support to land the
whole world in exactly the state of crisis we are in now.
There are always enough people, and not necessarily communists, bleeding hearts, or lefties, to put together mutual
aid food and medical assistance networks, ad-hoc supply
chains, volunteer fire departments, and GoFundMe campaigns in response to the deficiencies produced by the
normal workings of capitalism. There is no shortage of
existentialist humanist values. In fact, we are bombarded
with this every day from the charitable acts of billionaires
featured prominently in news media, to heart-warming
stories of communities coming together to help front-line
workers in essential businesses. What is showcased as the
pivotal role of philosophy in crisis is the articulation of
a meaning that goes no further than what is given by the
everyday workings of necrotic capitalism.

Now, it may seem unfair to take Cleary's comments on
philosophy here to task. After all, she discusses Beauvoir
and the role of philosophy in three short paragraphs and
as part of a popular column in a newspaper—hardly the

place to present a comprehensive philosophical account of the role of philosophy in crisis. At the same time, pieces like this one in *the Irish Times* constitute the popular—if not academically rigorous—refinement of established ideology. Following Althusser's assessment of the unity of news and communications media, educational institutions, religious institutions, the political system, and other sites of culture as always unified under the ideology of the ruling class,[3] to engage with popular pieces like Cleary's is to engage head-on with the tip of the spear of the ruling ideology and with that which shapes social identity to contribute to the reproduction of the economic basis of necrocapitalism.[4]

Turning again to how Beauvoir's philosophy is called up as a way of coping with COVID-19, I am reminded of those passages in *One Hundred Years of Solitude* where, suffering from an insomnia plague that results in memory loss, Aureliano Buendía begins marking the objects in his laboratory with their respective names. A terrifying realization occurs when José Arcadio Buendía, Aureliano's father, recognizes that a "day might come when things would be recognized by their inscriptions but that no one would remember their use."[5] The marks, to be useful, reveal a use, a purpose, and a meaning. And the horror is that they may not.

Necrocapitalism challenges us to do more than select philosophical reflections and use them like sticky notes on the world. We are charged with providing alternatives to theories of the COVID-19 crisis that obfuscate its material conditions. One way to spell this out for the space of philosophy is to insist on philosophical reflections that help us think through meanings not given by the same limited and fatal imagination that has made crisis and death an ordinary feature of the world for most people. It requires excavating meanings with the tools of philosophy conditioned by a struggle to alter the basis of all that we see surfacing before us in crisis. Yes, lives are disrupted by containment measures and by death. Like the people of the town of Macondo in *One Hundred Years of Solitude* suffering the insomnia plague, life under COVID-19 has become difficult—we forget how to do things that once occupied our daily lives, and we are limited in what actions we can take and how we plan for the future. The present has imposed on us a new routine and we wonder what it means for ourselves, our families, and our communities. Connecting humanist aspects of Beauvoir's existential philosophy to what is happening in the world right now falls short of satisfying the need for meaning and understanding for people who find no consolation in rehearsing the same pattern served up to countenance the common tyranny of capitalism.

And, in this case, doing so displays a way of conceiving the role of philosophy as an activity that abruptly and uncritically stops at the point where there is opportunity to extricate thinking from the unremarkable humanist supplications we have always been told will make a better world. The truth is that Beauvoir's philosophy is not so thin as that. Beauvoir came to see the work of philosophy and her philosophy as more than humanism:

> Were she to write The Second Sex "today," she also wrote in 1972, she would now ground

women's alterity in a more "materialist" and
not an "idealist" manner: "I should ground the
rejection and oppression of the Other not on
the antagonism of consciousnesses but on the
economic basis of scarcity," she said.[6]

This is more in line with the type of investigation that centers the material conditions of capitalism and recognizes
the need to connect philosophizing to those conditions.
Marxism itself played a central role in Beauvoir's philosophy and it was something she engaged with, throughout her life and in her philosophical work[7]—with, of
course, varying degrees of correctness in political orientation from the standpoint of contemporary revolutionary
Marxism. What we choose to emphasize as philosophers
itself reveals our pre-philosophical class, national, and
gender commitments. For those who are philosophically
inclined and fail to identify with the meanings and explan-
ations provided by philosophies expressing commitment
to the standing conditions of necrotic capitalism, philosophical activity divides the field of theory on the causes,
effects, and impact of the COVID-19 pandemic into those
that have a stake in returning to the normalized crisis of
necrocapitalism—inert humanist ideals and all—and those
that propose to liberate philosophical imagination from
its death-grip. Philosophers can contribute to the latter
by taking seriously the task of excavating meaning, connecting their activity to material causes and focusing their
interventions in ways that support unified action to end
the continued barbarity of necrocapitalism. We should
settle for nothing less.

NOTES TO CHAPTER 4

1. Joe Humphreys, "How can philosophy help us in this time of crisis?" (https://www.irishtimes.com/culture/coronavirus-how-can-philosophy-help-us-in-this-time-of-crisis-1.4205889).

2. Ibid.

3. Althusser, *Lenin and Philosophy and Other Essays,* 143–146.

4. Ibid., 154–155.

5. Márquez, *One Hundred Years of Solitude*, 40.

6. Kruks, "Beauvoir and the Marxism question," 246.

7. Ibid., 246.

CHAPTER FIVE

UNEQUALLY DISTRIBUTED VULNERABILITY

So far, we have had to wrestle with the difficulty of doing philosophy in the face of crisis. We have gestured towards a sort of capitalist imaginary that not only constrains the very possibility of philosophy pointing towards a communist society, but shapes philosophical interventions such that they can act as a naturalization of the capitalist order even when such interventions seek to disrupt its own logic. In Žižek we found a vague reimagining of the meaning of communism such that it becomes perfectly compatible with even right-wing forms of capitalist governance. In Agamben's response to COVID-19, we see a philosopher descend into a conspiratorial and childish inability (or unwillingness) to wrestle with the actual threat posed by the pandemic. So far our exploration of the philosophical response to COVID-19 has painted a rather sad depiction of the state of the discipline.

It is not enough, of course, to simply point to the failures of philosophy so far. All the previous chapters have attempted to point to the need for a communist politics that denies the realist terms of the capitalist imaginary and tackles this crisis in the context of moribund and decaying capitalism. Just as Lenin could intervene to demonstrate that imperialist aggression was a continuation (a refinement even) of capitalist development rather than an aberration that had appeared from nowhere, philosophers committed to a truly liberatory approach to philosophy must show the ways in which COVID-19 is simultaneously novel and inseparable from centuries of previous crisis. Both imperialism and pandemics force us to theorize at a global scale; they both demand that we wrestle with systems and logics playing out across the globe. They have also historically intersected. The so-called Spanish Flu of 1918 coincided with, was exacerbated by, and was in many ways inseparable from the First World War, one of the most shocking crises of imperialism at the start of the 20th century.

Now of course we know that Lenin's analysis of imperialism remains crucial for communist struggle today, not only because he was able to understand imperialism as a stage of capitalist development but also because he was able to draw out a concrete praxis from this realization. Lenin was able to demonstrate how international solidarity for national liberation struggles and revolutionary defeatist organizing against one's own imperialist state could allow for international proletarian resistance to imperialism. In short: Lenin not only allowed us to understand imperialism for what it truly is, he also equipped us with insights regarding how we might fight it. The philosophers we have analyzed thus far have largely erred in terms of their analysis of what exactly this pandemic is, and few have tried to point towards a useful political response. Žižek offers us a muddled redefinition of communism and Agamben's logic seems to end in the fascist protests occurring around the United States and Canada demanding a reopening of the economy. If philosophy is to have any value in moments like this, it must go beyond providing analytical clarity; it must point us in an actionable direction such that the clarity it offers might inform and refine political action.

One important public philosopher who has taken up this task of pointing us towards a political response is Judith Butler. On April 30th, *Truthout* published an interview between George Yancy and Judith Butler about the COVID-19 pandemic in which Butler attempts to theorize how mourning and vulnerability in the context of COVID-19 might help us understand a political response to the pandemic. There are two interesting features about this interview: First, there is the sense in which Butler comes close to providing a useful understanding of the relationship between the pandemic and capitalism while avoiding an actual class analysis. Second, there is Butler's failure to provide a means of moving forward outside of the bounds of liberal humanism. As far as contemporary philosophers go, Butler is fairly equipped to think about the global scope of COVID-19, having wrestled with global problems like imperialist aggression in her previous work on mourning and vulnerability.

Before thinking through the interview itself, we should briefly review Butler's earlier work on vulnerability and mourning, which had largely been based around a certain form of dependency built into human life and subjectivity. On a basic level she draws on Hegel to note a mutual need for recognition at the core of human consciousness.[1] She further develops this by noting the forms of physical dependence built into human relationships. For Butler, human life is defined by relationships to others; these relationships can be basic instances of material dependence of a mother and child or the forms of affirming recognition between lovers. It is in moments of death and loss that human interdependence is revealed. When we mourn the loss of someone in our life, we are transformed by their absence and we discover that who we are was defined in terms of our relation to them. With this relationship cut off, we are faced with a recognition of our own interdependency with those around us, and we are forced to face the fact that our very selves are bound up with the lives of others. Mourning can thus point us towards a form of solidarity with others by forcing us to recognize that we are not fully individual and autonomous selves but are constituted by the relations we are caught up in. Butler suggests that these insights are of global importance; she gestures towards the intense but badly resolved "mourning, fear, anxiety, rage" that surrounded the 9/11 attacks, and insists that insights of vulnerability can operate as "the basis of claims for nonmilitaristic political solutions."[2] While violence can force us to face the interdependence built into our very being, Butler notes that the response from states to international violence has been to displace this recognition, instead favoring a buffering up of national sovereignty. In this sense, the United States responded to the violence of 9/11 not through a recognition of its interdependence but through a securitization of the domestic and international order; the state response was defined not by facing vulnerability but by denying it through imperialist military action.

Given this political theory of mourning and vulnerability, it is unsurprising that Butler would seek to tackle the issue of COVID-19 as a public philosopher. George Yancy opens the interview by asking her to reflect on the relevance of vulnerability in our current situation, with special attention paid to the way that "vulnerability isn't equally distributed." Butler responds to this inquiry by going beyond the banal "we're all in the same boat" observations that Žižek offers. She notes that while there is a shared global vulnerability in the face of the virus, there is also a sort of differential vulnerability experienced most strongly by those who are deemed "vulnerable groups." In addressing this differential vulnerability, she writes:

> The vulnerable include Black and Brown communities deprived of adequate health care throughout their lifetimes and the history of this nation. The vulnerable also include poor people, migrants, incarcerated people, people with disabilities, trans and queer people who struggle to achieve rights to health care, and all those with prior illnesses and enduring medical conditions. The pandemic exposes the heightened vulnerability to the illness of all those for whom health care is neither accessible nor affordable. Perhaps there are at least two lessons about vulnerability that follow: it describes a shared condition of social life, of interdependency, exposure and porosity; it names the greater likelihood of dying, understood as the fatal consequence of a pervasive social inequality.[3]

It is in her recognition of this second lesson that we see her response to the pandemic rise above the responses of the philosophers we have looked at thus far. Butler, at least momentarily, goes a step beyond the apolitical universalism that assumes that this pandemic is playing out in a similar manner for all communities. This deserves recognition.

At the same time as Butler's own philosophical intervention provides some useful political insights, it is also cut short from providing a useful path forward precisely because of its inability to connect the crisis at hand to capitalism. Butler is correct to note that the pandemic uniquely threatens those who have faced various forms of marginalization resulting from state repression and economic exploitation, but she ultimately lumps these concerns together under the label of "inequality." This focus on inequality is a classic trapping of liberal social analysis. If the problem with our society is one of inequality, basic state reforms can address the problem through reducing inequality in various ways. For example, Butler's own assessment of the situation would seem to indicate that the problem of differential vulnerability might be at least partially resolved simply through universal health care, equal treatment of queer and trans patients in a health-care context, and better access to care for Black and brown communities. We as communists must push back against this focus on inequality, of course, by asking what sort of material conditions this inequality arises from. A key Marxist insight is that inequality results from the relationship between various classes to production. The problem with capitalism is not simply that a worker makes a lower income than a capitalist, but rather is that workers as a class are forced to sell their labor to capitalists as a class in order to enrich the capitalist class. A critique of differential vulnerability cannot simply emphasize abstract inequality, it must draw out the class relations and class struggle that produce this inequality. For this reason, Marx explains that communism cannot be a base leveling of income for the sake of equality, because such an impulse represents a crude sort of envy that seeks only to reduce all members of society down to a common level.[4] Despite the fact that she is able to trace some of the political and economic contours of the pandemic, Butler's insights here fall back into this crude liberal focus on equality as opposed to class struggle.

Having discussed the political nature of vulnerability amidst a pandemic, George Yancy moves things in a more action-oriented direction. He correctly notes that we are seeing "forms of economic instability that have always been there" and asks "how do we mobilize such mourning and grief" in the face of this crisis. It is in her response to this rather concrete question that we see Butler weighed down by the liberalism of her analysis. Instead of pointing towards a concrete political mobilization informed by mourning, Butler merely restates that we are living in a time marked by great grief in which uncertainty weighs heavily on the minds of workers and the masses. Here we might question why Butler seems to dodge the question of actual concrete political mobilization. Why is it that she simply redirects towards further analysis of how dire the situation is when pressed for actual political insight? Perhaps it might be that her own liberalism carries with it the burden of the capitalist imaginary that cannot envision a world where the political vulnerability we see now is actually resolved through political action. Perhaps precisely because of this imaginary, Butler herself is plagued by a "closure of thought" such that an answer to Yancy's question simply cannot be articulated. When asked what we ought to do about our situation, Butler only reiterates the scope of the present horror. In this sense, she seems to be unable to overcome a liberalism that leaves us "faced with only a choice of barbarisms."

As the interview progresses, Yancy presses Butler further in an attempt to finally garner some sort of political insight from her work. Yancy asks Butler to reflect on some of the forms of mourning that might emerge from the current pandemic. In response, Butler differentiates between a private mourning and a public mourning, noting that the "piles of bodies" we see in the media force us to attempt a form of public mourning that is simultaneously a mass mourning. We are faced with the deaths of those who are different from us, whose languages we cannot speak, who live in parts of the world we have never experienced. Death reveals itself on a truly global scale; a mass scale. Butler notes that:

> Learning to mourn mass death means marking the loss of someone whose name you do not know, whose language you may not speak, who lives at an unbridgeable distance from where you live. One does not have to know the person lost to affirm that this was a life. What one grieves is the life cut short, the life that should have had a chance to live more, the value that

person has carried now in the lives of others, the wound that permanently transforms those who live on. What someone else suffers is not one's own suffering, but the loss that the stranger endures traverses the personal loss one feels, potentially connecting strangers in grief.[5]

Butler thus gestures to a sort of global connection that can emerge from this pandemic as a result of mass mourning. Here she abandons her own astute observation that dependence is experienced differently based on class, race, sexuality, and ability; she instead falls into more liberal universalism and humanism wherein connection across and in spite of alterity is opened up. Mourning here becomes an opportunity for a trite recognition of shared humanity and vulnerability that transcends difference. If this humanism gestures towards a sort of global solidarity, it is a solidarity that is so universal that it not only transcends but erases contradictions and antagonisms that produce differential experiences of vulnerability. We are thus left with a feel-good recognition of mutual humanity and vulnerability that does little to challenge the status quo.

It is in this appeal to universalism that we see Butler not only fail to properly understand or respond to the present crisis, but rather naturalize the conditions that have produced it. We know that globally it is the working class who will be at the greatest risk of death from this infection, especially those deemed "essential" and forced to continue working in the face of potential infection. What good does it do for workers in the United States to see the bodies of workers in the Global South on TV and feel a sense of mutual loss that connects them to *all other humans* on the planet when some of those other humans are their class enemies? Instead, we ought to call attention to the fact that those workers have a similarity that transcends national divisions on the basis of their shared membership within the international proletariat. Their shared vulnerability is not purely on the basis of a universal human vulnerability but also on the basis of a particular vulnerability, as a result of class struggle and exploitation. We cannot simply point to the violence that the working class is being subjected to and state "well we are all human and facing a shared vulnerability right now." Instead, we ought to move away from universalist theories of humanity and point to the class divisions that are leading to differential experiences of vulnerability. The task at hand is not to point to mutual vulnerability that transcends difference, but rather to point to the differences that have exacerbated this crisis: class differences. Butler ultimately papers over the class contradictions at play through her focus on shared grief in spite of difference; she simply naturalizes the suffering that is falling most heavily on the working class by redirecting our solidarity away from a class solidarity between workers towards a liberal solidarity between all humans.

As communists we must offer a different approach. We cannot simply understand the crisis at hand as one of inequality. Instead, we must wrestle with the economic reality of the crisis. We must recognize that failed state responses have been a result of capitalist forms of governance that ensure the continued functioning of capitalist economies at the cost of workers' safety. We must emphasize that imperialism as a global order has exacerbated this crisis at the cost of the working class the world over. We must not paper over differences and contradictions for the sake of a shared sense of human grief; instead, we must draw attention to the differences that matter most. We must ask that workers mourn other workers, not a depoliticized image of humanity as a whole. We must emerge from this crisis not with a revived liberal humanism and commitment to inequality, but with a sense of proletarian solidarity that seeks to do away with the economic base that produces inequality in the first place. Perhaps Butler's own inability to see beyond the horizons of the capitalist imaginary can help us clarify our own philosophical interventions and point to the need for something that breaks with the same old liberalism that has produced and exacerbated this crisis.

NOTES TO CHAPTER 5

1. Butler, *Undoing Gender*, 19.

2. Ibid., 22.

3. Butler and Yancy, "Mourning is a political act" (https://truthout.org/articles/judith-butler-mourning-is-a-political-act-amid-the-pandemic-and-its-disparities/).

4. Marx, "Economic and Philosophic Manuscripts of 1844," MECW 3, 295.

5. Butler and Yancy, "Mourning is a political act," op. cit.

CHAPTER SIX
PANDEMIC FEMICIDE

THE PREVIOUS CHAPTERS HAVE CRITIQUED THE notable efforts and also the failures of popular philosophers to utilize theory in a way that clarifies the systemic machinations of capitalism at the heart of the pandemic, as well as the road forward for those of us whose very lives depend upon upending that system. The past two chapters in particular have analyzed the interventions of philosophers Judith Butler and Skye Cleary who offer up liberal humanist sentiments—for Cleary rooted in the feminist existentialism of Simone de Beauvoir, and in Butler's case a politics of "mourning and vulnerability." This Butlerian language of unequally distributed vulnerability and its attendant calls to a praxis of non-violence have become suffused throughout the contemporary feminist movement, but as Marxists we contend that only a proletarian feminism grounded in class struggle can adequately account for the gendered dimensions of necrocapitalism in general and for the COVID-19 pandemic specifically.

In addition to the philosophical interventions of Butler and Cleary, mainstream and liberal feminists across the globe have called for an analysis of the pandemic that takes gender into account. Some, like those in the (American-occupied) state of Hawaii, have even proposed an explicitly feminist policy for economic recovery; one that would include a universal basic income, state-funded childcare, and material support for survivors of the sex tourism industry. Other feminist organizers have scrambled desperately to draw attention to a predictable increase in misogynist violence in the home during lockdown and to open up more space, following the edicts of social distancing, for those forced to flee their homes due to this same violence. The Liberal Trudeau government in Canada has offered a $40 billion dollar Band-Aid for this gaping and festering wound, in the form of funding for women's shelters and sexual assault centers in order to assist them in adapting their spaces to suit social distancing guidelines. Then, on April 18th and 19th, Canada's worst mass shooting to date in the province of Nova Scotia, a shooting precipitated by misogynist torture and violence in the home, brought the issue of gender-based violence into the public eye. And while misogynist violence and patriarchal inequalities might be amplified by the pandemic, it is important to illuminate the ways in which they are inextricably wrapped up in necrocapitalism and have been from the time of capitalism's bloody birth. This chapter will lay the groundwork for a proletarian feminist analysis of the pandemic, offering clarity to some of the muddled theorizing of bourgeois liberal feminists.

In one notable and widely shared piece in *The Atlantic*, Helen Lewis points out that "pandemics affect men and women differently."[1] Lewis details increasing wage inequalities, the excess burden of reproductive labor in the home falling onto women's shoulders as daycares and schools close down, as well as the ways that stress and isolation can both intensify and catalyze violence in the home. While Lewis is right to draw attention to patriarchal inequalities and misogynist violence, her analysis stops short of rooting them in the capitalist mode of production, thus limiting any progressive response to calling for reforms to an already violent system. As Maoist writer and founder of proletarian feminism Anuradha Ghandy aptly demonstrates in her piece *Philosophical Trends in the Feminist Movement*, narrowing our analysis to women's unpaid work in the home limits and obfuscates a broader analysis of the role that women's labor plays in capitalist systems of production as well as reproduction. Here we can draw on numerous other feminist commentaries on the pandemic that have already pointed out the over-concentration of women workers on the frontlines of the pandemic, working feminized and thus devalued jobs as nurses, personal support workers, and cleaning staff.

As discussed in a previous chapter, child rearing and other reproductive labor is ideologically rendered as a "free gift of human nature" and is thus exploited by capital as much as possible, as unpaid labor in the home. But why is this type of labor, its use value abundantly clear, so definitively naturalized as non-work that we often cannot imagine it producing an exchange value, even as some of the very same activities traditionally imagined as part of the realm of reproduction (never mind that they have never been confined solely to the home)—from sex, to cleaning, to raising children—comprise major global industries from nanny and au pair services to maids and janitorial firms to the multi-billion dollar sex trade? Italian Marxist feminist Silvia Federici argues that reproductive labor began to "appear as a natural resource, available to all, no less than the air we breathe or the water we drink" precisely because it became understood as a biological function of women's bodies.[2] And although gendered divisions of labor have existed in many different types of societies, the ideological devaluing and invisiblizing of this labor by attaching it to the individualized female body is unique to the capitalist mode of production.

This patriarchal ideology, born in the united efforts of the feudal nobility and the rising bourgeoisie prior to capitalism's emergence, was sold to the peasants and the urban proletariat through various campaigns of terror and the widespread distribution of pedagogical violence, over several hundreds of years, throughout Europe and, via colonialism, to the peripheries. Federici's historical and detailed exposition of the European witch hunts, in which hundreds of thousands of women were murdered, is laid out in her book *Caliban and the Witch*. However, even prior to the witch hunts the use of misogynist campaigns of violence were deployed following the Black Plague in order to divide the peasantry and to suppress heretical religious movements. As Federici argues, the major demographic decline and the resulting abundance of empty land due to the Plague meant increasing power in the hands of peasant and proletarian labor, who could now threaten to pick up and move to new land or into the growing cities if the conditions were not in their favor. Moreover, women's control over their own reproductive systems through midwifery and herbal remedies mattered more than ever to the feudal economy hungry for more laborers to exploit.[3] In addition to the brutal and bloody suppression of what Federici describes as a "whirlwind of proletarian insurrections," the nobility and emerging bourgeoisie were able to unite in a campaign of misogynist terror that ultimately laid the ideological groundwork for the witch hunts that followed.[4]

In the current plague, we would do well to remember that it was these insurrections that led to the downfall of feudal regimes across Europe—feudalism did not simply wither away as a serendipitous side-effect of the plague. In other words, a plague can only kill off human beings, not an entire mode of production, even if some states are now willing to grant meagre welfare provisions. We would also do well to remember the immediate counterrevolutionary response of the feudal nobility and the bourgeoisie to the peasants and the growing urban proletariat. One part of the earliest responses was, as Federici details, "in France, the municipal authorities practically *decriminalized rape*, provided the victims were women of the lower class."[5] The gang rape of peasant women became a widely practiced "sport" across Europe, as the "youngest and most rebellious of the male workers" were invited to join the men from the ruling classes in acts of riotous violence that would have bestowed upon them an intoxicating sense of superiority and entitlement.[6] In addition, municipal brothels were opened across Europe (in every village and town in Italy and France), fortifying prostitution as a state institution with even the Church reluctantly approving of it as an antidote to the imagined orgies of heretic sects and the looming fear of sodomy and homosexuality.[7] Federici asserts that these twin campaigns bore the ideological fruit of the sexual objectification of women, "created a climate of intense misogyny," and "desensitized the population to violence against women, preparing the ground for the

witch-hunt."[8] Thus, we can see that rather than being natural to men's psychology, misogyny and sexual aggression
have been ideologically imposed by the ruling classes and
taught through centuries of pedagogical violence, where
even the most downtrodden men can come to know
themselves as superior to women, at least in the moment,
through acts of sexual violence. There are eerie parallels
today that I do not want to overstate, but I do wish to
highlight in US secretary of Education Betsy Devos's changes to Title IX regulations, effectively sanctioning rape on
American post-secondary campuses on one hand, and
Pornhub (a 2 billion dollar corporation built on the sale of
misogynist propaganda) offering free premium accounts
to Italians in the early days of the pandemic on the other.
Federici contends that the sexual politics imposed from
above after the Black Death were successful in rending
asunder the fabric of solidarity amongst the proletariat,
by redirecting young men's energy away from anti-feudal
insurrection and towards the widespread oppression of
proletarian women. It remains to be seen how increasing
rates of misogynist violence in the home will affect the
already fragile solidarity amongst the working class who
survive the COVID pandemic.

Misogynist violence in the home, both during COVID
and during other times, can easily be understated by liberal feminists as mere acts of individual men, who must
therefore be rooted out and incarcerated. But proletarian
feminists know that the ideology that supports this violence has been historically imposed from above, sold to
men through the propaganda of mainstream heterosexual
pornography and other ideological apparatuses. Why is it

then that we rarely see porn discussed and analyzed on the left as the bourgeois propaganda that it is, even as we relentlessly criticize bourgeois ideology in other forms of popular culture? Indeed, capitalist scum like Harvey Weinstein and Jeffrey Epstein were able to hide in plain sight, practicing their heinous violence, because of our societal inability to understand capitalism as sexually violent. We know that these two men are not alone in bearing the status of capitalist rapists, with longtime rumors circulating about British royal Prince Andrew; with the failed criminal prosecution of the former managing director of the International Monetary Fund, Dominique Strauss-Kahn for the rape of a Black hotel maid in New York; and, finally, with the looming American election where voters must choose between rapist Trump and rapist Biden. These are just a few examples alerting us to who really benefits when misogynist sexual violence is widely accepted and practiced by men of all classes, where the commodification and objectification of women's sexualities is widespread. It has become increasingly apparent that elite university campuses act as training grounds for young, rich, white cis men to hone and perfect their predatory techniques. And if these campus experiences are not enough, they can always travel abroad to popular sex tourism destinations in order to experience the added entitlement and intoxicating sense of superiority meted out during acts of imperialist violence.

While all of this analysis of misogynist violence is crucial to our proletarian feminist analysis, we would be remiss not to rigorously apply our critique to the patriarchal structural violence that has increasingly been laid bare during this pandemic. While in most countries the rates of COVID death have been higher for men than women, Canada is one of few countries where more women have died than men. This is because the majority of Canadian deaths due to COVID have been confined to long-term care homes. How can we understand this concentration of death in long-term care according to a proletarian feminist analysis? There are undoubtedly other forms of structural violence affecting women around the world during the COVID-19 pandemic, but we will turn to the glaring example of long-term care in the Canadian context in order to demonstrate the misogynist violence and patriarchal structure embedded into the very fabric of capitalism.

Within the imperialist center, it is hard to imagine people more cast aside by capitalist logic than the elderly and disabled. Unable to work, or at any rate, unable to work at the pace required by capitalist systems of time management that intensify production and generate the rate of profit imposed by corporate mandates, the elderly and infirm are pushed into retirement, supported by scant pensions or disability payments, which trap them far below the poverty line. Never mind the reality that many of us, including the young and able-bodied, are also unable to keep up with the manic pace of the capitalist workplace—from the floors of the Amazon warehouse to the line cooks flipping burgers at McDonalds—the working class is pushed to produce at a frenetic speed that increases the risk of accident, injury, and burnout. The elderly and disabled, deemed useless to the capitalist economy, and often disabled due to the working conditions they faced in that same economy as younger people, are increasingly unable to stay at home with younger family members who are themselves overworked and underpaid. A working-class household where family members increasingly work more than one part-time, temporary job at a time in order to make ends meet is not the type of household where any of its members have the time or energy to put in the significant amount of work necessary to care for elderly or disabled family members. Long-term care homes are then sold to families as an affordable option where grandma can receive the care she needs and be at home in a community of her peers. If the delusions of idyllic community living and compassionate care were flimsy in the best of times, the COVID crisis in long-term care has starkly exposed the necrocapitalist logic that structures our society's relationship with aging.

Capitalism has been a death cult from the beginning. As Marx wrote in the first volume of *Capital*, "capital comes dripping from head to foot, from every pore, with blood and dirt."[9] Federici, reading Marx's *Capital*, writes, "when we look at the beginning of capitalist development, we have the impression of being in an immense concentration camp."[10] From the Atlantic slave trade through to the ventures of the East India Company and other early multinational corporations, to the genocides of Indigenous peoples in the New World, to the mass slaughter of women in the witch hunts and the brutal suppression of European peasant rebellions in response to various forms of enclosure, capitalism was birthed in a vast sea of blood. This trail of violence has continued into the new millennium. Achille Mbembe writes of the necropolitical governance usually confined to peripheral zones filled with colonized and/or stateless peoples as "*death worlds,* new and unique forms of social existence in which vast populations are subjected to conditions of life conferring upon them the status of the *living dead.*"[11] However, the horrors of these colonial death worlds have again been replicated in the imperial centers, in the form of long-term care homes where those who are no longer useful according to capitalist rubrics of worth are sent to die.

During the pandemic, daily news reports have been steeped in horrific and gruesome details about the barbaric conditions of these homes. One of the first privately run homes in Canada to face condemnation in the press, Résidence Herron, was described by those who stepped in to assist after the home was reported as "abandoned," as "like a concentration camp."[12] The indignities and inhumanities that Herron's residents were subjected to were only the beginning in a now expanding list of injustices visited upon the elderly and disabled across North America under COVID-19. The descriptions of long-term care homes as concentration camps are far from hyperbole and the deaths that result are far from natural. Reports pour in from homes across the country about elderly residents being confined in urine-soaked beds, sometimes lacking bed linens completely, for so long that they experience "skin breakdown" and bleeding fungal infections on their genitals, along with reports of "significant fecal contamination" in some rooms.[13] Infestations of cockroaches, bedbugs, and other vermin have visibly worsened as standards of cleanliness have declined. In many of the homes residents haven't been bathed in weeks, a problem predating the pandemic in some cases, and an exacerbating factor for infection of bed sores and other wounds. If residents are lucky enough to get three nutritious meals each day—and many are not—these meals are often dropped off and left to residents who have trouble reaching them or feeding themselves, or they are force-fed or fed lying down, while they audibly choke and struggle to breathe, leading to at least one death witnessed by military medics who came in to assist in one Ontario home. Some are fed from "feed bottles" that haven't been changed or cleaned appropriately, leading to the ingestion of "foul and coagulated" contents while dirty food trays are left next to beds in other rooms contributing to a "foul food smell" that permeates a space already reeking of urine and decaying human flesh.

The elderly confined in these homes, living out their final days in a terror difficult to imagine, are often sedated with powerful benzodiazepines when they become "agitated or difficult." Reports paint a picture of residents crying for help for hours before anyone can see to them, of grandmothers left in their wheelchairs overnight because there are no staff available to move them into their beds, of traumatized patients saying that they "feel alone like they are in jail." When residents are seen, they are confronted by exhausted and traumatized staff suffering burnout and compassion fatigue, who treat them roughly and forcefully, ignoring their cries of pain. Other residents with dementia are seen confusedly wandering the halls like zombies, some infected with and spreading the virus, entering the rooms of other patients or storage closets, including those that hold medications and personal protective equipment, which haven't been properly locked or even closed. To prevent the wandering of other patients, walking aids were taken away in some cases and in others mattresses were placed on the floor so that it would be difficult for patients to get up. Contaminated medical equipment and personal protective equipment were used repeatedly by staff, who are warned by management that supplies "cost money." Some medications were reported to be months past their expiry date and other topical medications are inappropriately shared between residents. A lack of proper documentation and communication protocols between shift workers spread thin has put numerous residents "at high risk of dosing error." It is little wonder then that the virus has spread like wildfire through these institutions, killing off countless people. But as the pandemic ramps up they are not dying of the virus alone! They are also dying of neglect, most notably of infections from improper wound care—another recurring problem that predates COVID in many for-profit homes.

As many on the left have long pointed out, while death certainly comes for us all, the conditions of death are not distributed evenly—not even across the working class. We have long been aware of the realities of Indigenous women and girls stolen from their communities and families and often brutally murdered, of Black men and women killed by the trigger-happy pigs who patrol poor and working-class neighborhoods, of the structural violence of environmental racism and manufactured scarcity—from astronomically high cancer rates in Fort Chip downstream from the Canadian tar sands to Black families without clean drinking water in Flint, Michigan. The

COVID-19 pandemic is no exception in its differential meting out of death and violence. The stark reality is that there are more women than men in Canadian long-term care homes and this is why Canada is one of the few countries where more women have died of the virus than men. The overrepresentation of women in these homes is such that it cannot be attributed to women's longer lifespans alone. Making up 74% of the long-term care population, women are more likely to be sent to these homes because of the gendered division of labor wrapped up in capitalist logics. Women are much more likely to provide care in the home to their aging male partners than men are to their aging female partners. Yet another reason why more women are in long-term care than men can be attributed to higher rates of Alzheimer's and dementia among women, two conditions that often demand extra care. The reasons why women face these degenerative diseases at higher rates are no doubt complex, but one factor that medical experts have flagged for further study are high rates of women who suffer traumatic head injuries as a result of intimate partner violence. In fact, women survivors of domestic violence make up by far the largest group of people suffering traumatic head injuries but remain understudied by medical researchers who focus their energy and funding on male athletes instead. The risk of abuse at the hands of family members doesn't end with old age, however, as disturbingly women are at a much higher risk for elder abuse than men. The Canadian Femicide Observatory points out that elderly women over the age of 65 were most at risk for femicide, including intimate partner homicide, in the year 2019 compared to other age cohorts.[14] A widespread societal disregard for and repulsion towards elderly women, supported by misogynist and ageist bourgeois ideologies and capitalist metrics of worth that value human life according to productivity in the labor market, have marked elderly women as disposable, tossing them into the refuse bin of the necrocapitalist system.

Staff in these homes also face higher rates of COVID infection and thus higher rates of death. Even as they are lauded with empty declarations of heroism, these staff, the majority of whom are women, are routinely overworked and underpaid with many working more than one part-time position at more than one institution in order to make ends meet, thus spreading the disease between institutions. This, despite the fact that, almost entirely across the board, long-term care homes reported being under-staffed even prior to the pandemic. The scant staffing and the preference for part-time positions is a tactic used by management in for-profit homes to reduce labor costs and increase profit. Burnt out staff bear the brunt of this cost-effective decision-making as they experience declining morale, increased tensions and a lack of cooperation between staff members, compassion fatigue, and widespread fear of contracting the virus. These staff work long shifts without proper breaks, and when they return home they are forced to self-isolate because of their work with COVID patients, meaning that they are unable to unwind and spend time with their family members. What hasn't been as widely reported is that Canada's imperialist immigration and labor regime imports much of its health-care labor from peripheral economies such as the Philippines, through programs like the Temporary Foreign Worker program. Indeed, one third of all foreign-trained nurses in Canada are from the Philippines. Those who are on temporary visas face low wages and lack access to the meagre benefits other Canadian workers take for granted, including Employment Insurance, the Canada Pension Plan, and state-funded health care. Furthermore, temporary workers face even greater risks if they speak out about their working conditions or the mismanagement of the institutions they work for, because their immigration status is directly tied to their place of work. If they lose that employment, their visa is automatically terminated and they risk deportation or remaining in the country undocumented. While working in long-term care, these racialized nurses and support workers face routine racist harassment and bullying at the hands of other workers and even from the patients they are there to care for.

Calls for government inquiries into the conditions in these homes and for significant changes to the for-profit model of care have proliferated in recent weeks. However, Lenin's insight that the state is an instrument of the dictatorship of the bourgeoisie is once again starkly apparent when we follow the trail of money milked from these cesspools of human suffering. One of Canada's largest for-profit long-term care operators is a subsidiary owned by the Federal Crown Corporation that manages all public sector pensions, meaning that pensions of federal public service employees, the Canadian Armed Forces, and the RCMP are all supported by the blood of our elderly. In yet another sordid linkage, former Ontario Premier Mike Harris—responsible for many of the neoliberal cuts to public spending that paved the way for the predominance of privately-owned, profit-driven nursing homes—now sits as the chair of Chartwell Retirement Residences, which calls itself "the largest retirement living company in Canada."[15] It is highly unlikely that even modest calls for reform or even investigation into the conditions of long-term care homes in Canada will be championed by the state. This is precisely why we cannot fall into the trap of liberal feminist calls for reform. State institutions cannot be reformed in any meaningful way while capitalism persists.

Even if we are able to defeat COVID-19 through vaccination it will not be the end of our nightmare. Pandemics, widely predicted by experts in the field of public health, will happen again. It is not a matter of if but when. Imperialist globalization, in particular the multi-billion dollar industries of tourism, war, and resource extraction, with their tentacles reaching further into every crack and crevice of the globe, have already built the perfect conduit for the quick and easy spread of the next virus. This monstrous vision of mass death in long-term care is the inescapable future of each and every one of us blessed enough to make it into old age. This horror show is the inescapable future of all who are lucky enough to be disabled on the job rather than killed. Survivors of misogynist violence in the home may narrowly escape femicide only to land in long-term care as seniors, suffering from dementia exacerbated by traumatic head injury, a gift left over from an abusive relationship. All working people are headed towards these factories of death unless we unite, organize, and overthrow the capitalist system. In order to unite, we must also reject wholeheartedly the bourgeois ideologies and the sadistic violence that keep us divided as a class. There is no room in our movement for rapists, for those who terrorize their family members with misogynist violence, or for white people who weaponize their taken-for-granted innocence in order to sic bloodthirsty pigs on Black and Indigenous people in their neighborhoods. Those who engage in these acts of violence against other members of the working class are class traitors on the same level as the cops, scabs and strike-breakers, and soldiers in imperialist armies. This analysis makes clear that reformist calls for universal basic income, better wages for frontline workers, and an increase in "awareness" about misogynist violence in the home, while necessary for our survival in some cases, will not liberate proletarian women as a class. To end our suffering we must unite the working class and upend the capitalist system.

NOTES TO CHAPTER 6

1. Helen Lewis, "COVID-19 is a disaster for women" (https://www.theatlantic.com/international/archive/2020/03/feminism-womens-rights-coronavirus-covid19/608302/).

2. Federici, *Caliban and the Witch*, 97.

3. Ibid., 40.

4. Ibid., 45.

5. Ibid., 47.

6. Ibid.

7. Ibid., 49.

8. Ibid., 48.

9. Marx, *Capital*, vol. 1, 712.

10. Federici, *Caliban and the Witch*, 64.

11. Mbembe, *Necropolitics*, 92.

12. Aaron Derfel, "Public health finds bodies, feces at Dorval seniors' residence: sources" (https://montrealgazette.com/news/local-news/public-health-police-find-bodies-feces-at-dorval-seniors-residence-sources).

13. Unless otherwise noted, the descriptions of long-term care homes in this section are all taken from the Canadian military's report into five long-term care homes in Ontario (https://www.cbc.ca/news/canada/toronto/covid-19-coronavirus-ontario-update-may-26–1.5584665).

14. *#CallItFemicide* (https://femicideincanada.ca/callit-femicide2019.pdf).

15. Martin Regg Cohn, "Mike Harris expanded the privatization of long-term care" (https://spon.ca/mike-harris-expanded-the-privatization-of-long-term-care-doug-ford-is-discovering-that-wasnt-a-magic-cure/2020/05/05/).

B: DYSTOPIA

June 3 2020

CHAPTER SEVEN

DYSTOPIA OF THE REAL

THE PANDEMIC SEEMS TO POSSESS ALL THE CHARAC-
teristics of dystopia. Or, at the very least, a pre-dystopia:
the events of social breakdown leading up to the imposition of a dystopian state, in both senses of the word—a
new "authoritarian" State machine, or a return to the "natural" pre-State Hobbesian state of existence. Like *Dawn
of the Dead* or *28 Days Later* or *The Walking Dead* or *The
Girl With All The Gifts*. "The culture industry machine
has pre-transcribed such events in multiple movies, books,
and comics," J. Moufawad-Paul wrote in a blog post
about the pandemic: "We have been utterly saturated in
fictional pandemic paranoia, both fantastic and realist."[1]
Moufawad-Paul's statement about such pre-transcription
dystopian paranoia, however, was left uninterrogated,
serving only as an introduction to his analysis; he would go
on to talk about the broader trends of the pandemic rather
than interrogate the meaning of this pre-transcription.

But the apprehension of the pandemic as dystopian or
the preface to dystopia is becoming a common trope in
coronavirus discourse. More than one opinion piece has
declared that we are living in an actual unfolding dystopia, that social isolation and quarantine measures are directly out of some dystopian movie or novel, and that (isn't
it funny!) the real-world zombie apocalypse is "boring"
because we are all the extras, locked inside and glued to

social media, while the apocalypse rages around us and a new dystopian reality is on the horizon. Here it is worth noting, before we say anything else, that these analyses of the pandemic might be cute but that they largely miss the point. For one thing, they miss the ways in which the pandemic is experienced, globally, by the most marginalized populations (which are and will be far worse than for people who get to socially isolate without immediate harm to their existence) who do not experience it as "boring" but, instead, experience it with visceral fear and trepidation. As the previous chapter made clear, we don't have to travel very far to the margins to know about this fear and trepidation: those already trapped in situations of domestic abuse will experience social isolation as an isolation from support networks. For another, this supposed apocalypse that "we" are experiencing—that presages a dystopia—has been the way things are, as we have already discussed, for the vast majority of the world, and for a long time. Again, the discussion of the last chapter is timely: patriarchal violence, as with other depredations of capitalism, is endemic to the system—and is in fact "dystopian" for those who are its victims—with or without a pandemic. The reality of public homes for the elderly and infirm are merely revealing themselves as nightmare factories in the time of pandemic.

The necrotic characteristics of capitalism that were always with us do not go away in these times, as much as some want to pretend it is only now that we approach dystopia; they are in fact accentuated. George Floyd was strangled to death in Minneapolis, another victim of racist pig violence—violence that was business as usual before the pandemic. Regis Korchinski-Paquet was pushed off her balcony by Toronto pigs a couple days later. The dystopia is already here, was here before the pandemic, though it seems like state of emergency measures are taking advantage of what was already the state of affairs. But this is what capitalism always was and what it always will be. These are not "exceptional" moments, even within the "exception" of the pandemic; they attest to the fact that capitalist dystopia was already in effect and that maybe, just maybe, the situation of the pandemic could reveal that this dystopia was always in operation. In the prologue we indicated the ways in which the pigs were mobilizing as filibusters during the pandemic, but this is simply an extension of the capitalist normality—what the police are and what they want to be in settler-capitalist societies. If this is reality, what is the meaning of dystopia? Beneath this, what does this fictional notion mean in regards to the historical emergence of capitalism?

When Gerald Horne called the transitional period to capitalism "the apocalypse of settler-colonialism" he was being quite literal: the grisly violence of colonial occupation, genocide, and slavery was an apocalypse for its victims; the many nations subjected to this violence experienced an end of days. The libraries of Tenochtitlan, for example, were burned thus consigning multiple cultural lineages to limbo. Entire populations were eradicated, famine was engineered, and biological warfare pandemics were released on a scale that puts the coronavirus pandemic to shame. Thus, in a very concrete way, to speak of the pandemic as our first experience of a real dystopia belies the fact that such a dystopia has been the norm since the emergence of capitalism. Most of the world continues to live under the shadow of this norm, the deepest recesses of which are only accentuated by the pandemic. As Saidiya Hartman writes, "[t]he subterranean history of death and discontinuity informs everyday practice in myriad ways."[2]

With these facts about the concrete experience of dystopia and apocalypse out of the way, however, it is worth investigating the notion of dystopia and its tropes, since they lurk behind the various proclamations regarding the pandemic and the "common sense" apprehension of this pandemic. From biopolitical theorists such as Giorgio Agamben (already discussed in preceding chapters) to run-of-the-mill white nationalist libertarians such as Dan Dicks, dystopian tropes of state of emergency measures ushering in a totalitarian order loom large. But between the biopolitical "left" idealism and the reactionary conspiracy theories, the apprehension of the pandemic according to dystopian tropes is quite common. The questions that concern us here are: Why is this apprehension common? Why do we perceive this moment by helping ourselves to dystopian tropes, as if it is a "state of exception"? What does the notion of dystopia tell us about the capitalist imaginary?

Perhaps a key discursive element to the ideological formation of the capitalist imaginary is the concept of dystopia. It is from this concept, best represented as a literary genre, that we not only receive connected concepts, such as "totalitarian," but that capitalism justifies itself as a rational order of freedom in comparison to its anti-capitalist double. By presenting all attempts to transgress capitalism as determined by a dystopian logic, a fiction about capitalism's sanctity is constructed: all revolutions against the capitalist state of affairs, no matter how utopian, will result in nightmarish scenarios where freedom is sacrificed upon the altar of a Satanic anti-capitalist other. We have already discussed this notion of capitalism's other being monstrous. As with the attribution of mass murder to anti-capitalist movements, the dystopian discourse is a practice of displacement: by ascribing dystopia to its other, capitalism masks the very real fact that it is dystopia par excellence.[3]

Perhaps the most iconic dystopian novel is George Orwell's *1984*. Other works of dystopian literature are often judged based on their distance or proximity to Orwell's classic. As mentioned, one of the hallmarks of this genre is the trope of a "totalitarian government," the paradigm of which is *1984*'s Oceania. And yet the concept of "totalitarian" has never been a precise political category: outside of Cold Warrior historiographies and popular imagination it has lacked academic salience; it is the artifact of a propaganda that sought to draw dubious parallels between fascism and the siege socialisms of the former Eastern Bloc. Moreover, it seems rather silly once we consider the total purchase on reality that the capitalist "end of history" now possesses.

In 1949, the same year that he wrote *1984* as well as the same year that the Chinese Revolution led by Mao Zedong was victorious, Orwell compiled a list of "enemies" for the UK foreign office. This list of suspected communists was marked by the same all-encompassing rationality Orwell claimed to critique in his novel: it was enough to be a politically dedicated Jew, queer, or African-American to end up on Orwell's list. Paul Robeson, for example (and in an eerie parallel to current white supremacist discourse), was described as "anti-white." Thus, simultaneous to writing the book that would define dystopian fiction with its famous "Big Brother," Orwell had no problem aiding the "Big Brother" of imperialist states by suggesting who should be surveilled and controlled. Hence, the fictional dystopia of *1984* should be judged in light of the real dystopia in which Orwell consciously participated; dystopian fiction can be understood according to this contradiction.

Taking its cue from Orwell, the most common type of dystopian literature is a moral tale about the future gone wrong: the world was otherwise okay, chaos of some type ensues (maybe a pandemic?), a totalitarian government with absurdly authoritarian rules emerges to establish a vicious governmental order. Here, the fictional dystopian state is based on an imaginary where the dystopian is always othered but never completely other: it is too absurd to be comprehended, it is something the readers are presumed to be incapable of experiencing and to recognize as morally strange. Big Brother's regime is horrific, according to Orwell, for those who have the privilege of understanding Western democracy, but it must be understood as the future awaiting everyone who does not understand the perils of totalitarian socialist conspiracy. And thus, at the same time, it is the reality of Orwell's contemporary other, the citizen living in the Big Brother of the Eastern Bloc.

But whereas Orwell's moral tale was about a future

determined by the Eastern Bloc enemies of the Western liberal order, today's commonplace dystopias presume that this other existence is a bad future that might manifest following the breakdown of a presumably natural (capitalist) social order. (Again, from a pandemic?) Suzanne Collins's *Hunger Games* trilogy, for example, is a more recent popular example of this trope: an *other and future* situation where social order is secured by gladiatorial combat is a scenario that the reader is meant to see as strange, based on their experience of a society that would find this situation more vicious than the one in which they live. But if the reader already lives a life that has been rendered equally absurd by the vicious predations of global capitalism, how are the dystopian moral tales of Collins and others like her so surprising? Most of these Orwellian moral tales fail to grasp that the concrete history of the past several centuries is, for most of the world and as aforementioned, more dystopian than their dystopian imaginary would suggest.

Hence, the most common type of dystopian literature makes dystopia the province of a totalitarian future or of a totalitarian contemporary "other" state while, at the same time, obscuring the fact that for most people in the world a dystopian reality is just the way things are. Such a literature is ultimately reactionary because, by judging dystopia as something that is distant from what is "normal," it presumes that the normal is precisely the current order, which, for people living outside of the upper strata of imperialist countries, is truly dystopic. The most common type of dystopian literature, then, does not recognize the ways in which the current norms are the very totalitarianism they are projecting into a future-other state. Collins and authors like Collins write their dystopian narratives in a context that is only possible based on the super-exploitation of the world as a whole, where situations just as absurd as the "hunger games" are the rule of law. And all the proclamations about the COVID-19 pandemic being "dystopian" have simply plugged themselves into this discourse.

Indeed, the riots that spread across the US following the murder of George Floyd led to many of the same people who proclaimed the pandemic "dystopic" sharing pictures of the property damage and looting, declaring yet again that they had woken up to a dystopia. (More dystopic than what they had already declared dystopian?) Here the entire discursive fiction described above is revealed in stark relief. It was not the fact that the pigs could murder another Black person as part of business as usual, that the oppressed and exploited masses are living under a constant state of emergency, that was conceived as dystopian. Rather, it was the response to this actual nightmare reality that was perceived as alien, as "other" and outside of the norms expected by those who benefit from the normalized violence of the bourgeois order. And the state of emergency measures responding to the riots—police, national guard, and military policies of martial law—are treated as the forces of order responding to the chaos of dystopia rather than as a spectacular violent attempt to reassert the dystopia of the everyday.

In the middle of the 1960s the US sponsored, funded, and aided Suharto's coup in Indonesia, which resulted in a bloody, exterminatory regime. Because of this, the word "Jakarta" would become a by-word for CIA-led coups, used soon after in Brazil with the reactionary US-backed coup forces using the term "Operation Jakarta" as code for what they planned to do to progressives: "anticommunist mass murder and the state-organized extermination of civilians who opposed the construction of capitalist authoritarian regimes loyal to the United States. It meant forced disappearances and unrepentant state terror. And it would be employed far and wide in Latin America over the two decades that followed." As Vincent Bevins has recently argued, "the two events [in Indonesia and Brazil] led to the creation of a monstrous international network of extermination—that is, the systematic mass murder of civilians—across many more countries, which played a fundamental role in building the world we all live in today."[4]

The experience of such an extermination machine for those who survived systematic mass murder is more dystopian than the childish fantasies of *1984* or *The Hunger Games*. Moreover, it is not as if such an experience is atypical of capitalism. As we have already maintained, the litany of mass murders and torture under capitalism is so vast that to account for it is a task that is without end. Pick a place on the map of the Global South and there will be a similar story. To repeat what we quoted from Federici in the previous chapter: "when we look at the beginning of capitalist development, we have the impression of being in an immense concentration camp."

Hence, the dystopian is the perfect opening into understanding the topos and mechanics of the capitalist imaginary, that which delimits and atrophies the thought of those subjected to capitalism. Regardless of the wealth of empirical data that should demonstrate, beyond any shadow of a doubt, that capitalism is the most murderous and horrific system known to humanity, it is still normative to assume otherwise. Dystopian literature and film begins by assuming that the capitalist status quo is normal and that to imagine otherwise is monstrous. Dystopia is projected elsewhere when, in point of fact, it is already here, and this displacement is part of what makes capitalism truly dystopian: it commands and disciplines imagination itself. Once we understand this aspect of the capitalist imaginary—its command of the meaning of dystopia—we can understand its other mechanics and discursive elements. To be clear, it is not that dystopian literature and film by itself is a preeminent feature of the capitalist imaginary. The point is that an understanding of the concept of dystopia under capitalism is paradigmatic of its entire imaginary: the way it sees itself; the way its collective subject understands its reality. The reason why people could tweet pictures of post-riot streets in the US and declare them evidence of "dystopia" while not imagining for a moment that what precipitated the riots, or the fascist measures responding to the riots, could count as dystopian is evidence of this point. Riots, rebellions, revolutions: these are what the dystopian discourse of the capitalist imaginary perceives as monstrous—never the monstrousness of its own necrotic order, never this order's willingness to use all methods to reassert business as usual.

We would be remiss, however, if we did not address the fact that the dystopian genre predated its incorporation into capitalist ideology. Although it is the case that, now, dystopian literature and film is essentially, with very few exceptions, a genre that valorizes capitalism, this was not always the case. A more progressive type of dystopian literature existed before the variant that Orwell would make paradigmatic. Maybe this can point the way to how we can understand that the current global order is in fact dystopian. The way a communist imaginary generates its own notion of dystopia is what we have been talking about since the beginning of this chapter.

For example, Jack London's *The Iron Heel* (1908), which predates *1984* by four decades, was not an othered moral tale meant to reify the Western liberal order. If it possessed a cautionary dimension projected into the future, this dimension was about London's contemporary concerns: the dystopian future he described was simply the capitalist order he despised as a socialist; the future was intended to be a metaphor of the present. The dystopian order of *The Iron Heel* is thus a metaphor of a future unfolding under the rules of London's present; his argument, regardless of the book's faults (i.e., the prevalent machismo and sexism of an old school brocialist), was that the future dystopia is already present and must be transformed.

And yet for London the distant future imaginary is not dystopian but *utopian*. He constructed a near future dystopia that is analogous with the present but that is analyzed by a progressive imaginary—the more distant "Brotherhood of Man" (i.e., communism) that presents the story of the fascist "Iron Heel" as an artifact. Rather than treating the future as an othered extension of a breakdown of privileged mores, this kind of dystopian literature sees dystopia as the present order that might be redeemed in the instance of a future revolution. London claims that the political situation of his present possesses all the elements of a dystopia, that if it is not overthrown it will become fascistic. *The Iron Heel* is possibly the first literary exploration of fascism, decades before fascism was even a name for a political sequence. The "totalitarianism" in London's novel is simply an exploration of the present developing according to pitiless capitalist logic, out-maneuvering the socialists who struggled for a better world. It can only be grasped by an imagined future moment, the so-called "Brotherhood of Man," which possesses the perspective to understand the long state of emergency declared against class struggle (the eponymous "Iron Heel") as a dystopic historical sequence. To understand the dystopian, according to this conception, one must first imagine a utopian Archimedean point.

London's earlier conception of dystopia is thus already outside of the dystopian tropes that would be normalized by Orwell. For Orwell, there is no progressive imaginary that can grasp the present dystopia, because Orwell displaces dystopia into a future or othered order. For Orwell, the dystopic is that which challenges the state of affairs rather than the state of affairs itself: the Soviet Union, ghoulishly depicted communist revolutions. Orwell reified the economic and political order in which he lived and wrote, hiding the dystopian facts of his present (e.g., the brutality of British imperialism) within moral tales about farm animals.

The kind of non-Orwellian conception of dystopia represented by London is not unique to London. Stanislaw Lem's *Memoirs Found In A Bathtub* (1961) is a similar example of this kind of progressive dystopian story: a breakdown of the capitalist order, typified by the height of Cold War violence and paranoia, redeemed by a distant future socialist interlocutor who looks back on the wages of capitalism with horrified perplexity. "The metaphysical principle somehow merged with the materialistic, the earthly," writes the anonymous communist future anthropologist, perplexed by the archaeological remnants of our capitalist present, which have become entirely nonsensical in a classless society: "Worship of the deity Kap-Eh-Taahl … became one of the dominant cults of the time. This deity was revered throughout Ammer-Ka and the faith quickly spread to Australindia and parts of the European Peninsula … in Ammer-Ka the deity was generally called 'Almighty Da-Laahr.'"[5] Similar to London, Lem's dystopian order is a castigation of the present from a future perspective. Lem goes further, however, by making the conventions of the current order entirely incomprehensible from the perspective of an imagined classless future. Moreover, the present order Lem's imaginary socialist future castigates is the Cold War order whose victorious US narrative is in agreement with the Orwellian conception of dystopia: the paranoid regime of "Ammer-ka," which, aside from "worshipping" capitalism, was invested in Cold War intrigue.

The narrative that the future communist order frames are memoirs left by an agent lost within the intrigues of competing capitalist orders. The paranoid acts of the imperialist spy are elements of a pure dystopia, a political order that is conceived as nonsensical and properly dystopian by an imaginary future socialism that cannot understand market exchange as anything other than absurd. The dystopian narrative ends when the author of the "memoirs" encounters a corpse in a bathtub, its throat slit by a razor still clutched in its hands, and demands that this "traitor" corpse give it the razor so that the author can join it in suicide.[6] When judged from an imagined communist future, capitalism is a corpse that demands its subjects join it in suicide.

But this variant of dystopian literature, from London to Lem, is not the norm since contemporary dystopian literature by-and-large mimics the Orwellian version. Reflecting upon the way in which this other description of the dystopic apprehends reality, however, is important for understanding the genre. What London's pre-*1984* and Lem's post-*1984* anti-capitalist dystopias teach us is that dystopia is always about the present. The claim that dystopian literature is a meditation on the future is inaccurate; rather, dystopian literature is always the projection of a particular present imaginary upon imagined future scenarios. On the one hand, there is the tendency to present the future as the totalitarian result of a breakdown of the current state of affairs so as to reify business as usual and obscure the dystopian reality of the present; on the other hand, there is the tendency to present the near future as a metaphor of the way this state of affairs currently operates so as to expose the operations of actually existing dystopia. London's *The Iron Heel*, despite its many problems and antiquated vocabulary, is not only more relevant than Orwell's *1984* but also eclipses the work of Collins and other current authors of dystopia. The kind of dystopian literature that places itself in this tradition—that treats its "moral tales" as being more about the present than an othered future—will not obscure the everyday dystopian reality of the vast majority of the world's population. The capitalist imaginary, however, now possesses the monopoly on the dystopian. London might have been the first example of this genre, creating it mainly to reveal the ravages of capitalism, but the genre received its coherence through the capitalist imaginary. Following the capture of the dystopian best represented by Orwell, even later progressive attempts to ground the dystopian in the current state of affairs—such as Lem's *Memoirs Found In A Bathtub* and his *Futurological Congress*—are occluded by the Orwellian shadow. Dystopian literature is about the present, but not in the ways that London and Lem intended: it is a preservation of the present order by relegating all challenges to a dystopian fantasy, rather than a critique of the present, *as* dystopian. That which is dystopian is conceptualized as capitalism's other. We are forbidden from thinking otherwise even if actual dystopia is immanent. What London and Lem remind us of, however, is that the present order is dystopian, and so we should first examine the dystopian elements of the real.

The current situation in the United States of America is a
perfect demonstration of the ways in which the dystopia
of the real can be ideologically contained. The US is, in fact,
the perfect example of a dystopian order, precisely what
could be imagined by the great writers of dystopian fiction; even Orwell's dubious intervention ought to admit
that the US state of affairs best resembles the world of Big
Brother. The US dystopia functions as dystopia by export-
ing dystopia elsewhere. This exportation is both figurative
and literal.

On the figurative register, US nationalist ideology is
such that the majority of its subjects believe that they
live in the best country in the world—that everywhere
else is dystopic in comparison—and this is maintained
by both liberal and conservative discourses. Interestingly
enough, both liberal and conservative discourses each see
the other as a disruption to their respective patriotic fantasies. The liberals see figures such as Trump as a distor-
tion of an ideal America, a morbid disruption of the supposed values of the Founding Fathers. The conservatives
see liberal governments, such as the Obama or Clinton
governments, as barriers to the nation's glory: "Make
America Great Again." And yet both of these dominant
political discourses are unified in their belief that, even
when their opposite is in power, the US is the best country in the world in which to live and thrive ... and that
dystopia is elsewhere: every other country is believed to
be worse than the US (a belief reinforced by the waves of
Third World immigrants unleashed by the wars the US
generates), every other political possibility undermined by
a Cold War ideology that has convinced US citizens that

everything but US capitalism is a dreadful totalitarianism. Perhaps the pandemic is challenging this misconception, since the death tolls in the US are larger than anywhere else, but this seems unlikely: the US imperialist imaginary still imagines itself as the best place to live regardless of all empirical data; at best its liberal ideologues think that Trump is making the police and state forces white supremacist, as if they were not so since their very beginning.

On the literal register, dystopia is indeed exported by the constant military and economic interventions the US, as the most powerful imperialist nation-state, has commanded. The average US citizen can thus believe it is better to live in the US, for example, than Afghanistan without worrying that Afghanistan's current state is connected to the US-led "War on Terror" and the ongoing occupation. If this same US citizen bothered to consider the state of Honduras, to use another of many examples, they would doubtless draw the same conclusions and still refuse to accept that US intervention (along with other imperialist nation-states such as Canada) is the reason why life in Honduras is dystopic. Moreover, the ideology that permits this imaginary of US utopianism covers up the fact that those dystopian situations caused by the US and other imperialist nations (and the responsibility is also covered up) leads to immigrant lines of flight that, camera obscura, are taken to be evidence of US greatness rather than the result of US morbidity. Consequence is mistaken for cause: the vast numbers of immigrants and refugees are mistaken for a sign of the nation-state's greatness—"everyone wants to live in our utopia"—rather than an indication that, having made the world a living hell, migrants are simply following the lines of flight that capital has taken out of their countries and towards the largest imperialist parasite. The fact that this so-called "great" nation-state forbids these immigrants entry, though, does not undermine the ideology of US utopianism.

Now, in the midst of a pandemic, the US is demonstrating more than any other country (and despite all of the resources it has stolen from the Third World more than other imperialist nations) that it is incapable of protecting its citizens, that it will protect the economy first and foremost, that its medical system is one of the worst infrastructures in the world. *Even still*, dedicated US citizens believe, against all empirical evidence to the contrary, that they live in the best country in the world. Moreover, the current US regime is now demanding that the quarantine end, that the country become "open for business" again, and reactionary "Flu Klux Klan" groups are assembling to oppose social distancing, to claim the pandemic is a "socialist plot," while mobilizing for war with China. All of this despite the fact that it has reached the largest infection rates in the world. Hence, a rejection of health quarantine measures while simultaneously a construction of a cordon sanitaire around thought itself. The ideological containment is impressive.

Beneath this ideological containment, then, the US is in fact what Achille Mbembe calls a "death-world." Whereas other imperialist nations generate death-worlds elsewhere, and sometimes in their own settler-colonial interiors, the US is the only imperialist nation to date that is itself a death-world, a perfected dystopian order. The inability to use its imperialist super-profits to shelter its own citizens demonstrates how, unlike other imperialist nations, the US has descended into imperial auto-cannibalism. But the fact that it can persist as a death-world, projecting its necrocapitalist order back into itself while also generating the ideology amongst its citizens that it is the best country in the world, demonstrates the power of the capitalist imaginary to denigrate thought itself.

In the US, the most powerful capitalist nation-state, there is no universal health care, even though, because of its imperialism, it could afford to provide its citizens with this expense—a reality that results in vicious pandemic returns. Following the economic crisis of 2008, a massive number of US citizens were rendered homeless. In at least one city in the most powerful First World country, water is undrinkable and has led to an entire generation of disablement. In 2018 the US was ranked as the 10th worst country for women.[7] As a country that refused to give its former slave population the legal recognition of equal rights until the end of the 1960s, it still maintains a police force that hunts this population down in the streets, killing them with impunity. Despite the pandemic this murdering, as aforementioned, continues; it leaves no breathing space. Then there is the arming of a white garrison population mobilized to persist in "defending" themselves against anything that threatens the white fabric of the settler-state. A raving Christian Evangelical population that is opposed to birth control and scientific investigation. The list goes on: nobody possessing a modicum of sanity or choice should want to live in this death-world if they could be given a better option. And this was before the pandemic! *But this death-world is still chosen as the best of possible worlds* by those caught in its ideological containment.

Despite the fact that the choice of life in the US *is* a life that is terrible, it is still chosen by its proud citizens and proud would-be citizens. The US has made the dystopian order normative by projecting a utopian lie. The lie might be flimsy, but, once imagination has been evacuated of all substance, it possesses enough strength to displace the dystopian into the figurative and literal registers discussed above. The US order is an immanent dystopia projected as utopia, and this is both its strength and its horror. Perhaps the pandemic will reveal these lies, will undermine the horrific strength of the capitalist imaginary in the US, but this seems doubtful. Even now the riots have revealed these lies, but, as with Ferguson and the LA riots and many others, it seems likely that, without an organized and sustained movement, the capitalist imaginary will snap back into place. Those "progressives" proud of their settler-capitalist state are already declaring that the violence of the riots is the fault of "outside agitators" (according to the conspiracy-minded, on Putin's payroll) because "why would anyone riot in the greatest country in the world?" People will go back to being good citizens or desperate fugitives; business as usual will continue.

If the capitalist order has become necrotic, then the US is paradigmatic of necrocapitalism. As the most powerful center of global capitalism, the US best evinces the parasitism and degeneracy that characterize imperial nation-states at the vortex of capitalism's cancer stage. The fact that the US emerged as a genocidal settler-state that utilized mass murder and slavery to establish itself as an economic power is not what makes it unique. Here we are not saying that other imperialist nations do not preside over similar death-worlds, maintaining their own forms of parasitism and capitalist decay. (We should not forget, after all, that shortly after George Floyd was murdered in the US, Regis Korchinski-Paquet was murdered by pigs in Canada.) The uniqueness of the US political order is that it has not only presided over the death-worlds of colonial massacre and slavery since its inception—and continues to spread and support the proliferation of such worlds around the world through innumerable imperialist interventions—but that it has become a death-world itself while proclaiming itself the standard of life, happiness, and freedom. The same mechanisms are at play in the other capitalist nation-states of the imperialist blocs (and we must never pretend that Canada or the UK or whatever capitalist formation is a humane alternative), but the contradictions aren't as sharp and spectacular.[8] If the US is currently lapsing into a state of auto-cannibalism, then this tells us something about the fate of all imperialist powers in the global dystopia that is modern capitalism: the parasitism and degeneracy that is unveiled in regimes like Trump's is the path that all capitalist powers, to a greater or lesser degree, will eventually take. As the world burns around us and a real dystopian order is reinforced daily, there will be those imperialist subjects who will celebrate the extermination of existence as justified, good, and even holy. Even when they are subjected to a pandemic that their own precious state cannot contain. Even when riots rage around them, demanding justice for the oppressed, they will cling to their murderous manifest destiny.

We cannot escape the fact that dystopia is already here
and that it has been here for a long time. The reactionary dystopian imaginary pretends this is not the case by
reifying the present in a future totalitarianism. While the
progressive but realist dystopian imaginary uses the genre
to consciously critique the current state of affairs in the
hope of utopia, this is not the dominant trend of dystopian literature and thus does not feed into the dominant
ideological deployment of the dystopian. Even still this
progressive apprehension of dystopia persistently cracks
through the facade of capitalist utopianism with every riot
and rebellion. Despite the fact that those caught in the grip
of imperialist ideology, contained in its thought, can only
at best see imperialist states as the best of the worst, there
are always those factions of the oppressed and marginalized within these nation-states who, in agreement with the
perspective of the masses at the global peripheries, recognize this dystopia for what it is. Who will riot and rebel,
even in the midst of a pandemic. Although it is the case
that the pandemic has galvanized reactionaries to ignore
all the failures of capitalism, and to mobilize for the free
marketization of the coronavirus, many others have "suddenly become aware of [their] own putrescence ... forced
to live intimately with [their] own death, contemplating it
as a real possibility."[9] These others move in tandem with
those who always understood the nightmare reality of
capitalism, joining them in riot and rebellion.

Hence, the conscious apprehension that dystopia is

already the state of affairs *is* becoming prevalent: the continuing economic crisis that has rebounded upon the privileged nations, the absurdity of austerity measures, the rise of multiple fascisms in the heart of the so-called "civilized" world, the full flourishing of the exterminist tendency of capitalism, and now the pandemic. In response to this pandemic, we witness those who emerge to complain that their privileged way of life is being threatened by this "dystopia," upset that their breath is contained by face masks and confinement to their own homes. These are those whose understanding of dystopia and "big government" are determined by a notion of dystopia gleaned from the capitalist imaginary; they want a return to capitalist business as usual. At the same time, however, we are also witnessing those who emerge to challenge the deeper dystopia, who absolutely cannot breathe because they represent those the pigs have choked to death, and whose riots and rebellions actually challenge the state of emergency. And it is here, with this latter and actual resistance, that we can find evidence of an imagination beyond the capitalist imaginary: an act of imagination that demands we chart a course out of the dystopia of the real.

NOTES TO CHAPTER 7

1. J. Moufawad-Paul, "The bigger plague is capitalism" (http://moufawad-paul.blogspot.com/2020/03/the-bigger-plague-is-capitalism.html).

2. Hartman, *Scenes of Subjection*, 75.

3. By ascribing logic to capitalism as if it is a subject (capitalism does *x* or *y*) we are not lapsing into an idealism where we treat capitalism, a complex mode of production, as a thinking being. Obviously, the mechanics that function behind ideological formations are very real, produced and reproduced by institutions and structures, and often in conflict. At the same time, however, while there is a history of conscious capitalist ideologues working hard to create ideological formations at every level of society, it would be akin to conspiracy theory to try and trace these ideological formations to this or that government body in this or that capitalist nation. Ideological formations emerge over time, through a very messy concrete process, until they become what Marx and Engels called "self-determining concepts." We are less interested (at least for now) in providing a history of how this capitalist imaginary emerged than in examining how it functions now as a reified ideological form. Clearly, parts of it originated in active anti-communist think-tanks during the Cold War, but multiple Ideological State Apparatuses have maintained and reproduced it since then; it is part of the "common sense" of bourgeois hegemony. Hence, on the ideological level capitalism is a complex of multiple ideas and concepts that have become normativized through very complex historical processes. The ruling ideas of the ruling classes are most often reified, standing above us like the logic of the market itself, and it often seems as if capitalism is a thinking thing making its own decisions.

4. Vincent Bevins, "How Jakarta became the codeword for US-backed mass killing" (https://www.nybooks.com/daily/2020/05/18/how-jakarta-became-the-codeword-for-us-backed-mass-killing/).

5. Lem, *Memoirs Found In A Bathtub*, 7.

6. Ibid., 188

7. Ellen Wulfhorst, "US among 10 most dangerous countries for women" (https://www.reuters.com/article/us-women-dangerous-poll-usa-exclusive/exclusive-us-among-10-most-dangerous-countries-for-women-amid-metoo-campaign-poll-idUSKBN1JM02G).

8. It is often forgotten that Canada is also a vicious imperialist nation-state that possesses similar settler-capitalist characteristics as the US. Canada has its own novelty in regards to its imperialism: whereas the US embraces a destiny of intervention and macho militarism, Canada propagates the myths of "peace-keeping" and civilizational civility. Tyler Shipley's masterful *Canada In The World* (2019) is the best rigorous study to date of Canadian imperialism since its inception as a colonial project.

9. Achille Mbembe, "Universal right to breathe" (https://critinq.wordpress.com/2020/04/13/the-universal-right-to-breathe/).

C: UPRISING

June 11 2020–July 10 2020

CHAPTER EIGHT

PROTESTERS, "GOOD" AND "BAD"

A RECENT POLL, WHICH HAS CIRCULATED WIDELY across social media platforms, reveals that 54 percent of Americans believe that burning down a police precinct is justified in the aftermath of the death of George Floyd.[1] This poll shows what appears to be unprecedented support for the anti-police uprisings that have taken place over the last two weeks in the United States.

For us, it suggests that now is also an opportune time to confront the myth of the "good protester," which has served to buttress the status quo and neutralize political antagonism between the police and the communities they occupy. At the outset, we will stipulate that "good" protesters are not synonymous with nonviolent protesters. It is clear, especially in light of widespread police violence against nonviolent protesters who refuse to comply with curfew orders, that nonviolent tactics can reveal the antagonistic relationship between police and communities. The "good" protester, though, touts nonviolent conduct, legality, and close collaboration with police departments despite the fact that anti-police protesters seek to communicate the institutional racism, sexism, classism, and brutality of police—and thus the good protester (we're sure by now that the reader can insert the scare-quotes henceforth) works to deflect and obscure the antagonisms that other demonstrators seek to reveal.

We must first resist the temptation to invert the connotation of good protester, hence making the good protester the one who torches a police precinct and sets off fireworks to celebrate, as happened recently in Minneapolis. We contend that merely inverting terms like good protester or "outside agitator"—the latter meaning, in our terms, cops who live outside of the cities where they work—cannot effectively counter the predominant values these terms are assigned by mainstream, copagandistic discourses. Indeed, the dichotomy between good and bad protester is shorthand for a number of conceptual and practical distinctions that have profound consequences for direct action and for legitimation of the anti-police uprising—and for the demand for amnesty for all protesters involved.

For our point of departure, we will examine the dichotomy between good protester and bad—the latter who we also know these days as *outside agitator*, *antifa*, *white anarchists*, and other names. The general connotation is of an instigator who sows discord for nefarious ends unrelated to the demands of legitimate political dissent. We need not deny that movements that seek to reveal the antagonism between police and community—or, more broadly, oppressor and oppressed—encounter problems of adventurism and infiltration, and we need not deny that these adventurists and infiltrators aim to undermine the strength of social movements by inciting suspicion and distrust or undertaking risky or counterproductive actions. These problems can hopefully be dealt with within the movement.

We note, however, that when the good protester publicly pivots against the bad, they reiterate propaganda whose genealogy includes a legacy of racism and domination. As historians have shown, in the US, propaganda about outside agitators carries anti-Black, antisemitic, and counter-revolutionary connotations, which is unsurprising, given that the groups producing this propaganda sought to defend a racist, exploitative system. Even a cursory look at the period from the 1930s–1960s shows how the use of the figure of the outside agitator denied subjective agency to Black organizers (or the Black community writ large) while positioning them as manipulated— depending on the accusation—by Jewish and/or communist conspiracies. In short, the bad protester, especially as cast in racialized terms, functions to sow distrust and suspicion within social movements at a time when solidarity and trust are tantamount. Furthermore, it undermines legitimate grievances and anger at the brutality of the police, the legal system, and penal system by attributing them to illegitimate agents. The dichotomy of good protester and bad reinforces these negative connotations.

Of course, the genealogy of the bad protester runs further back than the 1930s. At the turn of the 20th century, we find that Americans attacked socialist, anarchist, and communist immigrants in xenophobic terms that would be readily familiar today. In *The Civil War in France*, Marx pillories how the bourgeoisie recoiled in horror as the Communards destroyed monuments and buildings as the army descended on Paris:

> The working men's Paris, in the act of its heroic self-holocaust, involved in its flames buildings and monuments. While tearing to pieces the

living body of the proletariat, its rulers must no longer expect to return triumphantly into the intact architecture of their abodes. The government of Versailles cries, "Incendiarism!" and whispers this cue to all its agents, down to the remotest hamlet, to hunt up its enemies everywhere as suspect of professional incendiarism. The bourgeoisie of the whole world, which looks complacently upon the wholesale massacre after the battle, is convulsed by horror at the desecration of brick and mortar![2]

From Marx, we can draw two conclusions. First, "professional incendiarism" serves as a pretext for a wider suppression of political dissent—which we glimpsed in reports that the FBI interrogated some of those arrested at protests (for actions such as curfew violation) about their political beliefs and affiliations.[3] Second, attacking so-called "incendiarism" shifts the public perception of violence away from the system's violence toward those fighting the system, as if *they* had introduced violence against social peace.

That said, let us assume, for the sake of argument, that the good protester is irreducible to this historical baggage. We could also set aside our own political framework and confront the good protester on their own terms. Such an approach has precedent in a recent article by Jennifer Kling and Megan Mitchell, "Bottles and Bricks: Rethinking the Prohibition against Violent Political Protest." There, Kling and Mitchell adopt the general parameters of the liberal concept of protest in order to show that on liberal premises there are cases—such as anti-police protests in Ferguson and Baltimore (2014–2015)—where "violent protest may sometimes be *required* to communicate about injustice" in a generally just society.[4]

In our discussion of Kling and Mitchell, we will need to temporarily set aside the problem of the good protester. Their analysis focuses on the more common distinction between nonviolent and violent protests. From a liberal perspective, violence is prohibited on the assumption that violence always undermines the rational communication of injustice. In addition, the prohibition on violence tends to extend to property damage (breaking windows, graffiti, burning down police precincts). Finally, the liberal concept also expects that messages communicated must have some degree of internal coherence or consistency.

In response to the liberal position, Kling and Mitchell then argue: first, that violence does not necessarily undermine the rational communication of injustice; and, second, that in some cases internal consistency may require violence to communicate the nature of the injustice at hand. The first point we will grant. When even 54% of Americans believe burning down a Minneapolis PD precinct is at least partially justified after the death of George Floyd, we need not reconstruct an argument that violence does not necessarily undermine communication.

To defend the second claim, we must introduce more precision. Kling and Mitchell certainly are not trying to argue that in all cases—for example, of anti-police protests—violence is *necessary* to communicate the message. This would place an unnecessarily dangerous burden on organizers. They stipulate early in the argument that there are moral and pragmatic concerns that would militate against violence. That said, Kling and Mitchell take aim at the conceptual argument that violent protest is illegitimate by showing that the liberal conceptual requirement of internal coherence leads to the conclusion that "(appropriately limited) violence is conceptually consistent with protest as a mode of public address"; and, second, that violence may be required—once certain moral and pragmatic considerations obtain—to convey the type of injustice protested.[5] On the first point, they cover a number of cases to show that nonviolence in itself is neither sufficient nor necessary to convey injustice communicatively. We will focus on the second.

For Kling and Mitchell, anti-police protests are a paradigmatic case where "consistency might require violence." Again, there are pragmatic and moral concerns that could be raised, but we are focusing on the conceptual argument about whether or not violence precludes communicating injustice—that is, we want to know whether or not protester violence could be legitimated philosophically. They argue that, if communication must be internally coherent or consistent, nonviolent protest contradicts the injustice of police violence. They write:

> For police to be tolerated, or even welcomed, as a benign, ordering element at protests against police brutality where the majority of the demonstrators are black sends a contradictory message about a central aspect of this injustice. It communicates that officers' actions are potentially predictable, provided black

citizens' behavior is not such that use-of-force
is warranted.[6]

That is, at a nonviolent protest against police brutality,
the fact that the police appear to uphold Black protesters' right to free assembly cuts against the message that
police regularly violate the rights of the Black community.
And, furthermore, as Kling and Mitchell point out, such
a protest also potentially reinforces the impression that
there must be some reason for the many cases of police
violence—that it was warranted by the victim's behavior.

In other words, for anti-police protest to be internally
consistent, it must demonstrate the antagonism between
police and community. We should note, again, of course,
that there are many pragmatic reasons why organizers
might choose not to use violence to do so (for example,
the risk, ultimately, of continued police violence, especially where protesters are not present in sufficient numbers). But organizers must consider tactics, where possible, that communicate the *antagonism* between police
and the community. In the past two weeks, it has been
clear that some nonviolent tactics serve to communicate
this antagonism—but we cannot lose sight of the fact
that these tactics follow in the wake of property damage,
looting (expropriations), and the bonfire and fireworks in
Minneapolis on May 28th.

By now it should be clear why the good protester is
reactionary or counter-revolutionary. The good protester
touts their activism as nonviolent, legal, and organized in
collaboration with the police—and thus they not only fail
to communicate the antagonism between policing and the

community, but they also openly renounce this antagonism. Finally, the damage done by the figure of the good protester extends beyond the immediate context of organizing protests. The dichotomy between good and bad protesters reinforces a concept of moral desert that assumes that protesters who are arrested and/or prosecuted are there as a result of their actions rather than widespread police malfeasance and violence. When other organizers are tasked with the legal fallout for the uprising, the good protester is nowhere to be found. Let us have done with the idea that there are good protesters and bad. We demand full amnesty for all protesters in the uprising!

NOTES TO CHAPTER 8

1. Matthew Impelli, "54 percent of Americans think burning down Minneapolis police precinct was justified" (https://www.newsweek.com/54-americans-think-burning-down-minneapolis-police-precinct-was-justified-after-george-floyds-1508452).

2. Marx, *Civil War in France*, 228.

3. Ryan Devereaux, "Brooklyn man was arrested for curfew violation" (https://theintercept.com/2020/06/04/fbi-nypd-political-spying-antifa-protests/).

4. Kling and Mitchell, "Bottles and bricks," 211. Kling and Mitchell adopt the assumption that the United States is a generally just society for the sake of argument. In their gloss on the term, they write: "A generally just

society is one in which citizens mostly respect the rule of law and the (acceptable, if not correct or perfect) principles of justice which underlie the laws. Although social, political, and economic institutions are not wholly well-ordered according to the relevant principles of justice, in protesting particular laws or particular applications and interpretations of the law, protesters are usually able to couch their messages in terms of widely agreed-upon principles of justice, and sometimes have success when they do so. However, unlike in Rawls's near-just society, injustices in a generally just society are more egregious and substantial, and may be woven into the political fabric of the society in such a way that the shared principles of justice are made less robust and thus more prone to conflicting interpretations by different groups within the society" (215).

5. Ibid., 211.

6. Ibid., 222.

CHAPTER NINE

ON SLOGANS

THE PREVIOUS CHAPTER CULMINATED IN OUR CALL
for full amnesty for all protesters. This opens up a bigger discussion about political slogans, because our interventions will have to develop as quickly as events do.
Above all, let's not forget that a good slogan is a tool, it
is a weapon—and it has to be the right tool, or the right
weapon, for the job.

In *On Slogans*, Lenin warns that too often "when history has taken a sharp turn, even progressive parties have
for some time been unable to adapt themselves to the new
situation and have repeated slogans which had formerly
been correct but had now lost all meaning—lost it as 'suddenly' as the sharp turn in history was 'sudden.'"[1] Now
here we are, perhaps in the midst of a sharp historical turn.
While the COVID-19 pandemic failed to manifest as truly
"unprecedented" in the months where necrocapitalism
revealed the full extent of its grim but ordinary logic, in the
wake of George Floyd's public execution the broad masses
of workers and unemployed are now seizing the initiative
and are rallying to break through the murderous deadlock
of late capitalist normalcy. The question of which slogans
to deploy is therefore the question of whether or not we
will overshoot, or be left behind in our attempts to swim
with the masses and crystallize their demands in a way that
has requisite force and capacity to catch and spread widely.

An effective slogan, whether revolutionary or reactionary, needs to be timely and forceful in its ability to capture popular affects, desires, and hopes. One of the more hilarious facets of the Trump 2020 campaign is precisely that it keeps fumbling the football in terms of slogans. In the lead-up to the 2016 election, the Trump campaign cribbed "Make America Great Again" from Ronald Reagan, and this slogan proved effective at the time because it was a lightning rod for white resentment. The problem of course is that once in power and seeking reelection, Trump faced a dilemma: either he had delivered on his promise, and America was great again, in which case he needed a new slogan—or America was not yet great again, and he had therefore failed to deliver on his promise. Trump naturally opted for the first solution, unveiling the much shittier "Keep America Great," before the pandemic and the surge in publicly documented police violence reduced it to ashes. Now, caught between the claim that he made America great and the demonstrable fact that it is not great—it is literally burning and cops are rioting everywhere while about a thousand people still die of COVID-19 per day— we have the recently unveiled "Transition to Greatness." The problem with this slogan is that it can't catch on in the same way MAGA did; it doesn't fluff resentment and it admits that greatness failed to transpire on Trump's watch. Small wonder then that Trump still pathetically tweets "Make America Great Again" in a clear display of political vacuity, or magical thinking, or both. A good slogan also can't be too abstract. As Lenin teaches in the aforementioned pamphlet, "the substitution of the abstract for the concrete is one of the greatest and most dangerous sins in a revolution."[2] Taken literally—which is to say, shorn of the white resentment they seek to mobilize—Trump's slogans suffer from precisely this flaw: what the fuck is "greatness" and when will we know that we have it?

Regarding such abstractions, however, let there be no mistake: "fuck the police" is a correct slogan at the level of generalities (because fuck them—look at how they behave, not just during insurrectionary periods but during periods of necrocapitalist "calm" too!). Similarly, "All Cops are Bastards" gets the job done if the point is to inoculate the community against "Officer Friendly" type propaganda (in recent weeks we've witnessed officers taking a knee in solidarity with protesters for the photo op, only to stand up and beat them down later). But at this moment, in the heat of ACAB Spring, the slogan "defund the police" resonates in a way that these others do not. It is forceful and timely, it crystalizes popular resentment, and it has caught on. The slogan now inspires countless social media discussions, memes, even mainstream think-pieces. Most importantly, "defund the police" indicates a concrete policy measure; though radical when measured against increasingly militarized police forces worldwide, it is at least conceivable (after all, haven't neoliberal policies just been one long series of public defundings?) in a way that the more radical, but long-term and ideologically correct, slogan "abolish the police" is not. The real proof is in the concrete political initiatives the slogan is driving (and that are driving the slogan), such as the Minneapolis City Council pledge to defund and dismantle the police force. (Take note that the strength of "defund the police" is also apparent in the fact that it has provoked a rather flaccid but nakedly, literally reactionary counter-slogan, "defund universities," from the usual quarters.)

One should never rest content with any slogan, however; that was precisely Lenin's point. "Defund the police" should be spread far and wide at this particular moment, since there is a great opportunity to radicalize the exhausted everyday folks who are as yet too afraid to dream of abolition. But watch out for its co-optation, and be ready to shift gears. The problem is inherent in the fact that "defunding" implies the continued existence of the state whose existence the cops are there to protect. If we're going to defund, let's take the struggle further and not miss the opportunity to wrestle our public institutions out of the hands of capitalist cronies whose property regime breathes terrible life into the police terrorizing our communities and making us all unsafe. Coming back then, finally, to our slogan—full amnesty for all protesters—we can see its force too, and its radicality. With widespread rioting, it's now more vital than ever to tap into popular rage and not to cede an inch to the state in terms of our moral right to make demands. And for diversity of tactics to have any meaning—for it to overwhelm, to render inoperative, to strike fear, to really *work*—we of the masses of workers and unemployed have to truly embrace it, and stand in solidarity with any and all who are singled out as "bad protesters."

NOTES TO CHAPTER 9

1. Lenin, "On Slogans," *Collected Works*, vol. 25, 185.

2. Ibid., 191.

CHAPTER TEN

ON LIBERAL ACADEMIC POLICY

IN THINKING THROUGH NECROCAPITALISM AND THE COVID-19 pandemic, we have come to grasp that the dystopia that has been portrayed in literature and film as a reality of some other place—a dark, violent, absurd, totalitarian future—is being challenged by oppressed people who face it as today's reality, not a distant, displaced dystopia. People have risen in protest against the dystopian reality of white supremacy that takes the form of commonplace police violence and murder of Black and Brown people and the poor. Dystopia is here and that fact necessitates that we meet it head on. As protests rage, police precincts are righteously torched, statues glorifying slavers and tyrants topple, and police escalate violence against the most vulnerable, we have argued that supposed protests that renounce the contradiction between police and oppressed people—be it through preaching non-violence, legality, or outright collaboration with the police—are reactionary in part because they obscure the injustice of police violence. The mythology of the good vs. the bad protester reinforces the displacement of dystopia in the capitalist imaginary by inaccurately setting up the present as a place where the harmony of non-violence, legality, and community-police partnerships are suddenly interrupted by violent rabble, outsiders, troublemakers, and vandals. The demonization of protesters that are meeting injustice head on and resisting the violence of the capitalist status quo culminates in the arrest and destruction of their lives—yes, protesters are facing life in american gulags for destruction of police cruisers—and their bodies. Thus, the demand for amnesty for all protesters, not just the "good" ones, in these uprisings undermines that myth and is a way of thinking beyond the limits of the capitalist imaginary that recognizes the present dystopia of capitalism and connects concretely to the struggle of the oppressed against it.

This struggle is taking place in the streets all over the world, and as the whole of settler society in the united states is rocked by acts of resistance; even the gilded, palm-tree lined streets of West Los Angeles—the most privileged, predominantly white, and wealthiest region of Metro Los Angeles—have been a locus of rebellion, with activists making a point of bringing the protests to that part of the city. It is in West Los Angeles, at the University of California, Los Angeles (UCLA) that students in solidarity with Black students participating in the protests wrote and delivered an email petitioning accounting professor Gordon Klein to offer a "no harm" final, which would have no negative impact on grades for students. The letter asking for this consideration referred to the effects of the murder of George Floyd by Minneapolis police on May 25th and the subsequent and ongoing rebellions. The students wrote:

> We have been placed in a position where we must choose between actively supporting our black classmates or focusing on finishing up our spring quarter … We believe that remaining neutral in

times of injustice brings power to the oppressor
and therefore staying silent is not an option.

In their email, students made it clear that their goal was
not to cancel final exams but only to ask for leniency in
grading, given the important, transformative social events
taking place right now.[1]

Professor Klein's reply to these students included a
series of off-the-mark racist contrivances including the
idea that Black students are disingenuously asking for special treatment (it was white students making this petition),
his supposed inability to identify Black students given
the online format of classes (the request was made for all
students), the supposed objective inability to determine
who is truly Black because some students are mixed, and
taking Dr. Martin Luther King Jr.'s comments about skin
color out of context and weaponizing them to promote
the racism that Dr. King opposed.

Students quickly launched a *Change.org* petition asking for his termination at UCLA: "We ask for your support
in having Professor Klein's professorship terminated for
his extremely insensitive, dismissive, and woefully racist
response to his students' request for empathy and compassion during a time of civil unrest."[2] With the petition
easily collecting over 20,000 signatures, UCLA responded
by reassigning Klein's classes and suspending him from
work pending an investigation into his racism.

With these students at UCLA we see a shockwave of
rebellion denying the lie of academia as a disconnected
intellectual refuge from the messiness of life, where
everyone is justly rewarded for their natural talent and

individual effort. Here, the students at UCLA call attention to the crucial connection between the world and the mind that, in the Marxist tradition, places the world as the source of ideas. That world is now at a moment of peak turmoil under necrotic capitalism: It is wrecked by a pandemic and by police violence matched only by the greatest dystopian imaginings. The students at UCLA recognize that the moment demands action and solidarity with the oppressed beyond what is possible with the status quo. The reactionary standpoint runs counter to this; it is invested in business as usual, and purports to separate mind from the world but defaults to imposing the practical strictures of the ruling class on those unprepared to resist them.

As we witness resistance unfold in the streets and on university campuses, it is not surprising to see that Klein's suspension was quickly trotted out by right-wing and conservative media as an example of the excesses of social justice hysteria, with publications like the *New York Post* and *The Washington Free Beacon* running stories with misleading headlines and distorting the facts to make it seem as if Black students are seeking a type of unfair special treatment and framing the university's decision to suspend Klein as a fanatical, ideologically motivated misuse of power and a threat to academic freedom.

In line with these reactionary talking points, liberal philosopher Jason Stanley took to twitter to denounce UCLA's decision to suspend Klein and demand his immediate reinstatement: "This is astonishing behaviour by UCLA, to suspend a professor for making a call about a final in their class. Reinstate immediately!"[3] Rather than consider the standpoint of the oppressed and their allies in this time

of social upheaval and the meaning of the students' call
to exercise leniency for those partaking in the uprising
(i.e., avoiding neutrality in a time of injustice that brings
power to the oppressor), Stanley dons his professor hat
and decries the power of the administration to go against
the wishes of one of their own: "Yeah the email is definitely not one that I can imagine sending to a student. But
to suspend them for it? Seems bizarre. Admin shouldn't
have such power."[4]

Stanley is correct to center this as a question of power,
which is also at the center of the mass protests against
white supremacy and police violence. But we are not
merely interested in interrogating power, but also capitalism. Power is something that is always wielded in the service of the material interests of a class and here we have
two powerful institutions: One is the police, with the
power to coerce and repress groups of people with violence according to the designs of the ruling classes. The
other institution is the university, with the power to do
the same in the space of ideology in a manner absent of
physical violence and with an outward appearance of political neutrality. These are part of what Althusser refers
to as Repressive State Apparatuses and Ideological State
Apparatuses, respectively.[5]

We view the current uprisings as a challenge to the
power that is in service of the ruling classes of the imperialist countries. What the ultimate outcome of these
uprisings will be is yet to be determined, but there is
no question that the police committing murder and the
repressive forces called upon to crush and discredit protesters demanding an end to police violence do not serve

the broad masses of people who bear the full brunt of the
tyranny and decay of necrocapitalism. But what about the
power wielded by the university?

Althusser explains that the ruling class cannot so easily extract the service of ideological repression as it can
with repressive violence because the "resistance of the
exploited classes is able to find means and occasions to
express itself there, either by utilization of their contradictions, or by conquering combat positions in them in
struggle."[6] And this resistance is just what is playing out
at UCLA. We harbor no illusions about the role of universities in imperialist, settler-colonial countries—they
are exactly what Althusser referred to as ideological state
apparatuses, and they advance social control in service of
the ruling classes. Yet, they are sites of class struggle and
the ideology of the oppressed can find political expression
within the confines of the enemy structure. It's a utopian
fantasy to imagine that this limited expression is a gate-
way to establishing these institutions in the service of the
oppressed using the legal avenues in the bourgeois state—
only revolution and building a socialist state can create
educational institutions that serve the people. Another
possibility is building independent educational institutions in liberated base areas in the context of people's war.
But the current struggle is different from those situations
and calls for support for those fighting it on the side of the
oppressed. That is why we demand amnesty for protesters.

Along the same lines, calling for leniency from academics for students involved in the uprising challenges the
supposedly neutral position of the university and is a way
of thinking beyond the limits of the capitalist imaginary

that recognizes the current dystopia of capitalism and connects it to the struggle of the oppressed. It is true that there are adjuncts and professors in academia that experience censorship and repression for staking out positions on the side of the oppressed against the grand mission of bourgeois educational institutions, and battles for their ability to express and disseminate their views are worth fighting. But to miss the political content of the action at UCLA and to fall in line with the viewpoint of administrative infringement on the supposed right of a racist professor to penalize students is no service to those educators who go against the grain of bourgeois academia. As an instrument of ideological repression, academia is porous and academics on the side of the oppressed must choose their battles with this fact in mind. Liberal principles of academic freedom cut both ways, and in a setting prejudiced against the oppressed it means they mostly cut the wrong way.

In the previous chapter we emphasized looking out for co-optation of political slogans like "Defund the Police" because it leaves open the possibility for the continued existence of the capitalist state that produces the problem of police violence against the working classes and the oppressed. To keep politics in command we need to be able to pivot quickly when the slogan outgrows its usefulness or misleads. It's important to do the same as we look out for ways to use existing contradictions in institutional power to win concessions—like leniency for those partaking in the uprising from the university—without giving the struggle up to liberalism and acting against the oppressed, coming down on the side of reaction out of a dogmatic adherence to liberal principles.

NOTES TO CHAPTER 10

1. Colleen Flaherty, "Saying the wrong thing" (https://www.insidehighered.com/news/2020/06/04/professor-resigns-after-criticizing-protesters-and-another-faces-calls-his).

2. Natalie O'Neil, "UCLA suspends professor for refusing leniency for black students" (https://nypost.com/2020/06/10/ucla-suspends-professor-for-refusing-leniency-for-black-students/).

3. Jason Stanley (https://twitter.com/jasonintrator/status/1274770175246708743?s=20).

4. Jason Stanley (https://twitter.com/jasonintrator/status/1274778518149304324?s=20).

5. Althusser, *Lenin and Philosophy*, 141–145.

6. Ibid., 147.

CHAPTER ELEVEN

MASS RAGE AND RISK

As we have attempted to wrestle with the relationship between the ongoing uprisings and our project of theorizing necrocapitalism, we have found ourselves analyzing the need for slogans that can articulate radical demands. In the previous chapter we also saw the way that these uprisings have revealed the political nature of the university as a public institution. In this sense, these uprisings have drawn our attention not only to the colonial and class function of the police themselves but towards a broader criticism of the civic institutions that compose the bourgeois state and its parastate non-profit milieu. In particular, we have drawn attention to the dangers of "good protester" discourse and some attempts to simply invert the good/bad dichotomy as applied to protesters.

While the discourse of the good protester versus the bad protester emerged immediately in response to the use of property destruction and militant tactics, there is also an emergence of a new form of this discourse that converges with current discourse around the COVID-19 pandemic.

An NPR article published on June 24th, 2020, declared in its headline that "Parties—Not Protests—Are Causing Spikes In Coronavirus."[1] This article summarizes findings regarding the spread of COVID-19 in the last few weeks and concludes that protests are likely not the cause of the increased spread in the United States. The article itself provides very little analysis of evidence for this being the case, but it echoes the sentiments reflected in a variety of other articles from outlets such as *Forbes,* which do analyze data to back up this point.[2]

On the one hand, this is good news. It is good to discover that protesters have not been in serious danger of infection as a result of protesting. On the other hand, we have to consider what sort of move this reporting is making in terms of sanitizing the protests. One of the chief concerns expressed by both state authorities as well as those concern-trolling on the right was that the uprisings in the wake of the George Floyd murder were going to spread the virus. This concern contained within it an obvious value judgement regarding how to prioritize various dangers. That is to say that this judgement assumed that the danger of COVID-19 was somehow more pressing than the danger of the daily police murder of Black people.

This value judgement is, of course, absolutely untenable. The same capitalist system that has produced our current system of policing and oppression of Black populations is the same system that has entirely failed to respond to COVID-19 in a meaningful manner. In fact, the failure to manage the current pandemic is itself racialized. *Wired* reported in May that "In Chicago, Black people account for 70 percent of deaths due to COVID-19 but make up only 30 percent of its population."[3] This reflects data more broadly on a national scale within the US. Because of this stark reality, over 1,000 health professionals signed an open letter encouraging the protests, on the basis of recognizing "opposition to racism as vital to the public health."[4]

The value of the open letter lies precisely in its ability to contest the value judgement that asked us to choose between protesting anti-Black police violence and taking the pandemic seriously. The letter itself acknowledged that protesters were taking a risk by taking to the streets, and in response to this risk it suggested that risk is sometimes justified. In fact, the letter went so far as to point to the ways that police violence would make COVID-19 transmission risks higher at protests, as a result of the use of chemical irritants that produce coughing and gasping for air. This was absolutely the correct approach to the question of pandemic safety at protests: do not deny the risk, justify it and contextualize it within broader structures of systemic injustice. Of course, the letter did not go far enough in this last regard, failing to connect the failure of public health to capitalism. Despite this failure, it pointed us in the correct direction and opened up room for more radical interventions that could draw those connections.

Nearly a month after this letter was published, we have seen liberal pundits begin to push the narrative reflected in the NPR headline: the protests were perfectly safe in terms of pandemic safety, and the protesters were never in any danger of COVID-19 transmission. This narrative responds to the safety concerns raised in opposition to the protests not by challenging the reactionary value judgements that such concerns are based on but by simply factually contesting the risk of infection. In this sense, there is an attempt to once again save the image of the "good protester" who does not risk public safety, does not disrupt the status quo too severely, and is worthy of approval from the ruling class. In this narrative shift away from

justifying risk-taking in the face of intense state violence
we find a repackaging of narratives meant to neutralize the
threat posed by these uprisings.

Again, we must insist that it is a good thing that protesters are not in fact at major risk of COVID-19 transmission, but we also need to critically engage with the way
that this information has been taken up by liberalism in
order to contextualize the uprisings. Beyond the sanitiz-
ation and neutralizing of protests, there is a form of individualism invoked within these narratives that obscures
the workings of the capitalist state in terms of allowing the
pandemic to continue to spin out of control. The NPR article, as well as several others that discuss the relationship
between spiking infection rates and the protests, point
blame at parties and individual private gatherings. While it
is true that these gatherings do lead to transmission of the
virus, this shift in blame still maintains a focus on individual action as the primary concern and the main vector for
transmission. This is a mistake.

In the wake of massive protests in Los Angeles, the
city responded by punitively closing down testing sites.
Similar actions were taken in Illinois and Florida as well.
These actions in response to the protests demonstrate the
extent to which public health is a secondary priority for
the capitalist state. When the population gets out of hand,
the state is willing to suspend life-saving testing services as
a petty punishment. We have also seen protesters throughout the United States confined in jails after mass arrests
and placed for long periods of time in buses waiting for
transport. In these contexts, social distancing has not
been possible and access to masks has been denied. These

examples demonstrate the extent to which the capitalist state itself responded to protests in a manner that directly aggravated transmission of the virus.

Given these forms of state negligence of public health, it seems that the liberal narrative to sanitize protests and displace the blame onto individual gatherings also operates as a means of obscuring state repression in response to the protests. Attention is drawn not to the ways in which the bourgeois dictatorship has used the protests as a justification for abandoning any pretext of upholding a neutral public good, but is instead shifted to another set of individuals. This narrative thus at once repackages some of the "good protester" justifications and erases the violence enacted against protesters and the real risk of infection that they faced precisely as a result of this state violence.

These uprisings are at the very least an instance of intense unsettling. They express a mass rage against a colonial capitalist system that is rotten to its core. The state response to them reveals a willingness to allow risk of infection itself to operate as a punitive measure, meant to punish those protesting and to operate as a deterrent to future protesters. This willingness to essentially weaponize the virus speaks to an utterly broken system of capitalism truly worthy of the name necrocapitalism. And yet, in spite of the obvious horror of this system, the liberal impulse is to draw attention away from state action and to try to assure everyone that these protests pose no threat to the capitalist order but are perfectly safe and civil expressions of frustration, with the exception of certain "bad actors."

The move to defend the protests on the basis of there being no COVID-19 risk at all plays into the idea that if such a risk did exist then the protests would not be justified. The simple fact of the matter though is that with uprisings there are always risks, viral or otherwise. What matters is that we recognize that the risk of the virus is not an apolitical reality separate from the racist policing of the capitalist state, but that it is a result of the same rotten conditions at the base of our society. The virus is as political as it gets, and it has been used as a political weapon against those willing to take to the streets. We must not downplay the risk protesters take but rather praise the courage of the masses willing to rise up against a society that would happily see them die of COVID as punishment for daring to fight back.

NOTES TO CHAPTER 11

1. Christianna Silva, "Parties—not protests—are causing spikes in coronavirus" (https://www.npr.org/sections/coronavirus-live-updates/2020/06/24/883017035/what-contact-tracing-may-tell-about-cluster-spread-of-the-coronavirus).

2. Tommy Beer, "Research determines protests did not cause spike in coronavirus cases" (https://www.forbes.com/sites/tommybeer/2020/07/01/research-determines-protests-did-not-cause-spike-in-coronavirus-cases).

3. Emma Grey Ellis, "Covid-19 Is killing Black people unequally" (https://www.wired.com/story/covid-19-coronavirus-racial-disparities/).

4. Mallory Simon, "Over 1000 health professionals sign a letter" (https://www.cnn.com/2020/06/05/health/health-care-open-letter-protests-coronavirus-trnd/index.html).

CHAPTER TWELVE

"CANCEL CULTURE," "OPEN DEBATE," AND MORE LIBERAL DISCIPLINE

IN PAST CHAPTERS WE GRAPPLED WITH THE CURRENT uprisings that swept through cities across the United States, but also in Europe and Canada, against deadly police violence and anti-Black racism. In particular, we devoted attention to the language surrounding the uprisings in terms of slogans, the demands of student organizers at UCLA and the racist response from faculty, as well as an open letter from 1,000 health professionals urging that efforts to confront racism be recognized as vital to public health. Each of these instances were examples of various groups of people making sense of the uprisings and forming some sort of written response articulating actionable demands, in order to create some basic change—leniency in grading university course work, addressing racism in the health-care sector, granting amnesty for arrested protesters, and defunding the police.

The above, of course, only covers a limited scope of the disparate written directives pouring into the public sphere that are attempting to put words to the widespread sense that some sort of change is necessary. Corporations are capitalizing on the moment by writing vague and flowery statements on their support of "Black lives" in the abstract. Social media influencers are making teary-eyed public apologies for racist remarks, or at least apologies that the racist remarks made anyone feel bad if not apologies for the racism itself. Student unions, universities, even government bodies are all releasing communiqués with vague promises to "listen." In the midst of this flood of words, where it suddenly seems like everyone and their (racist) uncle has something to say about "Black lives," not only does it seem like very little actual listening is happening, but there has also been a particularly atrocious attempt by a group of liberal academics, a significant number of whom are philosophers—as well as writers, artists, and people who are famous for having shitty ideas[1]—to use this moment to make calls for "open debate"[2] and, of course, justice.

A number of excellent responses to this whiny drivel have been disseminated through online publications, blogs, memes, and tweets, and so we will not waste anyone's time or the contents of anyone's stomach regurgitating the numerous flaws, fallacies, or inanities that make up this desperate call for attention. Nor will we waste much time reiterating what others have already pointed out about the signatories: that many (like Rowling and Singal) are outspoken TERFs, that others have made entire careers out of propagating Islamophobia, that more than one signatory has mounted a public defense of a rapist,[3] or that others, like Bari Weiss, have spent much effort engaging in exactly the kind of "cancel culture" the letter pretends to denounce (apparently cancel culture is ok provided it is aimed at Arab intellectuals who speak out about Palestine). Author Viet Thanh Nguyen responded to a request to sign the letter by claiming (correctly) that it was a liberal letter and that he does not identify as a liberal. In his blog post, David Palumbo-Liu takes up Nguyen's response and asserts that, "'Liberal letter' does not do justice to the document." He claims instead that the letter is "horrible," "aggressive," and "illiberal."[4] But those of us who are invested in revolutionary politics recognize that it is precisely the liberalism of this letter, and liberal ideology in general, that are so horrible. In fact, "it is a liberal letter" should be a response that we recognize as conveying horror, since liberalism and its attendant political economic formation, capitalism, are the drivers of immeasurable violence, destruction, and exploitation across the planet.

As communists, we know that it is important to attend to written and spoken expressions of thought that proliferate in various forums because we know that these declarations both shape and are shaped by ideology. We know that one of the functions of liberal ideology is to obfuscate the violence and exploitation inherent in the capitalist mode of production, coating it in the gloss of "equality," "freedom," and, yes, that word again, "justice." But for the vast majority of people forced to labor incessantly for their very survival, freedom and equality are mere illusions. Furthermore, justice is impossible in a system that values profit over everything else, profit at any cost. The letter also drips with vague and glossy language about "democratic inclusion," "the free exchange of information and ideas," as well as "justice and freedom"—values that are apparently the "lifeblood of a liberal society." As communists, we know that the real "lifeblood" animating the capitalist system is the labor of the proletariat.

We will return to blood metaphors in a moment. First, it is necessary to point out briefly, as others have already done, that this conception of "the free exchange of ideas" is completely devoid of any analysis of power. It is one thing for a billionaire, best-selling author to call for the "freedom" to spout anti-trans diatribes on her twitter account; it is quite another for the migrant farm laborer who faces threats of deportation to make similar calls—or worse, to even speak out about the dangerous working conditions and deplorable living arrangements she is subjected to. For the migrant laborer, the freedom to speak out about the violence and exploitation is important, but this right to speak is pointless if it fails to bring an end to the violence and exploitation. The revolutionary struggle to transform the material conditions that our laborer finds herself embroiled in is not something that can be secured through "exposure, argument, and persuasion" (these are the tools for securing justice that the letter upholds as virtuous). The laborer knows that her freedom is material and is something that must be struggled and fought for. Indeed, the police violence and anti-Black racism that have sparked the recent insurgencies are not something that liberal commentators can bring an end to through "exposure, argument, and persuasion," though a quick tour through social media is enough to let you know that they have tried to do just this! These realities can only be transformed through action: at minimum, the defunding of the police, but as others have pointed out, the revolutionary transformation of our political economic system is necessary in order to truly end the violence of a system that treats proletarian lives as disposable in ways that go beyond policing and include the prison-industrial complex, imperialist wars, and the near-total lack of any social safety net under neoliberalism.

Let us return to the signatories of the letter for a moment. What exactly is it that many of them have either accomplished or have hoped to accomplish with their speech? For a disturbing (but not surprising) number of signatories, their words have been instrumental in inciting, cheering on, or directly ordering imperialist invasions of Afghanistan, Iraq, Libya, and other countries. Some signatories to the letter—including Anne Applebaum, David Brooks, Roger Cohen, George Packer, Matthew Iglesias, and Fareed Zakaria—used journalism or commentary in the mainstream media to incite American imperialist ventures; the blood of innocent Iraqis is just one thing that they may fear being "cancelled" over. Others, such as Michael Ignatieff, Anne Marie Slaughter, Michael Walzer, and Paul Berman, used scholarly and philosophical creeds to make the same calls for bloodshed. We would be remiss not to include the very first signatory (alphabetically) to the letter, Elliot Ackerman, a former marine who got famous for writing memoirs about his experiences killing Afghans, in our list of imperialist warmongers who want to cancel "cancel culture." Worse still, the letter was also signed by David Frum, a speechwriter for the former Imperialist in Chief George W. Bush and the man who is said to have come up with the term "axis of evil." The true political implications of the letter, and indeed of liberalism more generally, are perhaps best represented by this group of signatories who are concerned with the metaphorical lifeblood of democracy—free speech—yet at the same time are foaming at the mouth to lap up the very real blood of innocent Iraqis, Afghans, Libyans, and others who may be encompassed in the ever expanding "axis of evil." It is convenient to call for freedom of speech when the speeches you make call for the bombing and invasion of entire countries. The letter asserts that, "As writers we need a culture that leaves us room for experimentation, risk taking, and even mistakes." We cannot help but wonder if this includes "mistaken" claims about weapons of mass destruction in Middle Eastern countries.

In his defense and clarification of the letter, Thomas Chatterton Williams claimed that "he was trying to think through how outrage over Mr. Floyd's death had become so intertwined with calls for change 'at organizations that don't have much to do with the situation George Floyd found himself in.'"[5] Anyone who has written more than one book on issues of race in America, and yet fails to see that the white supremacy that allowed a white police officer to murder George Floyd in broad daylight, in a public space with onlookers all around, all while wearing a righteous grin on his face, goes beyond just the system of policing, is definitely someone who has just a little more "thinking through" to do. White supremacy is entwined into the very fabric of American society and, through imperialist globalization, the entire world. It is this ideology of white supremacy that creates cheaper labor through the wages of whiteness, an ideology that after the "abolishment" of slavery (except as punishment for crime) has led to a massive underclass of unfree prison laborers who make everything from Victoria's Secret panties to McDonalds beef patties. Indeed, it is the ideology of white supremacy and structural anti-Black racism that has resulted, as aforementioned, in Black Americans dying of COVID-19 at disproportionate rates, up to 3 times the rate of white Americans. It is also worth noting that Chatterton Williams attempted to side-step criticism for the timing of the letter by claiming that, "we didn't want to be seen as reacting to the protests we believe are in response to egregious abuses by the police." An odd claim about a letter that begins by stating, "powerful protests for racial and social justice are leading to overdue demands for police reform, along with wider calls for greater equality and inclusion across our society, not least in higher education, journalism, philanthropy, and the arts," before going on to decry the climate of "ideological conformity" that they perceive as accompanying these same protests.

Allow us to close this chapter by returning to explore the metaphor of lifeblood that the letter invoked in its call for the "free exchange of ideas." Why this use of the term "lifeblood"? Metaphors about blood are popular across a wide range of political perspectives because of what these metaphors are able to do. Blood can be a metaphor that stands in for many things including kinship, nation, race, and other social and political groupings. Metaphors of blood can be used to connect or to divide. Blood is a powerful metaphor precisely because of its connection to the biological reality of human life, because it is something that we all feel a connection to since it flows through our bodies. Philosophers from Irigaray in her discussion of the red blood of the repressed feminine subjectivity (see her *Speculum of the Other Woman*) to Foucault in his history of the "society of blood" that preceded the "society of sexuality"[6] have drawn on blood metaphors to conceptualize various aspects of modernity. Indeed, Foucault conceptualizes pre-Enlightenment society as the "society of blood" because he claims that at that time the symbol of the "blood relation" functioned as a mechanism of power in a society where widespread famine, epidemics, and violence, "made death imminent."[7] But Fanon reminds us that blood goes beyond metaphor, that it has a material reality, in his statement that Europe was "founded on slavery, it has been nourished with the blood of slaves."[8]

In other words, the European "progression" to modernity, the birth of capitalism, could only happen through the very real spilling of the blood of the colonized and the enslaved under colonial economies of slavery, theft, extraction, and settlement—the necrotic foundations we have made clear from the outset of this project. In conversation with Foucault, Fanon is also instrumental in clarifying for us that the "famine, epidemics, and violence" described by Foucault, the immanent death that made blood an important signifier, never truly ended with the advent of the so-called "society of sexuality"; they were instead displaced onto the masses of the colonized and enslaved. Finally, Marx also evoked blood when he wrote that, "Capital is dead labor, which, *vampire*-like, lives only by sucking living labor, and lives the more, the more labor it sucks."[9] Indeed, it is the material reality of the blood of the colonized and the enslaved, spilled in imperial wars and invasions, that truly represents the "lifeblood" flowing through the veins of liberal capitalism. It is the exploited labor of the proletariat, labor that often results in the spilling of blood in unsafe work, overwork, extreme poverty, and the denial of state-funded health care, that is the true "lifeblood" animating the capitalist mode of production. It is this material blood that the letter disavows in its metaphorical use of "lifeblood" to describe the so-called "free exchange of ideas" that is apparently central to liberal democratic society. Never mind that the vast majority of people never really have access to this freedom under the conditions of capitalism. As long as petty bourgeois intellectuals are able to spin out whatever fantastical ideas they dream up, the rest of us can rest assured that liberal democracy is functioning as it should. Instead of fighting for the freedom to speak foolish words in open debates about various inane issues, we should prioritize fighting for the material freedom of all colonized, exploited, and oppressed people around the world.

NOTES TO CHAPTER 12

1. Tobi Haslett, "Irrational man" (https://www.bookforum.com/print/2603/thomas-chatterton-williams-s-confused-argument-for-a-post-racial-society-23610).

2. "A letter on justice and open debate" (https://harpers.org/a-letter-on-justice-and-open-debate/).

3. Some signatories have defended Harvey Weinstein and Jian Ghomeshi.

4. David Palumbo-Liu, "Why 'justice' and 'open debate' don't fit together in Trump's America" (https://palumboliu.medium.com/

why-justice-and-open-debate-dont-fit-together-in-
trump-s-america-c247add61fda).

5. Jennifer Schuessler and Elizabeth A. Harris, "Harper's
letter: artists and writers warn of an 'intolerant climate'"
(https://www.nytimes.com/2020/07/07/arts/harpers-
letter.html).

6. Foucault, *The History of Sexuality*, vol. 1, 147.

7. Ibid., 147.

8. Fanon, *The Wretched of the Earth*, 96.

9. Marx, *Capital*, vol. 1, 224, emphasis added.

D: PACIFICATION

July 16 2020–August 27 2020

CHAPTER THIRTEEN

POLICY AND PERMANENT CIVIL WAR

LET US BEGIN THIS CHAPTER BY ASSERTING THAT LIFE under any class society, especially capitalism, is "a protracted civil war."[1] According to this understanding, as Mark Neocleous points out:

> civil society is *always already at war*. On the one hand, and *pace* the myth of peace and commerce as congenital twins, there is the permanent war of capital. … On the other hand, there are the manifold permanent or semi-permanent wars against the various "enemies within": war on crime, war on drugs, war on poverty, war on unemployment, war on scroungers, and on it goes until the war that has been articulated as the one that will probably never end: the war on terror. All are code for the permanent pacification required in/of the bourgeois polity.[2]

Over a century ago, Karl Liebknecht grasped that the bourgeois state required an internal militaristic component "purely as a weapon in the class struggle, a weapon in the hands of the ruling classes," would fuse the police with "law-courts, school and church, [for] the purpose of obstructing the development of class-consciousness and of securing, besides, at all costs to a minority the dominating position in the state."[3] The point, here, is that the bourgeois state achieves its "peace" by an active process of pacification, which is both explicitly and implicitly violent. The class in command needs to keep pacifying the masses—that is, forcing the social peace of capital upon them—and this happens not only through outright violent policing, but in institutional and ideological management.

Hence, the *Harper's* letter discussed in the previous chapter reveals something we began to notice after our examination of the distinction between "good" and "bad" protesters, and which became clearer by the time we discussed the ways in which peaceful and "safe" activism was becoming reified by liberal pundits. This something is the emergence of a general policy of pacification and counter-insurgency. In the midst of rebellions erupting at a time of pandemic, we are being told that anything that approaches what Marx called the "ruthless criticism of all that exists" is going too far, especially when those engaged in this criticism are beginning to realize in their actions that "the weapon of criticism ... cannot replace the criticism of weapons."[4]

Despite the fact that actually existing capitalism (and its colonial/plantation roots) is the most violent reality the world has known, any apprehension of this fact will face pacification, especially if such an apprehension translates into practice. Pacification can be explicit, where rebellious movements are violently suppressed through policing, unofficial vigilante justice, assassinations, etc. But it can also be implicit, where the ideological domination of the capitalist imaginary enjoins us not to think outside the "reality" it defines as sacrosanct. Dystopian literature/film and its popularity, as we have already discussed, is a paradigm example of this disciplining of thought: it attempts to mask the horrendous predatorial aspects of the system by inventing facile fictions that are supposedly worse than capitalism's conception of reality; it projects the violence of this reality upon anything that would dare to challenge capitalism. The *Harper's* letter (paradigmatic of many other existing letters and analyses, and many more to come) is another disciplining of thought. The question then becomes, what is the nature of the counter-insurgency pacification that is manifesting in the wake of the pandemic and those rebellions that have broken out in the imperialist metropoles? What sort of policy of pacification is already in development? We cannot answer these questions yet, beyond pointing at police actions and the punditry of bourgeois ideologues, because events are still upon us. But we can begin to develop a general frame of analysis.

In *The Undercommons*, Fred Moten and Stefano Harney discuss the ways in which the consent mechanism of ruling class hegemony generates a techne of "policy" as a "resistance from above" to the "planning" and radical demands that come from below.[5] The structure of policy, of making policies to pacify recalcitrant populations, often functions much like capitalism's version of détournement (détournement being, perhaps, Guy Debord's only interesting notion), where the plans and ideas of the class-conscious oppressed masses can be appropriated, warped, and pacified within the boundaries of a reformist perspective. Where, to use an older revolutionary typology, "one divides into two" can be transformed into "two unites into one." The generation of policy, the way it functions to dampen and pacify the "general antagonism" towards capitalism—by attempting to transform radical planners into docile participants—is indeed a key characteristic of the way in which the bourgeois state needs to generate consent and make this consent common sense. And again, we can use that older revolutionary typology here: the way in which antagonistic contradictions are intentionally misconceived as non-antagonistic contradictions. For example, the contradiction between the proletariat and the bourgeoisie is essentially antagonistic; the ideology of reformism attempts to make this contradiction non-antagonistic, as if these two oppositions can be united under the auspices of liberalism. The same goes for the general antagonism generated by the hegemony of white supremacy.[6]

In any case, when it comes to the current rebellions in the US, this notion of policy and its capture of radical planning becomes starkly evident. The fact that Moten and Harney used the term "policy"—connected to the root word of "policing"—is even more appropriate when we observe the ways in which the diktat of policy literally has to do with the role of the pigs. That is, from the recalcitrant and rebellious masses there is the spontaneous demand to "defund" and even "abolish" the police. From bourgeois politicians and their ideologues, self-proclaimed pragmatists, liberal journalists, and all the "deputies" of policy, we are told that these demands really just mean demands to "reform the police," as it is utterly ludicrous for those plugged into common sense ideology to imagine a world without capitalism's repressive state apparatus. Politicians, community-minded reformers, and status quo ideologues embark on campaigns of inoculation. The *Harper's* letter was a shot across the bow of radical planning: "cancel culture run amok," the ideologues screech, "they are literally cancelling our beloved statues!" Proposals for community policing are announced, and the radical planners are invited to become participants in new state policy. Again and again and again.

The pandemic accentuates policy. There is a need to found new policies of state power that can account for the rebellions and reconcile them with the real state of emergency that emerged when recalcitrant populations rebelled in a global crisis. The state of emergency that responded to the pandemic is different from the state of emergency that responded to the riots; this difference demonstrates why the biopolitical analysis derived from Agamben and his ilk is nonsense. When the state responded to a health crisis, those opposed to this health emergency—those who wanted to reopen the capitalist economy—were treated as friends. They might have been mocked by some establishment politicians and journalists, but they were seen more as an uncouth cousin or embarrassing childhood acquaintance. State violence was not unleashed upon them; they were not even harmed when they marched on sites of state power, armed to the teeth and demanding their right to haircuts. The representatives of state repression were not bothered by angry white militias; such a manifestation was in tandem with them, because it desperately wanted to return to business as usual.

But we can imagine now, when the riots die down and are literally pacified, that there will be new policies derived from the ideological policing of those opposed to the police—who were policed by these police. In the hope that participating with the deputies of dominant state policy will bring change, the hopeful will become participants with policy—on community police relations initiatives, in a variety of reformist-oriented bodies—and yet, as Moten and Harney remind us, policy has a different understanding of "hope" and "change" (key slogans of the Obama regime, the perfect policy electoral mechanism), where hope for real change is channelled back into the capitalist imaginary: "this is the hope policy rolls like tear gas into the undercommons."[7] As noted from the outset of this project, capitalism possesses a strong purchase on our imagination; it is difficult to think outside of its boundaries even when we know that what lies within its boundaries is utterly necrotic. Hope for reform rather than hope for the monstrous impossibility of revolution—"monstrous" and "impossible" because these are the terms set by the capitalist imaginary—is indeed a pacifying tear gas. Why not become participants, since being intransigent planners of revolution is to hope for something beyond the limits of this imaginary? As Dionne Brand puts it:

> This we fear—this we know—that all of our thoughts will be rushed into editorial pages, used up in committee meetings; all the rich imaginings of activists and thinkers who urge us to live otherwise may be disappeared, modified into reform and inclusion, equity, diversity, and palliation.[8]

These are policies that will also connect with whatever post-pandemic capitalist reality awaits us. After all, just as the riots are being treated as an aberration, as a dystopian response to the rationality of liberal capitalism, COVID-19 is classified as a similar aberration. Although the coronavirus revealed capitalism's inability to deal with crisis—laying bare its rotting foundations while simultaneously exposing how willing the ruling class is to spend more money terrorizing and murdering its most marginalized populations than on Personal Protective Equipment for hospital workers—the capitalist imaginary functions to make us think that the contradiction is merely external. That is, we are meant to believe that there are no meaningful contradictions internal to capitalism itself and that it is quite capable of establishing a general equilibrium of capitalism and democracy, if only these pesky external forces hadn't shown up to ruin everything. According to this perspective, the problem is not capitalism itself but only that capitalism had to deal with an "unprecedented" virus and that any social formation would be affected similarly. The multiple contradictions between the oppressed masses and the state, which should be evident to anyone participating in or observing the rebellions, have been détourned from above by policy-minded liberals who complain about "outside agitators" or "bad protesters" or agents that come from outside of the social contract in order to ruin it for everyone else.

As Mao states in *On Contradiction*, though, the "fundamental cause of the development of a thing is not external but internal; it lies in the contradictoriness within the thing."[9] This does not mean that some external

contradictions are not significant (such as the existence
of COVID-19 and its pandemic antagonism with capitalist
states), only that they are not fundamental in uncovering
the identity of an object of thought. As Mao writes a little
bit later in the same treatise: "In a suitable temperature an
egg changes into a chicken, but no [external] temperature
can change a stone into a chicken, because each has a different basis."[10] Similarly, the exogenous existence of the
coronavirus and its effects upon various capitalist states do
not explain how these states were equipped to deal with the
internal health of their citizens; this external contradiction
merely revealed particular aspects of contradictions internal to capitalism. This is evident due to the fact that the
nation-states best equipped to deal with the pandemic
(though still failing at multiple levels) were ones that had
higher levels of social democracy and public infrastructure.
A socialist social formation, because its state would be
concerned with the protection of citizens rather than the
protection of the free market economy, would be even
better equipped to deal with a pandemic: with no pressure
to "re-open the economy," with a responsive and needs-
based system where housing and food is more important
than wage-labor, a pandemic would not rip through its
social fabric with the same velocity as it has within the
capitalist heartlands. When it comes to the rebellion in the
US, though, the internal contradictions of racism, of the
state's violence levelled upon the oppressed and exploited,
should be even clearer. The external contradiction of the
COVID-19 state of emergency was merely the incubation
chamber in which these riots, based on an already existing logic, erupted; the supposed external contradictions of

"outside agitators," though, were fabrications.

So capitalist policy will rush in to stabilize the internal contradictions by blaming every disruption of social life—as if it was not always already disrupted—on the externality of COVID-19. Recalcitrant populations will be reined in, will be invited into reformist initiatives so as to be transformed into participants, and austerity measures will be unleashed. Capitalism will pacify. What will be the new capitalist policies following the pandemic, once the teargas has cleared? What will we be invited into as participants so as to reopen the economy and paper over the internal contradictions that were briefly laid bare? How will the necrotic aspects of this mode of production be once again pushed under the surface, as we are demanded to transform ourselves into proper democratic citizens and thus to discipline our imaginations?

Just as it is difficult for those who participate in the capitalist imaginary (either willingly or out of "common sense") to conceive of a world in which a pandemic will not severely harm and greatly disrupt life, it is even more difficult to conceive of a world in which the police as such cease to exist. The assumption that society will fall apart—that chaos will reign supreme and that people will fall upon each other as if they had entered the Hobbesian state of nature—demonstrates the strength of this imaginary. The fact that these police rarely solve crimes (unless it's a bank robbery or the victim is a member of the bourgeoisie), that they have rarely helped victims of violent assault (including the sexual assaults that women routinely face), have escalated situations of violence in every situation in which they are involved, and in fact regularly assault and kill the most marginalized members of society, is dismissed out of hand, despite books upon books of empirical data. Instead, the deputies of bourgeois policy cling to the fiction of the necessity of their given state's repressive apparatus (along with its prisons and other carceral institutions), sometimes going so far as to claim that people making such radical statements are like "flat earthers,"[11] despite all the empirical evidence that demonstrates that the police do not "solve crime" but in fact police the parameters of criminalization. These parameters, of course, are determined by the real function of these police: the coercive wing (along with the military, prison guards, etc.) of bourgeois hegemony, the repressive state apparatus that protects the ruling class and its mode of production. But the capitalist imaginary's strength in this particular situation is that it can still convince people who are horrified by police violence that they are simply watching a spectacle of excess, that the bourgeois repressive apparatus can be reformed and made into a humane creature, because the fantasy alternative of a Hobbesian war of all against all is even worse. "Just look at the looting!"

But if we are entirely honest, even the calls to defund and abolish the police can still exist within the capitalist imaginary, just at the farthest edge where they push against the boundaries. Because what would it look like to defund and abolish the police when capitalism is left standing? Calls to replace the police with brigades of social workers seem to forget that the institution of social work has a long history of complicity with state power. Let us not forget, for example, the ways in which social workers and other "non-police" institutions were involved in the Sixties

Scoop in Canada, which relocated Indigenous children with settler families, thus pushing the violent assimilationist logic that defines the particular *race regime*, in Patrick Wolfe's terminology, to which Indigenous populations are subjected. Such social worker interventions necessitated collaboration with actual police forces, hence creating the kind of "war machine" amalgam (where various policing institutions interlink according to policy) examined by Mbembe.[12] Hence, it is not difficult to imagine that social worker institutions, still plugged into state power, will necessitate new forms of policing even if the old police institutions are dead. Shuffling around state institutions, saying one can replace another because it is more humane, misses the point of why the police exist in the first place. It also fails to recognize that the immanent settler garrison, in settler-capitalist formations, will rush in to replace the official police: racist settlers are armed and prepared to institute settler policy; the official police, in these contexts, was actually generated from an informal state of settler-colonial emergency.

The point here is that one cannot abolish the repressive state apparatus without first abolishing the state. And even thinking of such an abolition, and what must be constructed following it, leads us to think through other questions beyond the diktat of the capitalist imaginary. Because the violent necrocapitalist imaginary reins us in, demands we think abolition and the world beyond the pandemic according to the capitalist world order; abolitionist demands, delinked from a revolutionary program, can become the new policy. Angela Davis now demands that people vote for Joe Biden—just as she demanded

voting for Hillary Clinton and Barack Obama—and
people forget that she has been a reformist for a long time,
that she emerged as a representative of the Communist
Party of the USA and *not* of the Black Panther Party or
Black Liberation Army. A policy industry emerges around
these kinds of éminence grise; liberal pundits, who ignore
everything else such figures have to say, are more than
happy to cite their thoughts about electoral policy, as part
of a general ideological pacification.

Lenin's *The State and Revolution* is instructive here,
and it is worth noting that a number of Leninist radical
thinkers who contemporary abolitionists celebrate (e.g.,
George Jackson, Fred Hampton, Assata Shakur, etc.)
upheld this text, which argued that following the abolition
of the bourgeois state the proletarian state *ought* to set up
its own repressive apparatus to deal with the bourgeoisie.
But this much more radical abolitionist language always
slips the grasp of policy capture, especially if it leads us
to think about what the abolition of capitalism and its
bourgeois state will look like. We must imagine new ways
of thinking, where the structures of dominant power are
reversed and where we can conceptualize a defense of
socialism that does not allow bourgeois power to reassert
itself.

Indeed, the most radical articulations of abolitionism
identify abolition with communism, as Moten and Harney
do in *The Undercommons*:

> Not so much the abolition of prisons but the
> abolition of a society that could have prisons,
> that could have slavery, that could have the wage,

and therefore not abolition as the elimination of anything but abolition as the founding of a new society. The object of abolition then would have a resemblance to communism.[13]

But how do we get there? What series of abolitions need to be performed, how can they be pursued while combatting current state power, and how do we avoid the ways in which the necrocapitalist imaginary will rein in our actions and thought? These are the questions that slogans such as "defund the police" and "abolish the police" raise, and despite attempts of policy capture, they point towards a world beyond this imaginary, one that we can and should pursue if we are to live.

NOTES TO CHAPTER 13

1. Marx, *Capital*, vol. 1, 283.

2. Neocleous, "War as peace, peace as pacification," 16.

3. Liebknecht, *Militarism*, 38.

4. Marx, "Letters from the *Deutsch-Französische Jahrbücher*," *MECW*, vol. 3, 142; and "Contribution to the Critique of Hegel's Philosophy of Law. Introduction," *MECW*, vol. 3, 182.

5. Harney and Moten, *The Undercommons*, 76.

6. Moten and Harney's notion of "general antagonism" at first glance appears to be quite vague. Generally

defined as "[t]his sense of dispossession, and possession by the dispossessed," (Harney and Moten, 109) it may be more concretely defined as the contradiction between the oppressed masses and capitalism, though with emphasis on the particular US contradiction of the Black population and the settler-capitalist state. (Moten and Harney's 2020 interview on the *Millenials Are Killing Capitalism* podcast, it is worth noting, discusses this notion with more precision.) Marx's notion of the "protracted civil war," noted at the outset of this chapter, perhaps best defines this notion of "general antagonism." Moreover, the notion of "antagonistic contradiction" is useful to parse this terminology. The general antagonism is that antagonism which cannot be, in the last instance, non-antagonistic without hammering reality into the boundaries of reformist capture.

7. Ibid., 80.

8. Dionne Brand, "On narrative, reckoning and the calculus of living and dying" (https://www.thestar.com/entertainment/books/2020/07/04/dionne-brand-on-narrative-reckoning-and-the-calculus-of-living-and-dying.html).

9. Mao, *On Contradiction*, 6.

10. Ibid., 10.

11. K. Thor Jensen and Dan Avery, "A top economist compared Black Lives Matter leaders to 'flat-earthers'" (https://www.businessinsider.com/

top-economist-compares-blm-leaders-to-flat-earthers-and-creationists-2020–6).

12. Mbembe, *Necropolitics*, 85.

13. Harney and Moten, *The Undercommons*, 42.

CHAPTER FOURTEEN

POLICY AND PACIFICATION

There has been a concerted effort toward funnelling anti-police protests back toward representative institutions of government. The Uprising, which began with a burning precinct in Minneapolis and demands to abolish the police, was being rerouted into symbolic forms of recognition. Though the people had done some excellent redecorating of public spaces on their own, their demands had been translated by policymakers into token gestures of limiting the scope of police powers.

The process of pacification seemed—the past tense is deliberate—to be working. As state repression proceeded to mount cost upon cost of arrests and injuries, along with intensified criminal penalties to getting scooped up by police and hit with bullshit charges, the policy industry offered a truce: vote Biden and we get a politician who is more likely to be held accountable by social movements.

That the truce was offered by Angela Davis revealed contradictions in the anti-police and abolitionist movement as it has rapidly grown. On the one hand, to transform Davis into a Democrat is a highly selective and opportunistic representation of Davis's work. The same people touting her "endorsement" of Biden would not, unfortunately, on her authority, embrace Davis's avowal that "I still consider myself a communist. If I did not believe in the possibility of eventually defeating capitalism and in a socialist future, I would have no inspiration to continue with my political work."[1] Nor have they followed the development of abolitionist thought to its conclusion, which contradicts the very model of political "accountability" to which Davis seemingly adheres. For if we examine the abolitionist theory of the carceral system, it shows that party-affiliation has hardly had an effect on the growth and intensification of the reach of the police and prison repressive apparatuses. A quick glance at representative examples drawn from Davis herself, W.E.B. Du Bois, and Ruth Wilson Gilmore reveal as much.

Davis conceptualizes the origins of the prison-industrial-complex in the failure of enacting a comprehensive form of abolition democracy:

> First, the prison-industrial-complex is a result of the failure to enact abolition democracy ... DuBois [sic] argued that the abolition of slavery was accomplished only in the negative sense. In order to achieve the comprehensive abolition of slavery ... new institutions should have been created to incorporate black people into the social order ... slavery could not be truly abolished until people were provided with the economic means for their subsistence. They also needed access to educational institutions and needed to claim voting and other political rights.[2]

Du Bois contends that the white bourgeoisie and white working classes (we will leave aside here debates concerning their specific class character, e.g., petty bourgeois, labor aristocracy, or proletarian) brokered a form of white hegemony to forestall interracial proletarian struggle. Note how the police and the judiciary factor into the formation of whiteness:

> It must be remembered that the white group of labourers, while they received a low wage, were compensated in part by a sort of public and psychological wage. They were given public deference and titles of courtesy because they were white. They were admitted freely with all classes of white people to public functions, public parks, and the best schools. *The police were drawn from their ranks*, and the courts, dependent upon their votes, treated them with such leniency as to encourage lawlessness. Their vote selected public officials, and while this had small effect upon the economic situation, it had great effect upon their personal treatment and the deference shown them. White schoolhouses were the best in the community, and conspicuously placed, and they cost anywhere from twice to ten times as much per capita as the coloured schools.[3]

Finally, according to Gilmore, appeals to law and order emerged as a form of reconstituting political hegemony in the late 1960s and early 1970s, during a period that coincides with the implementation of neoliberal policies in state planning and spending. The "prison fix," then, serves to shore up a political economy faced with surpluses of finance capital, land, labor, and state capacity:

> The new California prison system of the 1980s and 1990s was constructed deliberately ... of surpluses that were not put back to work in other ways. Make no mistake: prison building was and is not the inevitable outcome of these surpluses. It did, however, put certain state capacities into motion, make use of a lot of idle land, get capital invested via public debt, and take more than 160,000 low-wage workers off the streets.[4]

Du Bois, Davis, and Gilmore provide a long history of the implementation of carceral practices and their imbrication in the formation of white hegemony—which, Gilmore notes, was reconfigured through neoliberal policy. In addition, the Democratic Party repeatedly pushed measures to intensify mass incarceration, with Joe Biden boasting in 1993 that "every major crime bill since 1976 that's come out of this Congress, every minor crime bill, has had the name of the Democratic senator from the State of Delaware: Joe Biden."[5] In sum, the contemporary Democratic Party is both part and product of the neoliberal, carceral, white hegemony that has shored up American empire for the past five decades. From an abolitionist perspective, then, it is incorrect to conclude that the Democrats would be more responsive or accountable to social movements.

The electoral call to order was then invalidated practically by the deployment of federal troops to Portland,

Oregon. Interestingly enough, this federal policy is not dissimilar from far-right strategies of focusing their mobilization efforts on perceived "liberal" strongholds.[6] By applying the antifascist concept of the three-way fight, we will argue that an electoral call to order mistakenly reduces what has become an open struggle for hegemony, on terms more conducive to far-right social forces, to mere agonism.

In *Philosophy of Antifascism: Punching Nazis and Fighting White Supremacy*, Devin Zane Shaw argues that settler-state hegemony in countries like the United States is "constituted by a dialectic between two predominant but conflicting social forces," that is, liberal or bourgeois democracy and white supremacy, "and each of these predominant forces mediates between other conflicting forces as well."[7] Bourgeois democracy and white supremacy comprise two corners of the three-way fight. Opposed to both is militant antifascism (or liberation movements writ large).

For Shaw (drawing on the work of Du Bois, Cheryl Harris, Davis, and others), "contemporary liberalism is willing to formalize or codify white supremacy insofar as the norms of the latter can be codified in color-blind terms," which, in abolitionist terms, means that anti-Black racism is today laundered in terms of "law and order."[8] And yet, contradictions remain within settler-state hegemony. Though imbricated in white hegemony, liberalism also funnels social movements into representative institutions or meets their demands framed in terms of formal equality or redistribution. The liberal "call to order" involves pulling social unrest into the normative framework of policy and representative governance. In Fred Moten's terms, the "call to order" attempts to organize fugitive elaborations of social life within the normative terms of order, productivity, or (we might add) efficacy, carrying the normative assumption that "the only genuine and authentic mode of living in the world is to be recognizable within terms of order."[9]

Liberalism thus attempts to reduce broader social antagonisms to agonism. In deploying federal troops in cities marked by strong local organizing and continued unrest, the Trump administration has refused to follow the unwritten norms of an electoral or agonistic call to order. (At this point, one must note that both the Department of Homeland Security and Customs and Border Patrol have, under both parties, had their mandates extended in what is known as mission creep). Whereas for the last four years we have witnessed a resurgence of insurrectionary far-right mobilizations, Trump's current policy is a direct form of mobilizing white supremacy's institutional forms, by attempting to buttress the police power of the state.

In other words, if it is correct that white hegemony has been stabilized and reconfigured under neoliberal carceral policy, then what we are witnessing is the destabilization of this hegemony, a destabilization of the present arrangement between bourgeois democracy and white supremacy. The liberal impulse recoils at open antagonism and yet again attempts to resolve it in policy. Here, against liberal activism, the proper response is to defend and spread what Harney and Moten call "fugitive planning." Policy is the management of demands from above because "economic management cannot win the battle that rages in the realm of social reproduction."[10] It involves the command over and displacement of planning, which involves "self-sufficiency at the social level, and it reproduces in its experiment not just what it needs, life, but what it wants, life in difference, in the play of the general antagonism."[11] Harney and Moten relate fugitive planning to what they call the undercommons, but their comments apply to the Uprising as well—a social movement organized against one of *the* intractable assumptions of the settler-colonial project itself, that police are *necessary* (which carries the unspoken connotation of "*necessary* to maintain white hegemony").

The first duty of the intellectual is to refuse to call the situation to order. The (literal) fugitive planning of the Uprising must move in the space between the liberal recalcitrance to defund or abolish the police and the federal policy of outright police brutality. The liberal call to order might pull the Uprising into normative terms of representative government, but it stultifies the planning on the ground, where liberation movements draw their strength and solidarity. The refusal of policy is not the absence of politics; it is politics through continued fugitive planning.[12] Abolitionism on its own terms, as documented above, needs to pull down neoliberal, carceral white hegemony like the so-called "sacred fence" surrounding the federal courthouse in Portland; settling for recognition within the terms of order is capitulation.

NOTES TO CHAPTER 14

1. Davis, *Abolition Democracy*, 21.

2. Ibid., 91–92.

3. Du Bois, *Black Reconstruction*, 573–574 (my emphasis).

4. Gilmore, *Golden Gulag*, 88.

5. Sheryl Gay Stolberg and Astead W. Herndon, "'Lock the S.O.B.s up'" (https://www.nytimes.com/2019/06/25/us/joe-biden-crime-laws.html).

6. As Shane Burley writes: "Far-right organizations head into liberal towns so as to inspire violence, both their own and whatever they think they can stoke in their opposition by creating threatening situations in which antifascist organizers are forced to respond." (Burley, *Why We Fight*, 99)

7. Shaw, *Philosophy of Antifascism*, 14.

8. Ibid., 177.

9. Harney and Moten, *The Undercommons*, 125.

10. Ibid., 74.

11. Ibid., 76.

12. Here we are not using the specific term *politics* according to Harney and Moten's use.

CHAPTER FIFTEEN

"THINK OF THE CHILDREN"

WE'VE REJECTED THE LIBERAL CALL TO ORDER, BOTH in the current conjuncture and in principle. Fugitive planning is our watchword; swallowing policy is capitulation. Naturally, then—though this might seem like a sharp turn—we're going to have to talk about our children.

Saying "our" here is deliberate. The Uprising was first of all a righteous explosion of anger, but it now envisions and fights for a future, and to speak of futurity is to speak of children. Some of us militating on behalf of the Uprising are actually parents or caregivers of children in some capacity. But each and every one of us makes a claim on the future of our community's children when we enter the three-way fight. Never want to have any children of your own? Care not to engage in child-rearing, or educating children, or anything of the kind? Other people's children are still your responsibility, and this is a responsibility that bears down heavily on you, maybe even especially heavily, from the moment you line up against the state.

As communists, we need to embrace and declare this futurity loudly. The terrain of children's futurity and social reproduction has for decades been dominated by cultural conservatism, despite important inroads made from the left via feminist and antiracist organizing especially. The conservative hegemony regarding children is among a constellation of factors allowing Trump and Biden, from both sides of the necro-liberal cartel, to appear credible to the wide public when they decry "anarchists" among the protesters, or assimilate protest to "anarchism" full stop. They seem to mean something like "active nihilism," not anarchism as any self-identified protester would likely understand it, but the point is clear: the Uprising is framed as purely destructive, and pure destruction is framed as anti-future—hence, as anti-child. Never mind that neoliberal policymakers and their cultural conservative enablers have done more, root and branch, to increase stress on families and undermine children's right to futurity than any "anarchist" boogeymen could accomplish in their wildest dreams.[1] The point is that "the child" is already mobilized politically, for better or for worse, and from a purely strategic vantage point we have to play on this terrain if we're to get anywhere at all.

Parenthetically, here too we find philosophy and theory in a culpable role where it could have done better. A number of academic edgelords have made a career out of giving full-throated voice to anti-natalism, misanthropy, and the political rejection of "reproductive futurism." David Benatar and Lee Edelman are cases in point, both because they represent different streams of intellectual radicalism (utilitarianism and queer theory, respectively), and because they trotted out their canonical anti-future arguments during the Bush Jr. years (!), upstream of all the cruelty and political incompetence of 2020.[2] Unless we want to entertain moralizing over women's reproductive choices, Benatar's liberal "pro-death" position in the first trimester of pregnancy is a nonstarter—and Edelman's call for queers to *be* the very scarecrows of disease and death depicted by cultural conservatives resonates little outside of spaces where Lacanian point-scoring is important. Such examples might be extreme, but precisely because they are, they alibi the conservative lie that "progressives" hate children, that they foment a "culture of death," and so on. Especially in the time of COVID-19, we need to be on guard against anything smacking of nihilism, resignation, or neo-Malthusianism—for beyond these lies white supremacy. It's time to accept that people reproduce and care for children, that race, gender, class and other factors have measurable demographic aspects—i.e., that "childhood," "parenthood," and non-parental forms of caregiving are intersectional—and that this is all woven into the political fight at a basic level.

Theory aside, the point where the call to order congeals as policy is where the topic of our children becomes most important. Quite simply, our children are being used against us to force-feed us policy. This is of course nothing new—a distressingly familiar refrain by this point—but it appears in stark outline in the context of the Uprising and COVID-19.

First off, the presence of freely rioting federal police and militarized local cops in major urban centers is a resounding blackmail against parents who would otherwise join in protests or any kind of public political action. Children themselves have been tear-gassed and maimed by police,[3] so are better left home. Parents or guardians who still want to brave the streets without them are therefore forced to find childcare, and if they themselves are arrested or injured this will also affect their children. There is a heavy disincentive to fight for your child's future when it could mean injury, death, or family separation through incarceration.

The cops are one thing; the education ministries are another. What's more representative of a "call to order" than "back to school"? The problem, of course, is that simply sending children back, as Trump and DeVos have suggested, is bound to be disastrous from a public health perspective. A more subtle policy play, *qua* call to order, is to give us a choice between our children's safety (and ours) on the one hand, and our economic prosperity or even survival on the other. In Canada, with only six weeks left until the start of school, plans for the coming year are still being rolled out. The province of Ontario, where the Ford government unsurprisingly didn't bother to consult teachers' unions, is perhaps a representative case. There will be medical-grade masks for the teachers and rules about who sits where and pisses and shits when and all that, but in sum, public school children will be back at it for full days, five days a week, in generally crowded conditions — and for younger students, masks will be optional. This is what families have to look forward to, *unless parents or guardians request that their child shift to online learning.* Bracket for a second the public health implications of this plan, which like a full return is almost certain to result in new outbreaks and a Fall lockdown since many parents will have no choice but to send their kids back in. What else is going on here? Many parents who can afford to, and can make arrangements, will try to keep their kids at home. This will of course come at a cost — literally financial for many people, in the form of caregiving costs, staying home from work, debt, and the like — but also in terms of "opportunity costs" in general and the broader political cost of isolating and diluting the energies of more radical or progressive affluent parents.

The choice is between potential sickness and death on the one hand, and siloing and discipline on the other. Anyone who can afford to will take a hit to their political energies; after all, "think of the children." What then can we do—we communists, faced with such cynicism from the state—when "our" children are in the balance? *At a bare minimum* we must internalize and propagate the slogan that *childcare can be a radical act*. Bearing in mind all the necessary health precautions and scientific advice about social bubbles, we need to commit to easing each other's burdens of care and enriching children's lives in a terrifying time. We must do this by committing to equitable, reliable, solidary forms of community care, at a distance from the state—effectively, childcare in the circuit of fugitive planning.[4] Strong care networks have the potential to ease if not defuse both the blackmail of the police and the blackmail of the education ministries. This will free up our political energies, which is something we owe to our children.

NOTES TO CHAPTER 15

1. See Melinda Cooper's *Family Values: Between Neoliberalism and the New Social Conservatism* (2017).

2. See David Benatar's *Better to Have Never Been* (2006) and Lee Edelman's *No Future* (2004).

3. Jemima McEvoy, "Moms, children among Portland protesters sustaining gruesome injuries" (https://www.forbes.com/sites/jemimamcevoy/2020/07/29/moms-children-among-portland-protesters-sustaining-gruesome-injuries/)

4. It should go without saying that parents or caregivers of disabled or neurodivergent children should receive special consideration and that arguments about solidarity networks apply to the care of dependent adults as well.

CHAPTER SIXTEEN

CHILDREN IN SCHOOLS, CHILDREN IN CAGES

WE TURNED TO THE SUBJECT OF CHILDREN IN THE previous chapter: to the weaponizing of our children against us to force-feed us policy—always a policy that subverts radicalism to an assimilationist "call to order." And we affirmed that the concepts of "the child" and "childhood" are political and intersectional with social class at the base. As such, they are mobilized by the capitalist class and its accomplices to advance their material interests. In the summer of 2020, education bureaus in the imperialist countries that were bent on pressuring schools to re-open placed families between the Scylla and Charybdis of risking illness and death by COVID-19 or shouldering additional economic hardship as families scrambled to provide at home education for children and make ends meet.

Consider, for example, the fallout of alarming photos shared on Twitter at that time, showing hallways crowded with mostly maskless teens at a North Paulding High School in Georgia, revealing the grim reality of schools reopening during a pandemic. After such photos went viral, it came to light that staff and students at the school were diagnosed positive for COVID-19 just prior to the school's reopening and that teachers were in contact with those infected: "Teachers at North Paulding say there are positive tests among school staff, including a staff member who came into contact with most teachers at the school while exhibiting symptoms last week."[1] And for families with parents and caregivers who work full time and with little or no access to computers and internet, switching to online at home instruction was not a reality.

Why did this happen? In the United States, at least, it happened in part to further the agendas of reactionaries, such as Betsy DeVos, who were looking to put into action programs that hurt poor children and families and assist the wealthy. The basic operations of settler capitalism in the United States have not frequently been investigated in terms of their harm to children. Continuing the pivot of this critique of necrocapitalism to children, we note that the United States has a long history of endangering children and using violence and the threat of violence against the children of oppressed people to advance the political and economic goals of the capitalist class and of the settler population generally.

The 1619 Project documents how settler laws governing the lives of African children during the colonial period in the Americas enabled the United States to become a slave country. A Virginia law enacted in 1662, for example, stated, "all children borne in this country shall be held bond or free only according to the condition of the mother."[2] Slave mothers gave birth to slave children producing a reality where "most enslaved women had to endure their children being forcibly taken from them."[3] Why? And for what? There is no way to give a complete answer here, but if we want to point to material conditions, the answer will likely involve profit. Historians like Edward Baptist, author of *The Half has Never Been Told: Slavery and the Making of American Capitalism*, and economists like Gavin Wright in his *The Political Economy of the Cotton South*, detail how American capitalism owes its initial success to the slave order imposed by settler law and commodified slave labor in the American South. Indeed, "there was a concrete relationship between African-American suffering and economic growth: the more that enslaved people were tortured, the more efficiently they produced the new global economy's most essential commodity."[4]

As Americans expanded their slave order into lands stolen from the Indigenous people of North America, they also expanded child endangerment and forced family separation for the natives, with the goal of advancing American class and settler interests. From the mid-1800s through the 1970s, US Government boarding schools forcibly separated Indigenous children from their families in order to "kill the Indian in him, and save the man." These are the words of American Cavalry Captain Richard Henry Pratt, who, after experimenting with disciplining captured Plains Indians by means of military drilling and torture at the Fort Marion prison in Florida, established the Carlisle Indian Industrial School in Pennsylvania to assimilate the Indigenous population.[5] Pratt's "school" served as a model for off-reservation assimilation centers where Indigenous children, once abducted from their families, were "beaten for speaking their own languages" and were prohibited from practicing their religion.[6] These assimilation centers nurtured a "culture of pervasive physical and sexual abuse … [where] food and medical attention were often scarce;

many students died."[7] Appropriately, a piece at *Everyday Feminism* describes these "schools" as "Guantanamo for Native Babies."[8] As mentioned above, these practices carried on well into the 1970s, and according to the National Native American Boarding School Healing Coalition, their impacts on Indigenous families include both loss of parental power and the near destruction of the extended family system. (The same processes happened in Canada with the Residential School system and other institutional forms of breaking up Indigenous families—such as the Sixties Scoop—which continue into the present.) Theoretically, it may be useful to think of these assimilation centers as a counterpart to the US's general policy, in Veracini's terminology, of necropolitical transfer: the military liquidation of Indigenous peoples.[9] For Veracini, *transfer* is how settler society is achieved by "cleansing" others. Transfer by assimilation is a way for settlers to "uplift" Indigenous people out of existence,[10] to make the land bare of any existential challenge to the legitimacy of settler society.

These basic historical operations of settler capitalism in the United States, involving harm to children and families, the establishment of a slave order churning out slavery profits, and destroying Indigenous lives and culture through assimilationist policy and programs to entrench settlerism, are vectors in the continuing and necessary movement of necrotic capitalism toward the ruin and immiseration of people whose lives and deaths are required to maintain bourgeois society at various stages.

Coincident with funnelling resources to wealthy families at the expense of poor ones via "Back to School" orders, no matter the death toll, is the current US policy of family separation along US borders. A policy that endangers children and destroys the families of some of the most vulnerable people in the world. This policy is carried out punitively to discourage immigrants from seeking asylum in the United States. Punitive US border policy regarding families and children dates to at least the mid-1980s, when the former Immigration and Naturalization Service (INS) began jailing so-called "unaccompanied minors" in detention centers along the southern border.[11] The notion of "unaccompanied minors" is macabre. Then, American border police used it to refer to detaining and deporting children traveling with family, including grandparents and adult siblings, but not with their parents (who may be back in their home country or already in the United States). Today, the US government creates "unaccompanied minors"—from the "Zero Tolerance" doctrine of the Trump regime, where asylum seekers crossing into the United States "illegally" are immediately subject to criminal prosecution—by separating children from parents and adults they may be traveling with and opening separate immigration cases for the adults and the children. From then on, the children are treated as "unaccompanied alien children" and placed into a detention processing track away from their family.[12] Children may never be reunited with their parents, and the United States government has no program or policy regarding reuniting families. American officials have in fact lost track of thousands of children, and there are no plans in place to determine where they are or what happened to them.

In addition to the horror of being wrested from family, children in cages at the US border are at high risk of COVID-19 infection. At the start of the pandemic, the United Nations Children's Fund called for the immediate release of all children in detention centers: "Many are being held in confined and overcrowded spaces with inadequate access to nutrition, health care and hygiene services—conditions that are highly conducive to the spread of diseases like COVID-19. An outbreak in one of these facilities could happen at any moment."[13] And research by the Yale University School of Medicine urges that children shouldn't be "detained for a long time or separated from their families," at least in part because "in addition to the already high risk for traumatic impact of parental separation, the coronavirus pandemic creates additional burdens and distress, exacerbated by fears about their own health and safety and that of parents and family members they have little or no contact with."[14]

Finding the most horrifying way to respond to this situation, the United States has implemented a policy of immediate expulsion, which denies all migrants, including children, due process and access to asylum law. The US government is positioning this policy as a public health initiative to protect Americans from COVID-19, but experts say that there is "no public health sense behind" this policy that "categorically targets one particular group who is not anymore at likelihood to essentially spread COVID-19 than other groups."[15] Yet children as young as 8 months are being expelled from the border, often alone, not knowing if they will be reunited with family.

This brazen inconsistency—between willingly putting children and families at risk with "Back to School" orders and claiming that immediate expulsion of children without due process and the protection of asylum law is due to health concerns—exposes the political reality of childhood under necrocapitalism today, where the lives of our children are lanced in multidirectional ways against us in class war.[16] We refuse to entertain the foolishness of anti-natalist attitudes and philosophy, a stark foolishness when we consider the legacy of American imperialism and how it has targeted the children of the oppressed to disappear us from the world. Childcare is indeed a radical act, and the care of all our children, at schools and in cages in detention centers, must be connected in our political program and platform as revolutionaries.

NOTES TO CHAPTER 16

1. Molly Hensley-Clancy and Caroline O'Donovan, "The truth behind a viral picture of a school re-opening" (https://www.buzzfeednews.com/article/mollyhensley-clancy/georgia-school-reopening-photo-paulding-county).

2. Mary Elliot and Jazmine Hughes, "Four hundred years after enslaved Africans were brought to Virginia ..." (https://www.nytimes.com/interactive/2019/08/19/magazine/history-slavery-smithsonian.html).

3. Ibid.

4. Baptist, *The Half Has Never Been Told*, 421.

5. Dunbar-Ortiz, *An Indigenous Peoples' History of the United States*, 151.

6. Ibid.

7. Mary Annette Pember, "Death by civilization" (https://www.theatlantic.com/education/archive/2019/03/traumatic-legacy-indian-boarding-schools/584293/).

8. Taté Walker, "The horrifying legacy of Indian boarding schools hasn't ended" (https://everydayfeminism.com/2015/10/indian-boarding-school-legacy/).

9. Veracini, *Settler Colonialism*, 35.

10. Ibid., 37.

11. Dunn, *The Militarization of the US-Mexico Border*, 46–47.

12. Amanda Holpuch and Lauren Gambino, "Why are families being separated at the border" (https://www.theguardian.com/us-news/2018/jun/18/why-are-families-being-separated-at-the-us-border-explainer)

13. "Children in detention are at heightened risk of contracting COVID-19" (https://www.unicef.org/press-releases/children-detention-are-heightened-risk-contracting-covid-19-and-should-be-released).

14. Alexa Tomassi, "Children are at higher risk for COVID-19 infection in border detention facilities" (https://medicine.yale.edu/news-article/24019/).

15. Reynaldo Leaños Jr., "COVID-19 at the border" (https://www.houstonpublicmedia.org/articles/news/border/2020/07/28/378675/covid-19-at-the-border-unprecedented-use-of-law-expels-migrants-as-quickly-as-possible/).

16. It is important to remember that bourgeois law,
including international human rights law and asylum
laws, is not the be-all-and-end-all of justice, and certainly
not the end goal of communist approaches to these topics.
Revolutionaries can use bourgeois law to both expose
the hypocrisy of the bourgeois classes and to strategically
win temporary reforms to advance the goals of the proletariat, but we harbor no illusions as to the revolutionary
potential of reforming or advancing bourgeois law as an
ultimate goal.

CHAPTER SEVENTEEN

VIRAL ATOMIZATION
AND THE FAMILY

THE PANDEMIC HAS FORCED US TO CONFRONT THE violence built into our socio-economic system, which ultimately does not care in the slightest for the well-being of children. The question of children must force us to also confront a classic issue of Marxist and feminist inquiry: the family.

Prior to the pandemic taking the world by storm, much attention had begun to be devoted to the question of the family within Marxist writing. The work of Sophie Lewis, whose book *Full Surrogacy Now* was released in 2019, has continued to generate buzz around the question of the family, with far-right pundits like Tucker Carlson fear-mongering about the Marxist plan to destroy the family. In this sense, the attempt to smear Marxism with a wholly negative and destructive view of social formations seeks to appeal to the view of Marxists as the bomb-throwing anarchist or agitator intent only on the destruction of the world as we know it.

As such rhetoric ramps up as a way to smear those who have taken to the streets to demand justice, we ought to take the time to analyze the ways in which the pandemic has forced the issue of the family to the forefront of our current social situation. We must also analyze the ways in which Marxism can point towards another possibility, another futurity, beyond the horizons of the capitalist imaginary, which constrains our very notion of possibility.

In the *Communist Manifesto*, Marx introduces the notion of the abolition of the family when he writes,

> Abolition of the family! Even the most rad-
> ical flare up at this infamous proposal of the
> Communists. On what foundation is the
> present family, the bourgeois family, based?
> On capital, on private gain. In its completely
> developed form, this family exists only among
> the bourgeoisie.[1]

Marx here notes that this claim, that the communists seek to abolish the family, is itself a way of creating derision towards the Marxist position, while also pointing out a crucial hypocrisy among those who would choose to attack Marxists for this position. Marx points out that the bourgeois ideal of the family is a reality only for the bourgeoisie themselves, and from this we can actually uncover a critique of the way in which capitalism is itself materially incompatible with the ideals of the family that it claims to defend. The conditions of proletarianization are in fact the source of the destruction of the utopian view of the bourgeois family, because the realities of proletarian life are incompatible with such a family. Marx and Engels write:

> The bourgeois clap-trap about the family and
> education, about the hallowed co-relation
> of parents and child, becomes all the more

disgusting, the more, by the action of Modern Industry, all the family ties among the proletarians are torn asunder, and their children transformed into simple articles of commerce and instruments of labour.[2]

It is, after all, the conditions of capitalism that would transform children from loved members of a family into economic instruments who will also sell their own labor. It is capitalism that forced parents to choose between time with their children and time laboring for a meager wage. It is capitalism that has itself chipped away at some idealized vision of the family and that has created conditions that preclude the possibility for any sort of proletarian family.

While much has changed since 1848, the conditions of the present pandemic can call attention to the extent to which the capitalist construction of family relations has become a source of crisis. The problem posed by the rapidly approaching school year is a problem that is produced by a failure of capitalist social relations to construct a viable family model for the vast majority of individuals who are outside of the capitalist class itself. For working parents, there are real reasons to hope for the opening of schools; working parents can hardly supervise children doing school from home if they are working outside of the home. Capitalism, in its attempts to give the workers the bare minimum needed to get by, has created the conditions of partially socialized education for children, allowing some of the work of education and care to be undertaken through public schools. Of course, this is not a communist socialization of care wherein the community itself shares responsibilities for care, but rather a concession that the capitalists had to make in order to ensure that they could have a captive workforce. As we approach the school year, many parents who have managed to somehow still hold on to work are faced with the prospect of choosing between work or educating their children at home. This is, of course, an impossible decision. Sending children back to school is a death sentence for many, but giving up income during this time can represent a more slow and insidious path to financial ruin.

Here we see the failure of the capitalist approach to care and the family. For the rich it is possible to take time from work and oversee the home education of their children, to have only a single source of income, to have access to the idealized heterosexual vision of the nuclear family. The stable family, a calm amidst the storm of a chaotic world, is only possible for the bourgeoisie under the best of times; during a pandemic this possibility is foreclosed to the masses, and the violence of that foreclosure is brought to the surface for all to see. Once the meager forms of social care that capitalism has allowed us begin to collapse, we see how much the possibility of the bourgeois family is denied to the workers. The disruption to the school system calls our attention to a form of familial violence which precedes this pandemic and is endemic to capitalist relations overall. Capitalism has destroyed the possibility of the family for the workers, and it has not offered any real alternatives.

This outbreak has also exacerbated things by creating a more intense form of social atomization; although again, such atomization predates COVID-19 and is built into the core of capitalist social relations and ideology. Social distancing has isolated us within our own homes in a rather dramatic fashion, but the capitalist notion of the family had already laid the groundwork for this arrangement long before we faced this virus. The concept of the nuclear family as the core unit of capitalist society has been tied together with a whole host of ideological appeals to familial autonomy. While the family is made up of multiple individuals, the unit itself is still regarded as an individual cell in such a way that it does not disrupt capitalist notions of individuality in the slightest, leaving the neoliberal Margaret Thatcher to declare that "there is no such thing as society. There are individual men and women and there are families." Thus the forms of distancing and atomized isolation we see now have always existed and have always been built into capitalist notions of the family. This atomization becomes particularly problematic during times of acute crisis, as it ensures that the forms of communal care amongst neighbors that could be necessary for working families to weather this storm are in fact precluded, because the aforementioned ideology of familial individualism has stopped connections of care and kinship beyond the nuclear family from being formed. Now is the time that many are wishing they knew their neighbors better, that they had some sort of support system beyond the immediate family, because once again capitalism is demonstrating that this idealized vision of the family is impossible for the vast majority of people who labor for a living.

The capitalist notion of the family has always been corrupt and hypocritical. Capitalism has always sought to mobilize a surface-level defense of "family values" from agitators and anarchists, while simultaneously eroding the possibility for such families to exist among the working class. The capitalists have always talked out of both sides of their mouth. Now here we are, in the midst of a historic crisis on a global scale, and the rot and decay of the capitalist family now confronts us head on. We see just how minimal the socialized care allowed by capitalist society really is, and we see how once it is imperilled, proletarian families are forced to make impossible decisions that put their very existence at risk. We see the individualism of capitalism leaving us with neighborhoods where on the one hand all are trapped in their houses away from others, but on the other most would not be communally interacting even if the pandemic were not here.

Pandemics are a collective sort of crisis. They confront us with the need for actions that individuals or individual families cannot possibly undertake. It is for this reason that they call our attention to the failures of a socially atomized society. And so, when reactionaries rally around the notion of getting the children back to school and of protecting family values, we can see the hypocrisy behind these appeals. When those advocating for something better are accused of wanting to destroy the family, we can insist that the only version of the family that capitalism has provided is not worth defending, and we can show that this pandemic has made that reality quite clear. We demand not merely the abolition of the present state of things, but the construction of an alternative.

It is tempting, in this moment, to try to point to the resurgence of mutual aid and other forms of communal organizing as the solution to these problems. Those who defend a prefigurative approach to politics often argue that we are building the alternative to the nuclear family in the here and now when we create these forms of care that transcend the nuclear family and create a connected and collective sense of mutual responsibility. While these forms of organizing may indeed propagandistically call attention to the failures of the nuclear family and its individualized regime of care, they do not replace it or do away with it based merely on their existence. Such organizing is crucial, but it is not enough. The capitalist notion of the family, which claims to defend the needs of children while demanding that they die from a horrific virus so that the economy can keep functioning, is built into the very core of ideological understandings of society and is reinforced materially through capitalist social relations.

What we need to draw attention to is not only the ways in which current organizing efforts can propagandize a new possible future, but also the extent to which truly equitable socialized care that moves beyond the nuclear family and reactionary homophobic ideas about reproduction is incompatible with capitalist relations more broadly. Capitalism itself has made the possibility of the bourgeois family only available to the few while providing no alternative family structure for the masses, leaving them to face impossible decisions and constant states of crisis. The pandemic then forces us to see not just how children are endangered by the capitalist and settler state, but also the ways in which the very social unit tasked with the care of children functions as a complete failure. Another possibility for care is out there, somewhere beyond the horizons of the capitalist imaginary, and we must continue to struggle for it. If a futurity is possible, if the lives of the children of the most marginalized and exploited are worth fighting for, then we must fight back against every reactionary appeal to the children and the family that would seek to pacify struggle.

NOTES TO CHAPTER 17

1. Marx and Engels, "The Communist Manifesto," *MECW*, vol. 8, 501.

2. Ibid., 502.

CHAPTER EIGHTEEN

MIGRANT LABOR IN THE PANDEMIC

IN IMPERIALIST COUNTRIES SUCH AS CANADA AND the United States, the entrance of bourgeois and petty-bourgeois women into the paid workforce has resulted in a phenomenon that some feminists have dubbed the "care deficit." In the absence of a robust welfare state that can provide child and elder care, and with the majority of unpaid household labor and care work still shouldered by women in most families,[1] women in the workforce has meant that a gap has opened up in the home. Never mind that many bourgeois women did not actually participate in the majority of the household labor during earlier iterations of capitalism or under feudalism—deferring much of the burden to maids, nannies, and house slaves—or that most working-class women have always had to labor outside of the home, as these maids and nannies as well as in the factories, mines, and fields.

During the brief years of economic prosperity in imperialist countries following World War II, the "privilege" of staying in the home was extended to middle and upper-middle class women of the working class, especially white women who were idealized as perfect wives and mothers in popular culture. When white liberal feminists began critiquing women's exclusion from institutions of higher education and the workforce, their lack of historical materialist analysis meant that they took their particular experience at one moment in history and in the imperialist center as the universal experience for all women throughout history and across cultures. Thus, access to birth control and abortion were prioritized as *the* struggle for women's reproductive freedom, while issues of forced or coerced sterilization of Indigenous, Black, and disabled women were completely neglected, at best, and even advocated for by some feminists as a solution to broader social problems such as poverty. Similarly, the rights of bourgeois women to engage in "sex work" by choice took precedence as *the* struggle for women's sexual freedom over the experiences of Indigenous, migrant, and trans women of color who were (and are increasingly) trafficked or economically coerced into a violent and exploitative industry. Moreover, the white and bourgeois biases of a liberal feminist analysis have meant that as increasing numbers of women made their way into the paid work force, liberal feminism failed to provide a solution to the care deficit that did not rely upon further exploitation and oppression.

As a result, the imperialist bourgeois family has become dependent upon migrant labor regimes. White bourgeois women are able to work outside of the home in professional and management positions, while migrant women raise their children and clean up around the house and migrant men take care of the landscaping and gardening. This is not a contradiction in the mind of the liberal feminist, for whom individual empowerment and success are the end goals of the feminist movement. A woman in the White House or as the minister of finance, a female CEO or "boss babe," are the symbolic victories that liberal feminists valorize over and above the collective struggle

for women's emancipation. For liberal feminists, collective struggles against women's oppression and exploitation
are less important than empowering individual women to
live their best lives. As Sakai reminds us in *Settlers: The
Mythology of the White Proletariat*, "it is the absolute
characteristic of settler society to be parasitic, dependent
upon the super-exploitation of oppressed peoples for its
styles of life."[2] What is true for settler society as a whole
is also true of white settler liberal feminism, whose "victories" in breaking the glass ceiling have been achieved by
standing on the backs of migrant and racialized women.

The working conditions of the women who work in
the homes of the bourgeoisie are notoriously terrible and
have only gotten worse as the pandemic exposes exactly
which workers are considered disposable. In the early days
of COVID-19, nannies and maids working for bourgeois
American families, largely racialized and migrant women,
were laid off from their employment suddenly and without warning.[3] For undocumented migrant women, "working under the table" means that employers were already
able to pay below minimum wage and exploit them for
long hours; now pandemic layoffs mean that, in many
cases, they cannot access official unemployment insurance or government relief. Furthermore, because of the
relatively sudden imposition of COVID measures, many
nannies were let go without the chance to say goodbye to
the children they had invested so much emotional energy
and labor into. Meanwhile, others were asked to continue
a relationship with the children without pay, via online
outlets like Skype, because they are "like family" and the
children understandably miss them. As of June 29th, the

New York Times reported that over 20 nannies in New York City, mostly older migrant women from Caribbean countries, had died of the coronavirus.[4]

In Canada, many nannies are in the country on temporary foreign worker visas that tie them to one particular employer and contract. That there is a separate immigration category (formerly known as the Live-In Caregiver Program) for this group of laborers is indicative of how foundational this exploitation is to the participation of bourgeois and petty-bourgeois women in the Canadian economy. In early 2020, some of these Canadian families employing temporary foreign workers irresponsibly continued to travel internationally, with their nannies in tow to look after their children, despite the looming pandemic and border closures leading to several non-citizen nannies being trapped in countries like Mexico and the United Arab Emirates. Other nannies have been forced to live with their employers in times of social distancing, leading to a resurgence of the abusive and exploitative live-in conditions that migrant women's organizations in Canada fought for years to eliminate from the Live-In Caregiver Program. Trapped in their employers' homes, these women are often roped into working around the clock without overtime pay because, once again, being "like family" means being exploitable for unpaid labor at any time of day or night.[5] Being "like family" can also mean being subjected to the sexualized and patriarchal violence, harassment, and abuse that are commonplace in many families.

While the entire immigration system in imperialist settler countries like Canada is based on the exploitation of labor, migrant women working as nannies and caretakers are able to be intensely exploited as *temporary* workers, rather than economic immigrants who are granted Permanent Residency, because the government has labeled this work as "unskilled." This labor is seen as unskilled precisely because it has been feminized and essentialized as a natural function of women's bodies by bourgeois patriarchal ideology. Indeed, many of the Filipina women working as nannies in Canada and other imperialist countries have high levels of education and training as nurses—a situation the government authorities in Spain were happy to exploit by granting temporary permission for these women to work as nurses rather than nannies when the pandemic hit and health-care workers were urgently needed.[6]

However, in-home care work, while making up a large portion of the work performed by temporary migrants in countries like Canada, is not the only type of employment that migrant and undocumented workers are concentrated into. As noted in an earlier chapter, migrant workers are over-concentrated in nursing and personal support work in Canada and the United States, Filipina nurses making up approximately one third of foreign-trained nurses in both countries.[7] In Canada, where the majority of COVID deaths have been associated with Long Term Care Homes, it is also important to point out the concentration of temporary foreign workers who work in these homes. But these are not the only migrants working in Long Term Care. Disturbingly, asylum seekers who are in the country awaiting their hearings at the Immigration and Refugee Board are also overly concentrated as workers in these homes. One can only imagine the horrors faced by these workers who have fled war, persecution, and right-wing paramilitary violence only to end up laboring in institutions of death. After months of activist push-back, the Canadian government "generously" offered a "pathway to citizenship" for an extremely narrow portion of asylum seekers (approximately 1,000) working as personal support workers in long-term care homes, to the exclusion of those working other essential jobs, such as food processing, factory work, or even other jobs at long-term care homes such as security guards.[8]

In Canada, temporary foreign workers also perform the bulk of seasonal farm labor. In both Canada and the United States, the mythology of the settler farmer who works tirelessly on his own small plot of land is deeply foundational to the national imaginary,[9] and so the labor of all the people necessary to the functioning of even a small "family" farm has been overshadowed and disavowed by this mythological figure. In Canada there are also major marketing campaigns by agribusiness lobbying groups that have shaped our perceptions of everything from dairy farming to egg farming to the production of Alberta beef as being the product of the local (white) family farm rather than big business. But it is not modest family farms that make up the bulk of the $111.9 billion Canadian agribusiness sector. Major farming corporations such as the Scotlynn Group and Greenhill are only able to generate their massive revenues (over $73.88 million in the case of Scotlynn) and expand their operations at an impressive rate because they rely so heavily upon seasonal migrant labor.[10] During the COVID-19 pandemic,

Canadian farmers have continued to import seasonal farm labor despite the border closures that affect other temporary workers, such as the nannies trapped abroad by their employers' family vacation. Horrific living and working conditions for migrant workers on Canadian farms led to thousands of migrant farm workers testing positive for COVID-19. It also led to the preventable death of three workers: 31-year-old Bonifacio Eugenio Romero, 24-year-old Rogelio Munoz Santos, and 55-year-old Juan Lopez Chaparro.[11]

But worker deaths are nothing new to Canada's farming industry in recent years. In 2012, a van transporting 13 migrant workers from Nicaragua and Peru collided with a truck in Hampstead, Ontario, killing ten of the men inside, and in 2014, worker Ivan Guerrero drowned while trying to fix a leak near his bunk house in Ormstown, Quebec.[12] Sheldon McKenzie, a Jamaican worker in Leamington, Ontario, died after suffering a severe head injury on the job in 2015, and Zenaida, a worker from Mexico whose last name remains unknown, was killed in a hit and run in Niagara last year.

The dangerous working conditions and extreme exploitation facing farm laborers is built into the very immigration system in Canada. Due to their temporary status, these workers are unable to access benefits such as health care or employment insurance (EI) despite paying into them, and during COVID-19 are ineligible for the Canada Emergency Response Benefit (CERB) offered to other Canadian workers if they are forced to quarantine. These workers also lack many basic protections, such as minimum wage laws, overtime pay, time off, and the right to collective bargaining. Because their temporary status in the country is tied to their employer they are subject to deportation if they quit or are fired. As a result, many workers are coerced into silence in the face of even the gravest violations of labor law. Already, multiple workers have faced deportation for asserting their rights during COVID. Erika Zavala and Jesus Molina were deported to Mexico in July for inviting two migrant rights activists to speak with them at their employer-provided housing in Kelowna, British Columbia.[13] Their employer claimed that this action was in violation of their strict no-visitor policy due to the pandemic, but Zavala and Molina stated that the activists, their friends, were delivering work clothing and culturally appropriate food, which their employer had neglected to provide. Another anonymous Mexican worker in Leamington, Ontario, was threatened with deportation after injuring his head in the bunk house and calling the Mexican consulate for help filling out a workplace accident report.[14] Yet another worker, Luis Gabriel Flores, was fired from his employment and threatened with deportation after he spoke to the media about his working and living conditions.[15] Flores tested positive with COVID-19 after several of his bunk mates also caught the virus and one, Chaparro, died. Flores spoke out anonymously to the media and told them that the living conditions on the farm made it impossible to social distance. He also told them that even after Chaparro and other workers started demonstrating symptoms of the disease, the employer continued to make them work and was slow to take action and get testing for the workers. By the time testing was granted, 199 workers on the farm run by Scottlyn Group had contracted COVID-19.

The treatment of migrant farm workers during a pandemic has been so atrocious that even the Canadian health minister Patty Hajdu has called it "a national disgrace."[16] Rather than granting permanent status to migrant workers, however—a move that would allow them the protections to assert their rights—the Liberal government instead responded by giving $59 million directly to employers, who we are meant to trust to spend this money on proper social distancing and other safety measures for workers. The government also promised more farm inspections, but since the beginning of the pandemic, farm inspections have been "virtual" and always by appointment, giving the employers the discretion to show only what they want to show. What have employers done to inspire such trust? According to a report compiled by the Migrant Workers Alliance for Change (MWAC), wage theft is commonplace in the industry and they were able to confirm reports of over $57,369.46 stolen from workers in the form of deductions and unpaid wages.[17] In particular, many workers have reported that employers have refused to pay them during the mandatory two-week quarantine period when they enter the country. For low-wage workers, missing even two weeks of pay means facing starvation and mounting debt. During this same quarantine period, over 539 workers reported inadequate access to food and 160 reported an inability to social distance in the employer-provided living arrangements. Once the quarantine was completed, MWAC reports that the living conditions worsened significantly for a number of workers. Indeed, a number of YouTube videos showing inadequate living conditions on farms have been shared by migrant rights organizations such as Justicia for Migrant Workers. Those who have contracted the virus are often not paid for the time they are sick.

Most egregiously, the Ontario government has released a plan for migrant farm workers that allows them to continue working even if they are COVID positive, as long as they are asymptomatic. Other employers across the country have infringed on the basic rights of their workers by pressuring them into signing agreements where they agree not to leave the farm and to allow their employer to use their wages to provide food and other provisions for them. The option for migrant workers is to sign the document or to face firing and thus deportation. The same restrictions, including the restrictions on visitors that led to Zavala and Molina's deportation, are not being placed on Canadian workers. Other egregious cases of differential treatment have been reported to MWAC, such as the case of migrant workers at Ontario Plants Propagation, who were asked to unpack a major shipment of plants from an American farm with a confirmed COVID outbreak while their Canadian co-workers were given the day off. For this risky work the laborers were paid an extra $2 per hour, bringing their wages for the day to a generous total of $8 per hour. Within a few days, cases of COVID-19 were present at Ontario Plants Propagation. Workers have also reported increased surveillance, intimidation, and threats from employers, and some have even had private security guards placed at their bunkhouses to control and monitor their movements. These facts make it obvious that the COVID measures put in place on Canadian farms are meant to protect Canadians from contracting the virus from migrant workers but not to protect the workers themselves.

Temporary migrant workers are also concentrated in meat and fish plants across the country. Cargill and JBS meat-packing plants in Alberta have been responsible for major outbreaks, comprising up to 30% (1,400 cases) of total cases in the province.[18] It is also estimated that between half and three-quarters of their employees are migrant workers. In April, Bui Thi Hiep, a Cargill worker originally from Vietnam, died of COVID-19, and two more deaths have been linked to the JBS plant. In New Brunswick, fisheries owners afraid they would not have access to their usual seasonal migrant workers hired children as young as 13 to work in their plants processing fish and lobsters.[19] By resorting to child labor the employers here have exposed the true function of the Temporary Foreign Worker Program. Although there are many adult workers out of work due to COVID-19, the plants are unable to attract them because the wages are below the measly rate offered by Employment Insurance and the CERB benefit. In the first volume of *Capital*, Marx spends a considerable amount of time elucidating the ways in which child labor is used by the bourgeoisie to drive down wages and to maintain a relatively docile workforce.[20] Similarly, the Temporary Foreign Worker Program, with its lack of rights and protections as well as the constant threat of deportation hanging over workers' heads, is designed to keep wages low and the rate of exploitation high.

In *Settlers*, Sakai details the multiple ways in which the white American working class has been treated as privileged over and above migrant, racialized, and Indigenous workers, who have in turn been relegated to the most dangerous, lowest paying jobs. By standing on the backs of this "Third World" workforce, the white working class has been able to form a labor aristocracy and has at times achieved wages and working conditions impossible for most workers in other parts of the world.[21] The "privileges of belonging to the oppressor nation"[22] have often been enough to encourage a "petit-bourgeois consciousness that was unable to rise above reformism" in the white working class.[23] As Sakai writes, "it was only possible for settler society to afford the best-paid, most bourgeoisified white work force because they had also obtained the least-paid, most proletarian Afrikan colony to support it."[24] And while many things have changed since the times of the slave economy—slavery has been reformed into the for-profit prison-industrial-complex, globalization and imperialism have exported many of the most dangerous and lowest paid jobs to the Global South, and the multiple recessions of recent decades have meant the shrinking of the middle class and the impoverishment of some segments of the white working class in the United States and Canada—it remains true that the worst paying, most dangerous, most precarious work in these countries is reserved for racialized workers who are often migrants, undocumented people, or asylum seekers. Furthermore, the immigration system in imperialist countries like Canada has been deliberately designed to "respond to the labor market" by creating entire groups of workers who lack access to the legal rights and protections granted to citizens.

It is imperative then that communist efforts to organize the working class in settler countries like Canada and the

United States focus extensive attention on this group of ultra-exploited and oppressed workers. As J. Moufawad-Paul is apt to point out in *A Critique of Maoist Reason*, these efforts necessitate the leadership of a revolutionary proletarian party.[25] The ultra-precarious, and by design temporary, position of temporary migrant workers means that organizing must often take place clandestinely[26] and not through a traditional union drive, since temporary foreign workers lack access to collective bargaining rights in Canada anyway. As Moufawad-Paul goes on to explain, because this and other sectors of the working class are made precarious, and because their work is often temporary even if they are citizens, the politically advanced elements of the working class will necessarily be drawn from disparate industries and job sites.[27] It is only through the revolutionary proletarian party, then, that the working class can find political unity in this context. As the COVID-19 pandemic intensifies this pre-existing exploitation and leads inevitably to the death and illness of countless workers who lack even basic protection under the law, the necessity for this type of mass organizing led by a revolutionary party is more urgent than ever.

NOTES TO CHAPTER 18

1. While this is certainly the case in a majority of heterosexual and nuclear families, we should not imagine that the phenomenon is neatly confined to the state-sanctioned unions of "the straights," as the queer youth

of the internet like to call them. Indeed, the same patterns are often replicated and reproduced in a myriad of ways in families that extend beyond the nuclear model—in poly families of all sorts and even within queer chosen families, where home and care labor remain feminized to a large extent.

2. Sakai, *Settlers*, 8.

3. Emily Bobrow, "For nannies, both a job and a family can abruptly disappear" (https://www.nytimes.com/2020/06/29/parenting/nannies-job-virus.html).

4. Ibid.

5. Marites Sison, "Filipino migrant workers in Canada worry about jobs" (https://www.rappler.com/world/us-canada/filipino-migrant-workers-canada-concerns-coronavirus-covid-19-pandemic).

6. Ethel Tungohan, "Filipino healthcare workers during COVID-19 and the importance of race-based analysis" (https://www.broadbentinstitute.ca/filipino_healthcare_workers_during_covid19_and_the_importance_of_race_based_analysis).

7. Ibid.

8. Colin Harris, "Some asylum seekers who cared for patients in pandemic to get permanent residency" (https://www.cbc.ca/news/canada/montreal/asylum-seekers-guardian-angels-covid-19-permanent-residency-1.5686176).

9. Sakai, *Settlers*, 8.

10. Migrant Workers Alliance For Change, "Unheeded warnings: COVID-19 & migrant workers in Canada" (https://migrantworkersalliance.org/wp-content/uploads/2020/06/Unheeded-Warnings-COVID19-and-Migrant-Workers.pdf)

11. Carmen Wong, "Migrant worker on Norfolk County farm who died of COVID-19 identified" (https://kitchener.ctvnews.ca/migrant-worker-on-norfolk-county-farm-who-died-of-covid-19-identified-1.4993736).

12. Edward Dunsworth, "Canadians have farmed out tragedy to the migrant workers who provide food" (https://www.theglobeandmail.com/opinion/article-canadians-have-farmed-out-tragedy-onto-the-migrant-workers-who-provide/).

13. Hilary Beaumont, "Coronavirus sheds light on Canada's poor treatment of migrant workers" (https://www.theguardian.com/world/2020/jul/20/canada-migrant-farm-workers-coronavirus).

14. Migrant Workers Alliance For Change, "Unheeded warnings" (op. cit.).

15. Alexandra Mae Jones and Molly Thomas, "Migrant worker who got COVID-19 says he was fired from Ontario farm for speaking out" (https://www.ctvnews.ca/canada/migrant-worker-who-got-covid-19-says-he-was-fired-from-ontario-farm-for-speaking-out-1.5046484).

16. Kelsey Johnson, "Mistreatment of migrant farm workers amid COVID-19 a 'national disgrace'"

(https://globalnews.ca/news/7113934/
canada-migrant-farm-workers-covid-19/)

17. Migrant Workers Alliance For Change, "Unheeded
warnings" (op. cit.).

18. Omar Mosleh, "These meat plant workers came to
Canada for a better life" (https://www.thestar.com/news/
canada/2020/04/29/these-meat-plant-workers-came-
to-canada-for-a-better-life-their-kids-worry-theyll-be-
infected-with-covid-19-at-work.html).

19. Callum Smith, "NB students as young as 13 fill
lobster processing jobs" (https://globalnews.ca/
news/6956295/coronavirus-n-b-s-student-lobster-jobs/).

20. I write "relatively docile" because although children
have always had less (or no) access to legal rights and
protections in the workplace and in general, we should
not imagine that children are without a proletarian consciousness and unable to organize themselves as workers.
Indeed, the large newsie strikes in the late 1800s in New
York City were organized and led entirely by working-class children. The fact remains that child workers
have historically and continue to experience intense
exploitation and oppression at the hands of employers
because of their lack of legal protections and because of
the uneven power relations between adults and children
in general.

21. Sakai, *Settlers*, 27.

22. Ibid., 13.

23. Ibid., 27.

24. Ibid., 13.

25. Moufawad-Paul, *Critique of Maoist Reason*, 95.

26. Ibid., 96.

27. Ibid., 97.

CHAPTER NINETEEN

THE IRRECONCILABLE

AND SO, THE PROTRACTED CIVIL WAR THAT CHARAC-
terizes class society, particularly the general antagonism of
capitalism, continues unabated even in times of pandemic.
This moment of emergency, as we have seen, simply
changes the intensity of the general antagonism. In some
regions—in some countries, at some levels within countries—policy functions to mute the antagonism through
an appeal to nationalism and health. In other spaces the
civil war becomes more acute, as the rebellions demonstrated. The situation of migrant labor, which we just discussed, is evidence of how this type of labor—essential to
imperial capitalism—continues to demonstrate that class
struggle is ongoing. The depredations migrant workers
already face are only exacerbated by the pandemic, just
as the conditions faced by illegal immigrants and refugees
have been exacerbated. As we noted, it was not as if the
condition of migrant labor was particularly humane before
the pandemic; rather, the fact of the pandemic revealed the
already-existing predatory and necrocapitalist characteristics of migrant labor. As we asserted at the outset, "every
capitalist state's necrotic underbelly is being exposed."

Despite this exposure, however, what makes capitalism
thoroughly necrotic is its ability to continue to profit even
when its violence is exposed and to weather the crisis by
reshuffling the economy so as to push its necrocapitalist

aspects upon its most vulnerable subjects. The fact that bourgeois and petty-bourgeois families can comfortably weather this crisis through migrant labor regimes indicates that the upper strata of class society are able to treat the pandemic like a holiday while their domestic, landscape, and agricultural workers are even more exposed to death. They can even comfortably afford personal educators, when necessary, like Roman patricians employing slave tutors.

Moreover, the economy is being reshuffled. Large corporations that can afford to persist throughout the crisis are instituting new austerity measures while preparing to take over the spaces lost by the small capitalists crushed by pandemic measures. Agribusiness continues unabated as migrants are still shipped in, safety concerns waived since these workers—not white and/or not citizens—have never been worthy of rights to health and equal pay. New security measures for the police are being rushed in, and neoliberal plans for job discipline are becoming normalized. Imperialist warfare and neocolonial extraction continue unabated, generating super-profits. At the beginning of July 2020 the stock market was higher than it had been for twenty years.

The adage that COVID-19 has been a "social equalizer"—oft-repeated by liberals, based on the abstraction that anyone can potentially contract the virus—is about as meaningful as claiming everyone has a fair chance to "make it" under capitalism. It is another platitude generated from a bourgeois vision of society as a contract between equal individuals, which the three-ring circus of the recent Democratic National Convention wants us to embrace as an alternative to the Trump regime's open embrace of inequality. It's largely another version of "Make America Great Again" but based on the liberal mythology of the US where greatness is in everyone getting a fair chance, a veritable Rawlsian utopia. Joe Biden's senile neoliberalism and Kamala Harris's carceral capitalism are openly celebrated as alternatives to "Trumpism." Elizabeth Warren was lauded by the podcast "Pod Save America" for having "BLM" spelled out in children's toy blocks in the background of her video: "We see you Liz," they tweeted, authoritatively recognizing her as a champion of Black Lives Matter despite being a podcast comprised of white cis men.[1] Alexandra Ocasio-Cortez, once seen as a great hope for social democratic renewal, tried to bring the corpse of the Sanders campaign back to life with appeals to social justice the Democratic mainstream cared nothing about. And Colin Powell, former member of the Bush Jr. regime, was given more time than Ocasio-Cortez in order to demonstrate that the Democratic Party of 2020 was angling to look like the Republicans of 2001. All of this in the wake of mass rebellions. All of this despite the imperialism that generates, along with ruined countries and lives, refugees and migrant labor regimes. All of this to provide an alternative to so-called "Trumpism," which is wagered as the prime evil rather than the violent necro-capitalist context in which the politically useless (but not useless in the *policy* and *policing* sense of politics) electoral spectacle plays out.

While it is the case that the pandemic has shed light on the predatory aspects of capitalism—that it has revealed the sham "think of the children" and "family values" discourses for what they are, that it has demonstrated the outright cruelty of labor exploitation that openly exposes the most vulnerable workers to disease, and that it has continued to profit greatly—official ideologues continue to generate the same garbage they blathered before the pandemic, though one senses an almost desperate tone in their proclamations. The likes of Charlie Kirk state without irony that center-right liberals are akin to Marxists. Liberals imagine that their regimes are rational calls to order and that to refuse to endorse even their most carceral representatives is to support a fascist alternative. Charlatans like James Lindsay write books about a social justice conspiracy that has taken over liberal society—and yet these books, which cannot even represent their subject material accurately,[2] are published by massive mainstream presses. Although we can look at these examples (and others) as proof that mainstream public intellectuals are, as a whole, unworthy of the name "intellectual" (they are willfully ignorant and/or opportunistic hucksters), the more salient point is that this entire faction of acceptable intellectual producers is struggling to convince their audiences that the only meaningful struggle is between the liberal and conservative wings of the bourgeoisie, or even between liberals and fascists, and that the third pole of struggle (anti-fascism, anti-capitalism, abolition, *communism*, etc.) is politically inadmissible, if not aberrant or "insane." The particular antagonism between capitalist siblings thus obscures the general antagonism between social classes.

Whereas some members of the liberal reptile press note the ills the pandemic has delivered upon, say, migrant workers, their analysis (following the class they represent) is that this is merely an exception to normal labor practices. The solution is an appeal to liberal rights, an appeal to humane labor practices, and blame is placed upon human error; management, which can be "good," was simply unprepared and did not have the resources to deal with the coronavirus. Hence, what the pandemic has in fact revealed as a deep problem with the system is blithely interpreted as a problem with the pandemic rather than with the system itself.[3] What the pandemic merely demonstrates is that, in the words of Jasbir Puar and yet again, "labor is an inverted form of warfare against a disposable population ensnared as laborers-consigned-to-having-an accident."[4] There were always other "accidents" that these "disposable" populations faced before COVID-19.

Hence, the general antagonism of class society is ignored in favor of a particular antagonism that conservatives ignore but that liberals claim they can fix: just get some more individual rights in there! But what anyone who has grasped the necrocapitalist aspects revealed by the pandemic must realize is that these depredations are not *exceptions* but are in fact novel normative developments of the bourgeois order. The violence inherent in migrant labor regimes (and other labor regimes) did not only manifest after the pandemic; the pandemic simply revealed the already existing violence of this facet of the protracted civil war. The COVID-related violence visited upon migrant workers is like the mustard gas released upon the trenches of World War I. While the ruling classes of the imperialist nations involved in the so-called "Great War" would eventually condemn the use of mustard gas but not the war itself (they still hold it up as sacrosanct and pretend it was identical to the Second World War's Allied fight against fascism when they cannot even agree on its meaning), revolutionaries understood that this war was essentially about bourgeois nations fighting over colonial territories while also being a war upon the international proletariat. (Lenin, Luxemburg, Connolly, and others walked out of the Second International when it endorsed this inter-imperialist monstrosity.) The horrendous use of mustard gas, then, was merely a violent epiphenomenal development of a war against the proletariat and colonized peoples. Violent COVID measures (meaning *lack* of protective measures) in these days of pandemic are thus the mustard gas that factions of the bourgeoisie roll out upon the hard core of the proletariat.

Liberal ideology thus approaches the pandemic as a problem that can be solved with individual responsibility, liberty and formal equality, and the rational agency of the bourgeois subject. Those economically privileged enough to work from home are seen as more responsible than those who must continue to work or starve, or whose work outside the home is necessary for the economy to continue functioning—who work long hours in a factory, whose children have to go back to a school system ill-prepared to meet the pandemic, and who often take crowded public transit to their sites of work. While liberal professions of "care" and "responsibility" are wagered as a panacea against a blithe reactionary attitude towards the pandemic, the same and similar platitudes have always been used to reify the protracted civil war. These platitudes are extended to the rebellions—both to the police and the

protesters. The police are chastised for being irresponsible or corrupt; their structural function as the repressive
manifestation of the bourgeois state, what Lenin called
"special armed bodies" of men and women, is ignored or
mockingly dismissed.[5] The protesters are exhorted to be
"responsible" in their protesting, as if this protesting were
akin to a debate amongst friends.

But this is precisely how liberalism and those largely
beholden to this kind of "common sense" way of seeing society react when faced with crisis. Before austerity
and alongside repressive measures, appeals to individual responsibility and rational citizenship abound. Class
struggle is denied; even worse, liberal ideologues proclaim
that any talk of this general antagonism is aberrant because
it is divisive in light of the social contract. Reactionaries,
on the other hand, openly engage with the protracted
civil war, though from a position that is complicit with
the capitalist state.[6] Hence, reactionary demands regarding
"bearing arms" are not treated as being in contradiction
with the state's monopoly of violence, but only against an
imagined state of affairs that would take away this right;
the right is conceived, in line with the settler logic of the US,
as being part of a standing white militia that is a legitimate
addition to the police and army—which is why the pigs
are not threatened by armed NRA goons. (Indeed, Kyle
Rittenhouse, the seventeen-year-old fascist who murdered
activists in Kenosha, was a "police admirer" who was in
fact not stopped by the police but was allowed to depart
the scene after having gunned down several people.)
But since a hallmark of liberalism is, as aforementioned,
to deny the general antagonism by making it about a

particular antagonism between different ruling class factions, the discourse of reactionaries is treated as vulgar and irresponsible but no more irresponsible than any faction of the oppressed masses who would dare to pursue class struggle.

Whereas reactionaries want both the state and armed white militias to have a shared monopoly on violence (a vision going back to the early days of settler-colonialism, where every settler was part of a standing militia and where scalp-hunters and filibusters engendered state expansion into the frontiers), liberals want only the official state to possess this monopoly.

Despite this distinction between liberal and reactionary articulations of the capitalist state of affairs, it is worth noting that even reactionaries truly want to believe—even in the midst of openly proclaiming fidelity to the state's side of the protracted civil war—that Marxists, anarchists, communists, and "ANTIFA" are ruining an imaginary national unity. Even for reactionaries, the recognition of the general antagonism only goes so far; classical liberal discourse also affects their judgment when it comes to the state. A strong state, what they want to impose, will be one of *reconciliation* once it does away with the rabble who are responsible for conspiring to foment national disunity. The Nazi regime, we should recall, worked to deny the general antagonism of class struggle by propagating the myth of national unity supposedly undermined by Jewish conspirators, Roma, and other non-Aryan and communist rabble. The notion that the state reconciles individuals into a common (manifest) destiny, and that class antagonism is just a myth perpetuated by extremists and conspiratorial bad actors (by even a Russian conspiracy!), is a point upon which reactionaries and liberals agree. Here it is worth recalling Lenin's insights regarding the state:

> The state is the product and the manifestation of the *irreconcilability* of class antagonisms. The state arises when, where and to the extent that class antagonisms *cannot* be objectively reconciled. And, conversely, the existence of the state proves that class antagonisms *are* irreconcilable.[7]

Reactionary approaches to capitalist hegemony might unconsciously recognize this irreconcilable fact of this state—which is why the persistence of an armed white nationalist settler garrison manifests in settler-capitalist formations—but they consciously proclaim that the state is reconciliation, even if it is fascist. Liberalism openly denies this irreconcilability and imagines the state as a social contract where liberals and reactionaries can live together in familial harmony, denying the irreconcilable and general antagonism.

So our job remains, as we have maintained since the outset of this project, to remind our comrades, friends, and fellow travellers of the necessity to foreground the fact of the protracted civil war and the meaning of the general antagonism. To treat liberals and reactionaries as our enemies, for they are both invested in this pitiless state of affairs. To revolt against pacification. The revelations brought by the pandemic must be understood as revelations of capitalism's already existing necrotic nature, not as something that can be dismissed by the policy apparatus of capture, diverted into reformist liberal avenues.

The problem, however, is that the necrocapitalist reality has also generated a particular kind of subjectivity that, while accepting the truth of the system, leads to a practical dead-end. That is, necrocapitalism tends to generate nihilist subjects. With the general antagonism transformed into a particular antagonism between liberals and conservatives, without an organized mass movement to combat this diversionary transformation, people who see precisely the meaninglessness of the necrocapitalist reality accept that meaninglessness is a fact of nature. To recognize that the protracted civil war is a real general antagonism, to see that there is nothing to make this general antagonism into a meaningful movement, and to also witness the diversion of this antagonism into the spectacle of a fight between liberal and conservative wings of the ruling class results in a hopelessness. Especially when the ideologues of this diversion have hammered into our heads that there is no alternative, no future, and no history beyond capitalist foreclosure.

NOTES TO CHAPTER 19

1. https://twitter.com/PodSaveAmerica/status/1296270750114918401

2. Samuel Hoadley-Brill, "The cynical theorists behind cynical theories" (https://www.liberalcurrents.com/the-cynical-theorists-behind-cynical-theories/). Since that

book was written, James Lindsay has drifted closer and closer to the far right. After positioning himself as an authority on critical theory (and eventually critical race theory), despite having very little grasp on his object of critique, he has since been dog-whistling antisemitic and "great replacement" conspiracy theories.

3. Here it is also worth noting that the term "necro-capitalism" has started to appear with more frequency since we began this project but that its appearance has largely been according to the way we warned against: as a new phase of capitalism, as something more than just a novel conjunctural revelation of what capitalism always was. For example, in July 2020, Mark LeVine wrote an article entitled "From Neoliberalism to Necrocapitalism in 20 Years," which asserted that "necrocapitalism" represented a new phase of capitalism rather than a characteristic of what capitalism has always been that is merely being foregrounded in this conjuncture. Such analyses risk endorsing precisely what liberals have been saying since before the pandemic: that we are in an unprecedented economic reality and that every current problem of capitalist depredation is "new" rather than part of an ongoing necrotic capitalist project that is sim-ply being revealed for what it has always been. Perhaps LeVine could have learned a thing or two if he had paid attention to this project, or even the original usage(s) of the term "necrocapitalism" (Banerjee in 2008, Holmes in 2017), but it was clear he largely wanted to make a very bland intervention that was wagered as unique in the face of pandemic.

4. Puar, *The Right to Maim*, 64.

5. Lenin, *State and Revolution*, 11.

6. In *Austerity Apparatus*, J. Moufawad-Paul writes: "Indeed, both Mao Zedong and Carl Schmitt argued that a coherent political order begins by drawing a distinction between friends and enemies. To argue that this demonstrates a unity of thought between the radical communist and the nazi, however, is rather simplistic; all it demonstrates is that coherent political movements are able to grow in power by recognizing antagonistic and non-antagonistic relations—who to recruit, who not to recruit, who to oppose and isolate, who to support and reinforce. The similarity is only formal: a militant political order that wishes to come into being must understand who and what would oppose its emergence, the class basis of its ethics. The substantial differences beneath this formal similarity are more telling: the friend/enemy distinction of the fascist is precisely the distinction opposed by the communist and vice versa." (Moufawad-Paul, *Austerity Apparatus*, 104)

7. Lenin, *State and Revolution*, 8–9.

E: CAPTURE

September 4 2020–January 15 2021

CHAPTER TWENTY

ON THE SO-CALLED "ANTIFASCIST VOTE"

In 2017, in the midst of the Unite the Right mobilization in Charlottesville, Virginia, Cornel West gave an unequivocal defense of militant antifascism. In 2020 he tweeted: "An anti-fascist vote for Biden is in no way an affirmation of Neoliberal politics. In this sense, I agree with my brothers and sisters like Noam Chomsky, Angela Davis, Paul Street and Bob Avakian."[1]

However, there is no such thing as an "antifascist vote." Antifascism is a form of group praxis that embraces a diversity of tactics, which gain their force through organizing and demonstrating. The electoral process functions, by contrast, to fragment social movements and isolate their participants. Antifascism doesn't defeat fascism at the ballot box; the fight against fascism demands that we organize better than them.

In 1973, Jean-Paul Sartre published a short but controversial essay, "Elections: A Trap for Fools" (which is a polite rendering of the French "Élections, piège à cons"). A more conceptually, though not linguistically, accurate rendering would summarize Sartre's central contention: elections are a form of serial organization that prevents transformational or revolutionary praxis. Seriality is a form of reified social mediation that treats individuals in abstraction. We would argue, in terms momentarily borrowed from Harney and Moten, that fugitive forms of social life are serialized when, as Sartre writes, "large social forces—work conditions under the capitalist regime, private property, institutions, and so forth—bring pressure to bear upon groups they belong to, breaking them up and reducing them to the units which supposedly compose them."[2] These autonomous groups are recomposed in serial forms of social organization within a practico-inert field; that is, social relationships are mediated by inert collectivities.

We have discussed throughout the many ways that necrocapitalism whittles down our imaginary to accept its narrow political possibilities. In this way, the general antagonism of necrocapitalism is reduced to the particular antagonism between liberals and conservatives. In this way, the systemic features of class domination appear as accidents of the rule of a particular party. The young Marx observed that "where there are political parties, each finds the cause of *every* evil in the fact that its opponent instead of itself, is at the *helm of state*. Even radical and revolutionary politicians seek the cause of the evil not in the nature of the state but in a specific *form of it* which they want to replace by *another* form."[3] When I enter into this serial structure my choices are already set by the terms of the institution. In the electoral process, the party might change, but the state as a form of class domination remains the same—in fact, its explicitly socio-political character is occluded. At the present conjuncture, as both US parties rally around "law and order," voters are presented with a choice between two different forms of implementing police and state power.

Voting is, for Sartre, a form of serialization. The liberal dogma holds that voting grants legitimacy to political rule; voting uses indirect democracy to delegate popular legitimacy and power to the representatives in power (and their parties). By contrast, Sartre argues that the voting system reifies the power of parties and the party system, which voters confront as individuals rather than groups. Furthermore, Sartre maintains that serial social forms mediate between individuals as Others. So, were I to vote, as an individual abstracted from group praxis I don't vote as a practical subject but rather as an Other whose interests are already mediated by oppressive institutional parameters.

In a typical American election year, immense amounts of political energy are funnelled toward strategies of influencing the Democratic Party, despite the fact that repeated attempts to move the party to the left have failed and party leadership has continued to tack to the center-right. Although the pandemic interrupted this process, it was quickly set back in motion during the Democratic National Convention. Unlike recent election cycles, however, the convention began amidst a widespread anti-police uprising and a growing white supremacist reaction, which Trump sought to both foment and commandeer. Trump both celebrated right-wing vigilantism and attacked the Democratic Party as, in terms borrowed from conspiracy theories, the electoral representative of radical Marxists and "ANTIFA" (the caps warrant scare quotes). Trump made a play to pull the Far Right into a system-loyal coalition with the Republican Party.

In typical election cycles, the Democrats present themselves as representatives of leftist social movements; as the story goes, an electoral victory offers an opportunity for the demands of these movements to be implemented in policy. The movement to defund or abolish the police demonstrates the actual antagonism between Democrats and social movements. Once the convention wrapped up, Biden, Harris, and their acolytes went on the offensive, attacking militant groups and delegitimizing militant tactics. As we argued in Chapter 8, at the conceptual level (setting aside moral and pragmatic concerns), for anti-police protest to be internally consistent it must demonstrate the antagonism between police and community. By contrast, the parliamentary left has largely fallen in line, attributing violence either to pathology or outside infiltrators; the possibility that property damage and the diversity of tactics have a significant meaning is flatly denied.

The present conjuncture lends support to Sartre's thesis that electoral politics is a process of serialization. By drawing a false dichotomy between legitimate and illegitimate protest, the parliamentarian left attempted to splinter the group praxis of these anti-systemic, anti-police mobilizations. With demobilization, the anti-police uprising is sapped of its political force and its members will end up serialized and isolated. Far from representing the movement, the parliamentarian left will be its undoing—to what end? To elect key cogs in solidifying and maintaining neoliberal carceral policy in the United States?

It is clear that Trump staked his political fortune on far-right social forces. But we must keep in mind that in city after city, defund/abolition protests have broken out and have been sustained — some now for over three months — in cities with Democratic mayors, in states with Democratic governors. These are places where, in the typical picture of grassroots political pressure, those in power are supposedly responsive to leftist social movements, and yet in broad outline, these politicians have done little beyond symbolic gestures that hardly approach the demands articulated by protesters and organizers. At best, Biden's victory stabilizes neoliberal policy without explicit far-right social characteristics. But there's very little chance that any faction of the ruling class curbs the present extension of an increasingly locally militarized police power and the infiltration of federal police powers throughout the United States — unless the continued strength of the uprising makes them curb this power.

Therefore, we must reject the thesis, maintained by the parliamentarian left, that there is a continuity between leftist social (and, in particular, anti-systemic abolitionist) movements and electoral politics. The electoral process is antagonistic to maintaining the power of the movement. The anti-police movement, therefore, doesn't owe anything to electoral parties.

NOTES TO CHAPTER 20

1. Cornel West (https://twitter.com/cornelwest/status/1301903251789414402?lang=en).

2. Sartre, "Elections," 200.

3. Marx, "Critical Notes," 348.

CHAPTER TWENTY-ONE

ON ABSTENTION, INFANTILISM, AND ORGANIZING

IF WE TOOK ADVANTAGE OF CORNEL WEST'S RECENT intervention to give a hard look at voting, interpreting it through the lens of Sartre's notion of seriality, the basic insight was to warn against the amorcelating or "serialization" of political energies through the ballot and electoralism, amounting to the de-fusion of the insurrectionary political group or movement.

No doubt some comrades will detect a note of "infantilism" in the insurgent notes we've sounded these past months. But make no mistake, our line is not that there is anything inherently problematic or impure about the *political tactic* of casting a vote. Many of us vote in small-scale, autonomous political groupings as a matter of course, and this can be both efficient and empowering. It is simply that we reject any fetishism of the ballot box. When, in *Left-Wing Communism*, Lenin famously castigated as "infantile" the principled abstention of the left Social Revolutionaries from parliamentary politics, this was in no sense a blanket endorsement of parliamentarianism. His defense was a qualified one; *tactical* and *strategic* considerations rather than abstract principles of the political good were at issue. The question, then, is whether those who defend voting do so on principle or for politically realist reasons. The follow-up question, if the latter is true, is whether voting *in a particular situation* actually holds up to the tactical and strategic criteria of a realist criticism.

A constant theme in our project has been the necessity to return to the actual conditions on the ground. In the present constellation of necrocapitalism, the serialization of political energies into the ballot amounts to "choosing" between hard right and center-right masters. This is a choice between an openly racist regime that will crush us under police occupation, and a regime that sees us, hears us, but will not hesitate to do the same (perhaps it will also hire drone operators from multiple marginalized communities, but we prefer our intersectionality without the imperialism). As such, with less than two months to go before the 2020 US election and fascism on the march, we repeat that there is no "antifascist vote." Even the oft-repeated claim that voting can be "harm reduction," minimally satisfying the tactical and strategic exigencies of Lenin's model, falls flat here. Bailing out a boat that is sinking so that it can stay afloat a little while longer, or so that a small number of privileged passengers can scramble for lifeboats, is hardly "harm reduction" in any meaningful sense of the term.

Nonetheless, there remains the possibility that if things are really all that bad my vote still *expresses something*; and that when we are stripped of our political efficacy we may nonetheless, as good Kantians, register our negation of the status quo on the properly moral plane. In 2020 such expressive politics, through voting at least, amounts to expressing that we very much would like the awful man to be replaced by a less boorish, less openly predatory awful man. Politically speaking, this is very little—arguably nothing—but such "expressive politics," pursued for example by Avishai Margalit in *On Compromise and Rotten Compromises*, is not meaningless. Personally powerless to oppose injustice, violence, apartheid, there is arguably a moral power in making even what we know to be a merely symbolic gesture. The wager is that this moral power might someday lend itself to political power, or at least keep the moral embers of political investment burning in situations where hope is on the wane.

The obvious rejoinder is that the real work is in organizing our communities politically, precisely against such a moralistic posture of impotence. Here, however, we need also to contend with the expressive power of *silence*, of non-participation, of "inaction." It's possible that not voting, as an expression of expressive silence, actually carries greater symbolic power than actively choosing a more palatable version of evil in a system that is widely recognized to be rigged. Jean-François Lyotard reminds us in *The Differend* that silence is "a phrase," i.e., an event of language that has a range of possible meanings. It's not like the message sent by not voting will always be heard, or heard unambiguously, or have any kind of power, moral or otherwise. But it takes very little effort not to vote, and unlike voting for the perceived lesser of two evils, it does not entail an expressive endorsement of the very system that is killing us.

Voting, then, amounts, in the current conjuncture, to *bad expressive politics* and *bad strategy and tactics* as well as serialization. It is worth saying a final word on serialization. The pandemic has sharpened certain contradictions and has helped bring them to light. But it has also drawn attention to serialization, both as ambient reality and as a broadly levelled recuperation strategy by those in power. What are schools, long-term care homes, workplaces, all privileged zones of tension in the pandemic, if not also serialization mechanisms? Seeming to bring us together, don't they end by disciplining us as atomized, neoliberal subjects? This they do by *intention*, by *design*. But the classic Marxist insight that capitalism produces its own gravediggers is apposite: any system that brings us together by way of breaking us apart has a built-in contradiction that can be exploited. If we are capable, in spite of everything, of coming together and working for a better future, then why would we waste that precious chance on electoralism?

CHAPTER TWENTY-TWO

DOWN GIRL IMPERIALISM

"To die for the people is weightier than Mount Tai," Mao Zedong once wrote, "but to work for fascists and die for the exploiters is lighter than a feather." In September 2020, J. Moufawad-Paul commented on the connection between capitalist electoral dogma and the performative mourning of US liberals over the death of Supreme Court Justice Ruth Bader Ginsburg.[1] The mourning is performative because it entreats us into accepting a liberating role for Ginsburg that, from the standpoint of the oppressed, she simply does not have. The piece refers to two cases motivating this view: Ginsburg's opposition to indigenous sovereignty in the case of *Sherrill vs. Oneida Indian Nation* (2005) as well as Ginsburg's coming down on the side of white supremacy (and ableism) when she referred to Colin Kaepernick and other professional athletes taking a knee during the American national anthem as "dumb and disrespectful." But there are other cases, such as *Daimler AG v. Bauman*, where Ginsburg prohibited relatives of victims and the survivors from bringing legal charges against Daimler AG when they conspired with the government of Argentina to torture workers at local Mercedes Benz factories during Operation Condor, the US-sponsored campaign of political repression and state terror in Argentina. And there's also *Homeland Security vs. Thuraissigiam*, which—in addition to condemning unknown numbers of

asylum seekers to death—allows the fast-track deportations that enable Trump's administration to separate families at the border by denying all immigrants, including
children, access to asylum law under the pretext of protecting Americans from COVID-19.[2] Restating the point
made in Moufawad-Paul's piece, Ginsburg was not a
friend of the oppressed; she was their enemy.

The connection of performative mourning to electoral
dogma in Moufawad-Paul's piece is the idea that without
Ginsburg, Biden's election to the presidency would be at
risk, bolstering the dead-end liberal narrative that voting
under necrocapitalism can fend off fascism. We've been
examining these and related ideas in the last couple of chapters, focusing on the role of voting in necrocapitalism and
its disarming, serializing effect on revolutionary groups
and movements that are fighting for systemic change, even
its failure as progressive expressive politics when compared to not voting. In this chapter, we continue to think
about the pitfalls of putting stock in the political systems
of necrocapitalism and turn to a particular intervention
on the death of Ruth Ginsburg coming from the liberal
petty-bourgeoisie of the imperialist countries claiming the
banner of feminism. This is the intervention of bourgeois
philosopher Kate Manne in a series of tweets anticipating
a misogynist response to Ginsburg's death and absolving
her of blame for the current situation in US politics.[3]

The situation in question is a vacant seat in the United
States Supreme Court and Donald Trump poised to fill that
seat with an imperialist politician of his choosing, resulting
in a 6–3 Republican majority. From the standpoint of the
non-revolutionary, parliamentary left represented by the

liberal bourgeoisie in the United States, this situation threatens existing and future laws serving the interests of a certain class of euro-american women in this country. The reason some people might think that Ginsburg is to blame for this situation is that she refused to retire during the Obama administration when Obama was in a position to appoint an imperialist politician to the chair occupied by Ginsburg—one with more appeal to liberals than one selected by Trump. To the liberal bourgeoisie in the United States these are multidimensional and weighty issues, which involve interpreting Ginsburg's choice to stay on rather than retire during the Obama presidency as a heroic and hard choice limited by Senate Leader and right-wing imperialist stooge Mitch McConnell's blocking of Obama's nominations to the Supreme Court. This is in contrast to the view opposed by Manne, which interprets Ginsburg's choice to not retire as a bad calculation on Ginsburg's part based on optimism that Hillary Clinton would be elected president in 2016, enabling her to retire in 2017 and have her chair filled by another imperialist politician, viewed favorably of course, because of selection by Hillary Clinton.

Manne's focus, however, is misogyny in the evaluation of Ginsburg's death and the political situation described above. Manne is the author of a bourgeois philosophy book on misogyny, *Down Girl: The Logic of Misogyny*, influential among euro-american liberals, white feminists, bourgeois philosophers, and those who aspire to and share the social identity of the imperialist country nonrevolutionary left.[4] In it, she defines misogyny as the law enforcement branch of a patriarchal social order,[5] and claims to propose an account of misogyny that situates patriarchy at the intersection of other systems of social control and that outstrips the naïve notion that misogyny is a type of subjective hatred of women and girls in the minds of misogynists. Manne is correct to conceptually connect misogyny to patriarchy and to recognize that patriarchy intersects with other forms of oppression. However, in the same way that the American Declaration of Independence claims that "all men (*sic*) are created equal"—while American liberalism in practice is white supremacy born out of the political and economic ambitions of euro-american settlers against the colonial powers of Europe through the genocide and dispossession of the native peoples of the Americas—Manne's philosophical work mentions the intersection of different strands of oppression but is born out of the political and economic ambitions of petit-bourgeois settler women whose material life sets them against the interests of women and persons generally oppressed by imperialism. Nowhere is this more evident than in Manne's consistent and plentiful defense of US imperialist politician Hillary Clinton in the pages of *Down Girl*, drawing on the narrow space of debate between American politicians, Democrats and Republicans, to produce examples of misogyny as petit-bourgeois settler women conceive it. Manne builds the case that Hillary Clinton was the target of hostilities by men involved in imperialist politics during her presidential campaign because she is a woman and because she violated the social norms of this group. In doing so, she cites examples of gender bias, expressions of disgust directed at Clinton, demands that Clinton be more warm and caring than male imperialist politicians, attributions of insincerity to her, and suspicion directed at her regarding behaviors that go unnoticed by the class of people involved when a male imperialist carries them out. In Manne's view, misogyny was a major contributing factor to Clinton losing the American election to Trump, upholding the view that Clinton was a "better presidential Candidate than Trump" and that misogyny kept the voting public in the United States from recognizing it.[6]

Manne's general claim is that powerful women, and women generally who seek the autonomy to exist according to non-patriarchal rules, are troublemakers and that patriarchy leverages misogyny point blank to prohibit that. What is missing from this formulation is the intersection—or the recognition that women, and powerful women, exist only in gender (power) relations mediated by class, nation, and ability. To go beyond toothless academic declarations of commitment to intersectional analyses we ought to ask: what is the political and economic content of Clinton's power and how does it relate to the powerless?

Spoiler Alert: the power in question is the political and economic power of settler capitalism in its imperialist, necrotic form. Hillary Clinton has effectively wielded this power—so admired by Manne as disruptive of patriarchy—to implement measures that have spread "a particularly virulent strand of Carceral feminism,"[7] expanding state repression of men, women, and people who don't fit patriarchal notions of abuse victims through the Violence Against Women act, a piece of legislation that ignores the roots of patriarchy as a system in connection to capitalism and instead builds upon it by increasing policing, prosecution, and imprisonment as the primary solution to violence against women. Taking this thinking internationally, in her capacity as Secretary of State for American imperialism, Hillary Clinton in 2011 threatened to cut off humanitarian aid to African countries that did not adopt American prescriptions on gay rights.[8] This action was prompted by Uganda's 2009 bill criminalizing homosexuality (a bill revealed to have been created by Ugandan lawmakers in connection with evangelical Christians from the United States).[9] The threat was lauded by LGBT activists in the United States and Britain, but LGBT activists in African countries responded differently, "with more than 50 African organizations working on LGBT issues in countries on that continent [signing] a statement indicating that premising foreign aid on a country's treatment of LGBT people was a dangerous move for LGBT people living in those countries as it would likely lead to more hostile treatment of LGBT people."[10] Moving from Africa to Central America, Clinton wielded imperialist power to continue the legacy of US terror in Latin America and to aid in the military overthrow of the democratically elected government of Manuel Zelaya in Honduras in 2009, a move that installed a right-wing dictatorship responsible for femicide on an unprecedented scale in that country.[11] Among the dead is Berta Cáceres, an environmentalist and Indigenous rights activist who in a 2014 video interview named Hillary Clinton as being among those responsible for legitimizing the military coup: Clinton, in her position as Secretary of State, pressured (as her emails show) other countries to agree to sideline the demands of Cáceres and others that Zelaya be returned to power. Instead, Clinton

pushed for the election of what she calls in *Hard Choices*
a "unity government." But Cáceres said: "We warned that
this would be very dangerous ... The elections took place
under intense militarism, and enormous fraud."[12]

Closer to home: "I voted numerous times when I was
a senator to spend money to build a barrier to try to prevent illegal immigrants from coming in," Clinton said
while campaigning in 2015. Specifically, she called for the
use of satellites and drones in addition to low-intensity
warfare checkpoints at the border. This is the power—the
class power of the bourgeoisie and the national power of
euro-american settlers, including the privileged women
who belong to those groups—that enables talk of Hillary
Clinton being a powerful woman. The reality is that to be
better qualified than Donald Trump at directing American
imperialism is not a feminist goal, and neither is holding
the office of president. As we discussed in the previous
chapter, there is no meaningful way to conceive of voting as
"harm reduction" at this stage in the necrotic development
of American capitalism. And if the history of American
leadership teaches us anything, it is that imperialism is a
total harm (à la total war) and that the relative incompetence and/or preparation of its leadership is a compass
for political maneuvering for classes of people with more
of a stake in perpetuating that harm than they have in
reducing it. The United States has had a Black president.
If the Democrats and people like Manne have their way, it
can have a woman president. It can have a gay president.
It can fill this office in every which way but those that
affect most of the people oppressed by the necrocapitalist
system where that office exists. In other words, there will

never be an anti-patriarchy, anti-capitalist, ant-imperialist, and anti-racist president of the United States.

And now we ask, regarding the enforcement role of misogyny under patriarchy, is there a way to make this important point in a way that takes into account the people who are violently subjected to the type of power that enables talk of Hillary Clinton as a powerful woman? Yes: one way to do this is to struggle in practice to uphold the standpoint in analyses of those whose practical demands for freedom and democracy are not served by the liberalism of the imperialist countries. If we wanted to do philosophy in a strictly bourgeois way, we could say that Manne's focus on Clinton is just the rhetorical avenue for a serious argument about patriarchy and misogyny. But we reiterate what we stated as early as the fourth chapter: what philosophers emphasize in their philosophizing reveals their pre-theoretical class, national, and gender commitments. And to this we add: to do philosophy after Marx's 11th Thesis as Marxists means doing philosophy with an awareness of those commitments as they intersect to produce philosophy, conditioned by our relation to both theory and to social practice. The commitment in Manne's philosophical work on misogyny is to what proletarian feminist Anuradha Ghandy characterizes as liberal feminism:

> It tends to be mechanical in its support for formal equality without a concrete understanding of the condition of different sections/classes of women and their specific problems. Hence it was able to express the demands of the middle

classes (white women from middle classes in the
US and upper class, upper caste women in India)
but not those of women from various oppressed
ethnic groups, castes and the working, labour-
ing classes.[13]

Consistent with liberal discourse, Manne cautiously refers
to the experience of Black women in the United States,
granting the privileged status of white women and their
complicity in misogynoir, but she stops short of the concrete understanding that Ghandy writes about because the
specific problems facing Black women are co-extensive
with the content of the power that enables talk of Hillary
Clinton as a powerful woman. So, we are treated to a bare
mention of problems and cases instead of a critique of the
material reasons for those problems and cases. Many of
the features of Ghandy's account of liberal feminism are
unfortunately exhibited in Manne's *Down Girl*: "it does
not question the economic and political structures of
the society which give rise to patriarchal discrimination.
Hence, it is reformist in its orientation, both in theory and
in practice," and ultimately aligns with the most conspicu-
ous representatives of American imperialism.[14]

It believes the state is neutral and can be made
to intervene in favor of women when in fact the
bourgeois state in the capitalist countries and
the semi-colonial and semi-feudal Indian state
are patriarchal and will not support women's
struggle for emancipation.[15]

These commitments to the capitalist state and to the social identity of the petty bourgeois classes of the imperialist countries turn what could have been an important investigation into the role of misogyny under patriarchy into a defense of agents of those sectors of capitalist society—the government, its judicial arms, and the mass base for liberalism—most responsible for upholding patriarchy and legitimizing misogyny for persons who don't fit into the liberal mold, persons who serve a different subordinate social role necessitated by the capitalism that produces the material life of liberal feminists.

So, who is served by this philosophy, and by this imperialist feminism? It is not the women of Honduras. It is not the LGBT people of Uganda and other African Nations. It is not women at the illegitimate border with Mexico who are pursued by Hillary Clinton's drones to be separated from their families by Ginsburg's laws, enforced by Trump's goons. It is not even women in the United States whose social reality is not expressed by capitalist liberalism or who are ignored by powerful women because their gender identity is non-conforming to liberal feminism or it intersects in "inappropriate" ways with their class and national standing, who are subjected to greater criminalization and police violence by the carceral feminism of women like Hillary Clinton, Ruth Ginsburg, and Kamala Harris. But, hey, on the bright side, it does positively serve bourgeois liberal women who seek validation of their experiences in their attempts to occupy positions of capitalist power in a global system of oppression.

Returning to Manne's tweets on the death of Ruth Ginsburg: Manne is concerned with the apparent punishment of a woman, Ginsburg, who failed to behave according to the strictures of patriarchy interpreted in terms of her imperialist country liberalism. Ginsburg's power is like Hillary Clinton's power—it is the power of the United States government, and everything that goes with it including capitalism and patriarchy. Ginsburg had the audacity to die and is criticized for it while male politicians die all the time, and no one calls them out for it—or so the reasoning goes. It is misogyny because it happens *because* they are women. In the case of a proletarian feminist critique of liberal feminism this reasoning fails to apply because proletarian feminists are seeking political and economic power for women and people whose gender intersects with strands of oppression not recognized by liberal feminism. The reason women like Hillary Clinton and Ruth Ginsburg are criticized by the oppressed is that liberal feminists attempt to pass them off as liberators when, in reality, they are our oppressors and relate to us in the same way that any male imperialist, Democrat or Republican, does—by wielding the power of capitalist patriarchy. From the proletarian standpoint, we want women wielding proletarian power to liberate us from the tyranny of necrocapitalism. Misogyny, if it is the law enforcement arm of a system of patriarchy, cannot, in the idealist sense of bourgeois philosophy, be disconnected from people in a material context. Patriarchy is intertwined with the material production and reproduction of social life complicated by racialized national oppression and ability-based oppression, and its enforcement wing, misogyny, is connected to this complex. This means that a supposedly liberating feminist ideology can

serve to enforce misogyny on women whose woman-
hood is racialized, intersecting with their national being
and their ability as subaltern in a social system. When
oppressed women are ignored, silenced, put down, told
their criticisms of women in imperialist positions of power
are "counterproductive" by liberal feminists, we have that
type of misogyny in practice.

During this project we have examined the way in which
the capitalist imaginary limits critical thought and erodes
the capacity to think through new political and social
possibilities. It fragments social movements against white
supremacy and police violence, channeling their energy
into bankrupt ballot-box activism, and during a pandemic
it cries for a return to the dystopian "normal" of capitalism. Thinkers too enfeebled by the capitalist imaginary and
those who have a material stake in it continue to repack-
age and rebrand the same failed strategies concealing the
workings of necrotic capitalism even as they perpetuate
them. The death of Ruth Ginsburg is being positioned
as an additional tragedy during a pandemic and the rise
of fascist forces worldwide, in order to gather support
for voting to maintain the status quo of necrocapitalism
during the 2020 American presidential election. Many of
the same arguments peddled by liberals during the 2016
election about the possibility of casting an "antifascist
vote" are being dredged up again to put down mass anti-
racist uprisings in favor of passive acceptance of the order
imposed by the ruling classes. In this context, we must be
aware of liberal efforts to weaponize opposition to misogyny in a way that harms proletarian feminists—whether
it is by putting them down, or pretending they don't exist,

or by making it seem that there is no principled feminist opposition to the necrotic system represented by Ruth Ginsburg or that a critique of women's role in upholding capitalist patriarchy is unequivocally misogynist.

NOTES TO CHAPTER 22

1. J. Moufawad-Paul, "Another negative obituary" (https://moufawad-paul.blogspot.com/2020/09/another-negative-obituary-ruth-bader.html).

2. Dara Lind, "Leaked border patrol memo tells agents to send migrants back immediately" (https://www.propublica.org/article/leaked-border-patrol-memo-tells-agents-to-send-migrants-back-immediately-ignoring-asylum-law).

3. Kate Manne (https://twitter.com/kate_manne/status/1307110210155274241?s=20).

4. We will refer to this book in a limited capacity here, but a type of trigger warning is warranted for those who might want to pursue the source material. The book is packed with imperialist country chauvinism, settler chauvinism, racism, neo-nazi anticommunist tropes, and apologetics for violence against women and people from the imperialist periphery, which may trigger survivors of the violence wrought by Hillary Clinton and euroamerican liberal women generally.

5. Manne, *Down Girl*, 63.

6. Ibid., 278.

7. Nair, "Marry the state, jail the people," 104.

8. Ibid., 109.

9. Abby Ohlheiser, "Uganda's new anti-homosexuality law was inspired by American activists" (https:// www.theatlantic.com/international/archive/2013/12/ uganda-passes-law-punishes-homosexuality-life-imprisonment/356365/).

10. Chávez, "Pushing boundaries," 89.

11. Mark Weisbrot, "Hard choices: Hilary Clinton admits role in Honduran coup aftermath" (http:// america.aljazeera.com/opinions/2014/9/hillary-clinton-honduraslatinamericaforeignpolicy.html). For more information about the coup in Honduras, in which Canada rather than the US would eventually take the lead imperialist role, see Tyler Shipley's *Ottawa and Empire: Canada and the Military Coup in Honduras* (2017).

12. Greg Grandin, "Before her murder, Berta Cáceres singled out Hilary Clinton for criticism" (https://www.thenation.com/article/archive/ chronicle-of-a-honduran-assassination-foretold/).

13. Ghandy, *Philosophical Trends in the Feminist Movement*, 39.

14. Ibid.

15. Ibid., 39–40.

CHAPTER TWENTY-THREE

ON LONG CRISES
AND SPEEDY RECOVERIES

THERE IS A STRANGE TENDENCY AMONG CERTAIN radicals to highly overemphasize the competence of the ruling class generally, and the competence of the state apparatus that serves their interests in particular. The power of the state is vast, and it clearly functions to consolidate class rule through its organs of violence and oppression. Daily we are reminded of this violence through extrajudicial executions at the hands of police and through the life-destroying effects of the criminal "justice" system. And yet, despite all this power, we also know that capitalism is prone to crisis. This is an inherent feature of capitalism. This is the reason why we insist that necrocapitalism is not some new form of capitalism; rather, it is an analytic for understanding the decay that is built into the very nature of capitalism and all class societies. While we are daily reminded of the power of the ruling class and the tools at their disposal, moments of crisis can reveal the dysfunction within the ruling class itself while also allowing us to see how those class forces unify in defense of the status quo during moments when the present state of things is most pressing.

In October 2020, US President Donald Trump announced that he had tested positive for SARS-COV-2.

Twenty-four hours ago, it was announced that he was being airlifted to Walter Reed Hospital. Initially, there were reports of his vitals being in serious condition, and it was discovered that numerous GOP politicians in contact with him had tested positive. It is moments like this when we realize that the ruling class and their state representatives are not all-powerful, and when we understand the truth behind Mao's insistence that the reactionaries are paper tigers.

To note that all people, including the leaders of global empires, are in fact mortal is utterly banal. This is a realization that anyone could come to. What is interesting in this context is the extent to which the incompetence of Trump, the US American state, and the unhinged coalition of petty-bourgeois and bourgeois elements supporting him were responsible for Trump's predicament in October. The state response to the crisis of COVID-19 varied from at best acknowledging its existence while failing to take systemic action to stop it, to at worst denying the reality of the pandemic and intentionally endangering the populace. Among Trump's base there was widespread conspiratorial thinking regarding the virus, with some insisting that the virus did not exist at all, while others insisted it was harmless and that the economy must open up. The US American right rallied around reopening, insisting that the costs of an expanded pandemic were justified in order to save the economy. The lens of necrocapitalism analysis enables us to see the extent to which the reactionary political forces revert back to the most base forms of Moloch worship during times of crisis. Furthermore, we now see how this frenzied drive towards irrationality and human sacrifice as a response to capitalism's own inevitable crisis has failed entirely as a strategy. The leader of this crazy cult temporarily ended up in a hospital bed while more and more of his close confidants and political allies tested positive for this deadly virus. Paper tigers indeed.

And yet, despite this obvious testament to the incompetence of the most reactionary aspects of the capitalist state, that moment revealed something about the unity of the capitalist class in times of crisis. In recent chapters we discussed both the liberal mobilization of performative grief in the face of the death of political figures, as well as the limits of voting for achieving any actual change. Our current rather acute moment of crisis overlaps with these concepts in a few fascinating ways.

Liberal claims that Trump represents a uniquely fascist and uniquely dangerous aberration within the realm of bourgeois politics have been central to the vote-shaming strategy employed to pull more radical forces in line with the Democratic Party. As happens every four years, we hear constant demands that we fall in line and cast a vote for yet another moderate neoliberal Democrat because the alternative poses an existential threat to the norms of democracy. While it is true that Trump has eroded liberal norms at a particularly rapid pace, it does not follow from this that a bourgeois electoral strategy would be sufficient to repair the erosion of these norms. As communists, we understand that the erosion of liberal norms is a result of reactionary defense mechanisms that occur within capitalism during moments of particularly distinct crises. Regardless of whether Trump is an instance of this fascist reaction crisis, we must insist that the conditions that allow the emergence of such a fascist reaction are themselves found within the very conditions that produce the norms and political order of liberal republicanism that the Democrats claim to hold in such high regard. Liberals, of course, remain blind to this reality and to the extent to which their own politics are inseparably intertwined with the conditions that allow for the emergence of fascsm. Thus we find ourselves endlessly shamed for being "unwilling" to compromise in the name of "practicality" or national unity in the face of a supposedly unique threat.

And yet, it is in this moment where this threat is endangered by our current pandemic that we see the liberal rhetoric fall apart. We might suppose that if these liberals were in fact genuine in their belief that Trump represents an existential threat then we would have seen them expressing some excitement at the fact that he was temporarily endangered by this virus. We did not, of course, see this response from those who chastise us for failing to oppose Trump "by any means necessary." Instead, we witnessed the total opposite reaction, as these same liberals wished Trump a speedy recovery and insisted that those who oppose Trump must take the moral high ground and wish the best for the president. In that moment of crisis, wherein nature itself threatened the well-being of a man they spent years decrying as uniquely dangerous, the liberal political class rallied around the president's well-being.

It is not merely that the pathetic liberal commentariat who endlessly chatter and moan for a living were calling for unity in support of Trump's health; we in fact saw the actual politicians who were then contending for state power back off their opposition. Biden himself chose to pull the attack ads from his campaign while Trump was incapacitated from the virus. During that moment, when the "opposition" candidate could have consolidated his campaign and taken advantage of the current situation, he chose to back off for the sake of the liberal ethics of "civility." There are two immediate lessons that we can learn from the reaction of liberals. One acts as a sort of corollary to our previous observations regarding the incompetence of the ruling class, and the other expands our understanding of the weakness of electoral strategies in the face of reaction.

First, we might note that while the reactionaries are in fact paper tigers, undermined by their own incompetence and their own drive towards irrationality in the face of crisis, it is also true that the ruling class on the whole is willing to unify when the consequences of this incompetence become too significant. That liberals suddenly went from seeing Trump as an existential threat to seeing him as a vulnerable person whose health we must rally around revealed the hollowness of their political outlook. Trump did not, in fact, represent the greatest threat to their politics, and they knew this. They recognized that, at the end of the day, their own politics and his politics serve the interests of capital, and they recognized that the legitimacy of the head of the capitalist state is crucial for the maintenance of capitalist social relations more broadly. What is more dangerous than Trump, according to the liberals? The possibility that the masses might come to celebrate the downfall of the leader of the American empire, regardless of who that leader is. In their calls for unity and civility they undermined their own rhetoric and endless ideological banter in order to defend a man who would happily have seen them die from the very same virus. It is tempting to misdiagnose this weakness of liberals as a sort of pathetic overcommitment to principles of civility, but this would be a mistake. It is not that liberals are weak or cowardly in the face of reaction, it is rather that they are on the same side as the reactionaries themselves. Our present moment brings this into clear focus.

The second lesson to learn from this moment relates again to the question of voting. If the liberals were correct that voting was the only way to oppose the fascism of the Trump administration, surely we would hope that the candidate we were told we must vote for would actually take every step within his power (which far exceeds our own) to overcome Trump. And yet, there we were with Biden refusing to take the actions necessary to secure the election. We saw, once again and for the millionth fucking time, that bourgeois politicians are not and cannot be held accountable to the masses and cannot be used as a tool for fighting off the most violent aspects of capitalist decay. Biden himself cannot be seen as a tool for fighting off the necrocapitalist decay that marks our time, as his current regime post electoral victory demonstrates.

In a sense, that moment of Trump's temporary infection is profoundly useful because it demystifies so much of liberal political ideology. It lays bare a hypocrisy that many radicals have failed to see beyond, and it draws our attention to a certain dual nature of the ruling class; a simultaneous weakness as a result of sheer incompetence, and a horrifying willingness for consolidation of political forces that are supposedly at odds with each other.

At the same time, we also witnessed a certain pathetic reaction from the radical left in response to Trump's infection. The chorus of social media voices unable to contain their excitement at the current situation speaks ultimately to the weakness of the organized left. A movement so weak that it has to cheer on the role a virus plays in the political struggle is a movement that must seriously self-reflect on the meaning of power and the means of attaining it.

If Trump had succumbed to the virus it would not have been a victory for the left. It would have surely spurred on violent reaction as a host of assassination conspiracies would have cropped up amongst the reactionary right to explain the situation. These people already believe the virus is a manufactured bioweapon; they are poised to engage in political violence should things turn badly. Furthermore, the elation of the radical left at Trump's current predicament played into the liberal hyper-focus on the uniqueness of Trump as a threat to progressive politics. True radicals ought to understand that Trump as an individual was in many ways insignificant. He was a chosen figure who represented forces and interests that will continue on even now that he is no longer president. What is at play is much more systemic than the life of a single person.

So let us look at that moment, a moment when the most morbid and stunning aspects of capitalist decay threatened the official representatives of the capitalist class, and recognize both that our enemies are often utter fools but also that they are willing and ready to set aside differences in defense of the status quo. Let us also realize that we gain nothing from cheering on the fall of our enemies to a virus, other than momentary catharsis. When that catharsis subsides, however, we are left recognizing the weakness that led us to seek out such a release of frustration in the first place. Power is found in organization and in the masses, not in lifeless virus particles, which are utterly indifferent towards the world around them. Power is built. There is much work to be done.

CHAPTER TWENTY-FOUR

NIHILIST RECONCILIATION

IF THE POLITICAL POWER NECESSARY FOR CHANGING the world is not to be found "in lifeless virus particles, which are utterly indifferent towards the world around them," and if it is not to be found in the US electoral machine or useless political figures like Ruth Bader Ginsburg, who are also utterly indifferent to the world, then where is it to be found and how is it to be built? Although we have a lot of thoughts on the answer to that question—many of which have been revealed or are implicit throughout this project—to even ask it is to also recognize a kind of thinking that needs to break from the capitalist imaginary.

In some ways, we have come to think like an indifferent virus. Or, rather, the kind of thinking that is most prevalent in the imperialist metropoles—even amongst progressives—is one of denial or nihilistic indifference. This is not the result of the pandemic, nor is it the result of the fascist movements pushing reactionary leaders into power, but was already emerging as a characteristic of necrocapitalism before the pandemic and emergent fascism. Again, the pandemic merely revealed the already existing depredations of a decaying system that has been morbidly violent from the beginning; emergent fascism is evidence of this decay. As these depredations came more and more to resemble the death throes of the system itself, and as coherent and sustainable revolutionary organizing vanished from the imperialist metropoles, the proclamation of the "end of history" became a proclamation of "no alternative" and even "no hope" for those who could not see beyond the boundaries of the imperialist strongholds in which they resided.

Within this cancerous and necrotic capitalist reality, denial or nihilism manifest as the only possible attitudes, as long as we think within its confines. Denial might take multiple forms, but these forms are over-determined by fascist and liberal perspectives, both of which are invested (in their own ways) in saving capitalism from collapse. Inordinate focus on the US elections is a form of denialism; specifically, a denial of our ability to organize and create another world. But such focus also demonstrates a nihilist attitude, an indifference to organizing political power because it has been drained of meaning.

Nihilism also takes multiple forms: (1) its own fascist variant as the nadir where collapse is embraced as judgment against those deemed weak (who let the virus, to cite one example, "dominate" them rather than "dominating" it); (2) a liberal individualism of giving up and accepting, with a pseudo-zen magnanimity, that armageddon is fait accompli; and (3) an anti-capitalist variant of loss, mourning, raging in the face of inevitable environmental and social collapse. It is this last species of nihilism that should concern us most, since it represents the power of contemporary crisis capitalism to infect the imagination of the left.

Indeed, nihilism is an attitude that is harder and harder for anti-capitalists in the imperialist metropoles to avoid.

We have witnessed multiple failures and have been socialized to forget or dismiss any success. We lived through the
trauma of the collapse of the great revolutionary projects.
We were fed the false hopes of movementism and were
incapable of recognizing that these fragmented projects
were doomed from the outset. We witness a world crawl-
ing towards the edge of destruction, maniacally pursuing
mechanics of species suicide. We understand that everything about capitalism is a lie, we know that it cannot save
itself from itself because of its logic, but our imagination
is such that the possibility of rupturing from this necrotic
sequence is unthinkable. Within the reality demarcated
and described by the capitalist imaginary, another world
is impossible—and it is very difficult to pursue the revolutionary slogan, famously proclaimed in May 1968, that
the revolutionary imaginary is about *demanding the
impossible.*

Faced with the vast graveyard that the world has
become, nihilism, when judged within the constraints
imposed by capitalism's vision of reality, certainly feels
like a viable option. According to the capitalist imaginary, resistance is impossible or (as the Orwellian discourse coupled with Cold War ideology has promoted)
will result in a more horrific state of affairs. Hopelessness
becomes normative amongst would-be militants who are
separated from the world-building projects of revolutionary communist parties. Even militants who join such
partisan projects might drop out and give up when events
do not proceed as quickly and as smoothly as they would
like. While there is indeed a petty-bourgeois variant of
this hopeless nihilism ("nothing matters so I might as

well enjoy what little time I have while complaining that capitalism has pushed the world into a death drive") it is common amongst the exploited and oppressed masses as well. The working class is taught that there is no future but drudgery and meaningless labor, that workers' failure to rise above their circumstances is their fault alone—because they are not creative enough, because they lack the incentive, because they are not thinking enough positive thoughts.

But it is the pseudo-progressive strain of "left" nihilism that attempts to push this sentiment enforced by capitalist ideology as a viable anti-capitalist option. Lee Edelman's *No Future* is a perfect example of the petty-bourgeois wallowing in capitalism's death drive, presented as radical. So-called "queer nihilism" (along with "nihilist communism" and "anarchist nihilism") emerges from Edelman's morbid acceptance of the capitalist imaginary. Nihilism is the "common sense" of necrocapitalism, even when it presents itself as critique.

The apotheosis of contemporary nihilism is that strange sub-region of speculative philosophy known as anti-natalism, a philosophy that claims to prove, as the name of an anti-natalist article puts it, *why it is better to never come into existence.*[1] Represented by philosophers such as Théophile de Giraud, Peter Zapffe, David Benatar, Julio Cabrera, and horror author Thomas Ligotti, anti-natalism asserts that non-sentient existence is preferable to sentient existence, sentient existence is in essence pain and harm, consciousness is a monstrous evolutionary aberration, and thus it would be better if humans simply ceased to exist. As Ligotti summarizes this philosophy:

For the rest of the earth's organisms, existence is relatively uncomplicated. Their lives are about three things: survival, reproduction, death—and nothing else. But we know too much to content ourselves with surviving, reproducing, dying— and nothing else. We know we are alive and know we will die. We also know we will suffer during our lives before suffering—slowly or quickly— as we draw near to death. This is the knowledge we "enjoy" as the most intelligent organisms to gush from the womb of nature. And being so, we feel shortchanged if there is nothing else for us than to survive, reproduce and die. We want there to be more to it than that, or to think there is. This is the tragedy: Consciousness has forced us into the paradoxical position of striving to be unself-conscious of what we are—hunks of spoiling flesh on disintegrating bones.[2]

On the speculative level, this philosophy is influenced by a materialist understanding that the history of conscious human existence, as well as the history of any form of sentient life, is both a tiny blip in the long ancestral history of matter and takes up minuscule space in a massive unthinking universe. The upshot of this very large materialist insight is that we should not think that humans possess an especial destiny, that they are better than other forms of life, or that we are the center of existence. Anti-natalism, however, adds a warped ethical injunction to the insight that non-sentient existence is older and larger than sentient existence; namely, it asserts that the former is preferable to the latter. Such an assertion, though, confirms the anthropocentric conceit since its reversal merely reaffirms what the initial insight attempted to undermine: the centrality of human consciousness. Human consciousness again becomes a central focus, though one that is problematized rather than being exhorted to be de-emphasized.

Hence, to assert that we come from nothing and exist for nothing is not enough for anti-natalism. These assertions again become puzzles. Ligotti complains that "[n]o philosopher has ever satisfactorily answered the following question: 'Why should there be something rather than nothing?'" and then asserts that such a question "suggests our uneasiness with Something."[3] And yet, if we reject the privileging of anthropocentrism we should recognize that "from nothing and for nothing"[4] are answers to this question—answers that allow us to think an existence broader than human consciousness. The only reason that this age-old question is a puzzle is because it emerges from an anthropocentric framework. Such a framework is precisely what allows anti-natalists to focus on the monstrousness of human consciousness, the claim that existence is pain, and to move on to privileging the non-existence of humanity over its existence. By focusing on a utilitarian calculus of pain and pleasure, and claiming that pain (and harm) is normative to human existence, David Benatar asserts that "there is nothing bad about never coming into existence, but there is something bad about coming into existence, all things considered non-existence is preferable."[5]

On the speculative level, it is an exercise in futility to argue against those dedicated to the axiom that the non-existence of humanity (and indeed all sentient life) is preferable to its existence. Charges that anti-natalists should simply commit suicide if they truly believe in what they argue are usually met with scorn: due to the programming of human consciousness, and in the words of the character Rustin Cole from *True Detective* (which was based on anti-natalist philosophy), they "lack the constitution" for suicide. Besides, what do the suicides of a handful of misanthropic philosophers matter when the problem they feel like they are diagnosing concerns all of sentient existence? Hence, following Zapffe's so-called "last messiah," anti-natalists can simply argue that they work to "bear witness" (again, as Rustin Cole puts it), to argue this truth to the rest of ignorant, conscious humanity, and to struggle for the solution of mass sterilization where all of humanity will agree to eradicate itself. Nihilist utopianism.

It cannot be denied, after all, that reality is horrendous and that, even if we side-step David Benatar's argument about "asymmetry" and argue that some pains and harms are simply part of life, not an insurmountable category of being (psychological and emotional pain, the fact that we will become ill and experience various level of distress simply because we are mortal and fragile), there is still the fact that the vast majority of the world does experience extreme harm and pain. Natural disasters, famines, wars, genocides, vicious labor conditions, immiseration, and multiple forms of pain and harm characterize the living conditions for the majority of humanity. Moreover, the unfolding facts of environmental devastation and a pandemic attenuate all of the above problems, resulting in a very bleak looking future that is drawing nearer every day.

But these terrible facts of material existence are facts that multiple radical social theorists have grappled with, have agonized over, but they have concluded that the solution is to struggle against them and change society so that such predations and their effects can no longer exist. Many of these social theorists were and are not starry-eyed utopians unaware of pain and thus deceived (as anti-natalists would have it) into thinking such pain and harm was not a big deal; many of them either originated from, or embedded themselves in, those marginalized populations that have experienced the worst aspects of social-historical violence. For example, Christina Sharpe writes about "the ways our individual lives [meaning individual Black lives] are always swept up in the wake produced and determined, though not absolutely, by the afterlives of slavery."[6] According to Sharpe, this "wake" inheritance continues to globally affect Black lives into the present, where the trauma of the past persists as a material memory upon the body of the present. "Racialization and colonization have worked simultaneously to other and abject entire peoples so they can be enslaved, excluded, removed, and killed in the name of capitalism," writes Indigenous scholar Jodi Byrd: "These historical and political processes have secured white property, citizenship, and privilege, creating a 'racial contract,' as Charles W. Mills argues."[7] Sharpe and Byrd are just two contemporary scholars, each occupying a position of social marginalization, amongst a litany of radical social theorists who have experienced and explored the multiple horrors of capitalism and its colonial roots, whose response to a visceral experience of marginalization is to demand an end to the mechanics of oppression, exploitation, and predation. Indeed, the vast majority of social theorists and organizers who originate from populations that have experienced the most abject pain and harm do not argue for the obliteration of sentient life even though they understand, intimately and viscerally, what this pain and harm actually means.

Therefore, what is truly monstrous about anti-natalism is not the supposedly profound "truths" it reveals; it is that it is an ontological confirmation of the imaginary of necrocapitalism. Most of these anti-natalist philosophers are not individuals who have experienced the abjection of contemporary global capitalism—who have lived in what Mbembe calls the "death worlds" of the current conjuncture—and, in fact, most of them belong to quite privileged and largely comfortable demographics. To demand that humanity embrace extinction, when those who have been historically threatened with extinction have always struggled against it, is worse than cynical. In the context of the pandemic, an anti-natalist might argue that we are merely dealing with the non-sentient planet wiping out sentience and that this is a "good" thing. Or perhaps they would take it as evidence of the pain and harm that is a normative part of existence, confirmation that we should cease to exist rather than struggle against it.

Past nihilisms functioned as confirmations of the dominant orders of meaning by assuming that all meaning was lost with the loss of these orders; they rarely attempted, outside of polemical and aesthetic statements, to be conscious and theoretical celebrations of nihilism. Nietzsche described these past nihilisms as *ressentiment* or self-hatred. Of course, being the "nineteenth century dirtbag philosopher"[8] that he was, Nietzsche's answer to nihilism was an occulted bourgeois triumphalism. But he was correct insofar as all forms of nihilism are produced by melancholia, *ressentiment*, and cynicism. Contemporary iterations of nihilism, however, are the most melancholic, resentful, and cynical nihilisms to date, despite—or perhaps *because of*—their attempt to present themselves as theoretical assemblages. Anti-natalism takes this necrotic wallowing to the speculative level, reifying the current order's hatred of existence.

To be clear, anti-natalism is a minor philosophical position. In fact, its proponents enjoy this minor status because they feel it confirms that they possess the kind of profound insight that only a few enlightened intellectuals could ever hope to attain. In this sense, it is also an elitist position and thus anti-mass, as its own dismissal of the insights from the oppressed masses demonstrates: such insights, for the anti-natalist, are delusions of the herd. They are, in a weird sense, inverted Nietzscheans who have somehow managed to copper-fasten the elitism of his philosophy with the *ressentiment* he despised. So why should we take their claims seriously? Largely because, as noted above, anti-natalism is the apotheosis of contemporary necrocapitalist nihilism. It represents a kind of trope in contemporary thinking, a trajectory of the thought of the necrocapitalist subject. It is where the thinking encouraged by this conjuncture leads: an indifference that is so far gone it celebrates its indifference by imagining it is profound.

Although proponents of the bourgeois electoral circus argue that refusing to participate in the spectacle of elections is callous indifference, and thus evidence of a nihilist attitude, might it in fact be the opposite? After all, once we examine these electoral systems with even the smallest amount of critical thought we are presented with an avalanche of absurdity. Aside from the limited options, aside from Lenin's joke that they are conventions where the bourgeoisie competes amongst itself to best misrepresent the people, aside from the fact that any and every elected regime has done nothing to make the world better but has in fact continued exploiting, oppressing, and straight-out murdering the majority of humanity ... Aside from all this, they are always compromised by the bounds of bourgeois democracy—they cannot even guarantee the limited grounds of bourgeois reason! Legitimized political parties court the most powerful members of society and demand that the marginalized just get on board, refusing to listen to any of their demands. People wait in line for hours to vote only to discover their vote won't be counted. Entire populations have their democratic rights suppressed; rumors are spread of illegitimate non-citizen voting while nobody cares about those citizens who are barred from voting. And all of this happens while imperialist states disparage and destabilize the conventions of voting in other nations. To find meaning in such a concatenation is impossible, and everyone who even thinks about it for more than a few minutes is forced to realize how meaningless it is. We would have to be nihilists regarding everything else about social existence to care about the electoral system: nothing really matters, and nothing will change, but we might as well vote since there is nothing better to do.

Meanwhile, the government of Alberta defunded and privatized its provincial medical system right in the midst of a pandemic.[9] Meanwhile, Joyce Echaquan died livestreaming the abuse she endured in a Quebec hospital because she was an Indigenous woman,[10] and the only result was a dialogue about reconciliation and a debate about whether systemic racism actually existed. The death tolls continue and, in the face of this death, there is denial (such as the absurd Barrington Declaration) and there is nihilism. But there is also outrage, and maybe this outrage can generate something productive. Something that goes beyond collaboration with the electoral circus; something beyond necrocapitalist thinking.

NOTES TO CHAPTER 24

1. This is the title of David Benatar's essay "Why it is better to never come into existence," which was reworked as a chapter in his book *Better Never To Have Been*.

2. Ligotti, *The Conspiracy Against the Human Race*, 11.

3. Ibid., 71.

4. Meillassoux, *After Finitude*, 110.

5. Benatar, *Better Never To Have Been*, 348–349.

6. Sharpe, *In The Wake*, 8.

7. Byrd, *Transit of Empire*, xxiii.

8. Mitropolous, *Pandemonium*, 32.

9. Jenn Russell and Charles Russell, "Alberta Health Services to lay off up to 11,000 staff, mostly through outsourcing" (https://www.cbc.ca/news/canada/edmonton/alberta-health-services-job-cuts-tyler-shandro-1.5760155).

10. "Indigenous woman captures hospital staff's abhorrent behaviour right before she died" (https://globalnews.ca/video/7367875/indigenous-woman-captures-hospital-staffs-abhorrent-behaviour-on-video-before-she-died).

CHAPTER TWENTY-FIVE

THE MISLEADING NATURE OF "TRUMPISM"

WRITING ABOUT THE AMERICAN PRESIDENTIAL ELEC-
tion from a militant perspective has many pitfalls. One,
that Marx long ago pilloried, would be to present all social
ills as the product of the opposing party, for this is the
deliberate myopia of all bourgeois electoral campaigns.
The other is to reverse cause and effect (or, more generally, to think them non-dialectically), by treating candi-
dates as if they command and manage their electoral bases.
Instead, we should consider elections as a snapshot that
captures the momentum or motion of social tendencies
and forces. When the likelihood of a Biden victory grew,
pundits and commentators began to assess the prospects
of the American empire. There is a trend, perhaps growing, to frame the years of Trump's presidency with the
vague and misleading term "Trumpism." The term certainly preceded the 2020 elections (it has already found its
way into academic discussions), but it might serve a particular purpose now that Trump was deposed from power
by electoral means.[1]

At present, Trumpism is said to designate a particular type of political style—demagogical nationalism, divisiveness, perhaps an explicit taste for cruelty—which
could potentially affect American politics for decades to

come. The upshot of this analysis is that liberal and social democratic antifascists cannot merely declare that something they decried during the Fall as authoritarianism, totalitarianism, or fascism was defeated by voting alone. This was a common error among Canadian critics and some activists after the electoral defeat of Maxime Bernier's People's Party of Canada in 2019; far-right groups quietly regrouped elsewhere.

But what looks like the mainstream recognition of the ongoing threat of far-right tendencies in the United States turns out to be the opposite. The use of Trumpism, though it might not demarcate the Trump regime as an aberration in American politics, severs these far-right tendencies from their roots in American history—indeed, even from recent history. First, Democrats become able to treat the far right as the fault of the Republicans, rather than as predicated on the conditions of American power that Democratic politicians have for decades tolerated, abetted, or supported. Second, the usage of Trumpism reverses cause and effect: Trump's political rise and fall is faulted for the rise of the far right, rather than being seen as part of a broader set of social tendencies and forces. Though he attempted to court some factions of the far right, as entries on the *Three-Way Fight* blog show,[2] we cannot consider the relationship between Trump and these factions to be one of simple top-down command of leader and base. Nor can we consider them to be merely reliably system-loyal.

At the same time, this courtship should not be given undue weight at the expense of considering his popular appeal. It must be noted that in the midst of the pandemic (which his administration failed to manage) and the antipolice uprising (which Trump opposed but never managed, to use his own term, to "dominate"), that he received at least six million more votes than in 2016. Indeed, that Trump received more votes as the incumbent than as the supposed anti-establishment outsider (a rich characterization for a billionaire, whether on paper or in reality), should indicate that we must look not at perceived outliers—Trump against other politicians who observe the unwritten rules of decorum, or the far right as opposed to other political currents in society—but at the underpinnings of American empire itself.

The basic premise of our project on necrocapitalism is not that necrocapitalism is a departure from capitalism but that we are in a moment that brings capitalism's contradictions into sharper focus, if not intensifying the contradictions.

One would think that as the United States reported over nine million cases of COVID-19 and 200,000 deaths therefrom in the Fall of 2020, that Trump's candidacy would be more imperiled than it was. The raw numbers simplify a complex story. Of course, Trump drove misinformation about the pandemic, and after his own recovery, extolled a kind of voluntarist will to "dominate" the virus. But again, these are features of a broader right-wing response to the pandemic, with appeals to herd immunity, and the cultivation of a sense that the petty bourgeoisie are entitled to services and goods from the before times despite the pandemic.

One possibility is that Trump's support, still persisting after Biden's election, is based in part in a reaction to the antipolice uprising. Without minimizing that aspect, we should also examine how Trump's base understood his administration's efforts to handle the coronavirus and how they self-reported their financial status in relation to the pandemic. Exit polls published by the *New York Times* asked voters how they viewed US efforts to contain COVID-19; of the 18% who said very well, 86% voted for Trump, while the 33% who answered "somewhat well" also overwhelmingly supported Trump (at 78%).[3]

Before we rush to judgment (there's no need to act like liberal critics of the far right who treat it as merely a manifestation of atavism or ignorance), let us consider two passages from Angela Mitropoulos's recent *Pandemonium: Proliferating Borders of Capital and the Pandemic Swerve*:

> What prevailing understandings of neoliberalism have obscured is the importance to capitalist extraction and accumulation of a political-economic boundary between the *demos* (the ostensibly proper subject of political representation and law-making) and the practices of managing (properly) productive populations.[4]

And:

> During the pandemic, while much of the risk of the disease was displaced onto private households—and therefore the patterning of (heritable) assets and liquid wages—those households were linked through an assumed racial genealogy to larger (national and geopolitical) taxonomies of populations and the management

of their health and welfare. However, the viability of locked-down households was physically contingent upon and linked by the unpaid and low-paid work in which women, migrants, and Black and Brown people predominate.[5]

Rather than dismiss those who incorrectly believed that the US efforts at containing COVID-19 were going well (to some degree) as ignorant Trump voters (given their overwhelming support for him), we ought to attempt to understand their significance in light of Mitropoulos's work. If neoliberalism is premised upon a political-economic boundary between the *demos* and a broader class of productive populations, and if pandemic management has functioned through buttressing those differences under Trump's administration, then for this group the system was and is indeed working well. To reflect upon these exit polls from another angle: 44% of the electorate reported no financial hardship due to the pandemic, and a majority voted for Trump (56%); the other 55% trended more strongly in the other direction. Associating social division or divisiveness with Trumpism is making Trump take the weight for vast social inequalities produced by neoliberal policy. Pin it on Trumpism and alibi the conditions that enable it.

We don't want to make too much of exit polling. It does not include the disenfranchised parts of the working classes and those who refuse to participate in electoral politics. It presumes to discern political trends from the unsound premise that political decisions are made from the perspective of the potential legislator-voter. We merely wanted to provide a different look at data, one that doesn't indulge in divining auguries of the mythological white working-class everyman's demands or demonize some particular minority group for its perceived atavistic tendencies (though we must highlight the fact that white voters as a group play some serious white identity politics, and this is normalized as the supposedly neutral attitude of the "universal legislator").

As critics of Trump have noted, his administration consistently worked to curb or remove the rights of large parts of the workforce. It might be, though, that some critics were more irked by the spectacular forms of disenfranchisement of voters and the willfully malicious use of detention and deportation. For, if Mitropoulos is correct, the Trump administration's policy was a particular (though relatively more explicitly white nationalist) implementation of neoliberal ideological and institutional infrastructure. Biden didn't run as an alternative to the underlying neoliberal policies, but rather as the candidate who would maintain neoliberal policy—to adopt his comments about police violence—in forms more likely to maim rather than kill. California, which overwhelmingly favored Biden, also passed Proposition 22, which classifies app-based drivers as independent contractors rather than employees—a huge setback for workers' rights.

We must not allow liberal critics to isolate, in a kind of ideological *cordon sanitaire*, only some uses and abuses of neoliberal policy as "Trumpism," when Biden is now working to shore up neoliberal hegemony through the prolonged crisis, supposedly of COVID-19. The crisis is part of capitalism itself.

NOTES TO CHAPTER 25

1. Of course, his administration had months to implement policy between Biden's election and inauguration, as well as spread baseless rumors about electoral fraud—a theme we will touch upon in later chapters.

2. See in particular the 2020 work of Matthew N. Lyons, Devin Zane Shaw, and Kristian Williams on *threewayfight.blogspot.com*.

3. "National exit polls: how different groups voted" (https://www.nytimes.com/interactive/2020/11/03/us/elections/exit-polls-president.html)

4. Mitropoulos, *Pandemonium*, 13.

5. Ibid., 11.

CHAPTER TWENTY-SIX

SLAVERING IN THE OUTER DARK

DESPITE THE CHARGES OF ELECTORAL FRAUD, IT WAS widely recognized that Joe Biden became the President of the United States in 2021. He received sufficient electoral college votes and a wide margin in the popular vote. Trump and his enablers took a hard anti-democratic line in response. They still refuse to concede defeat, having launched a preposterous barrage of legal challenges intended to change the outcome of the election, encouraged reactionaries to storm the Capitol, and endured another impeachment process. Trump also made some characteristically lurching, inept moves, which were being interpreted as preludes to a coup even without the events of January 6, 2021. It is now unlikely that Trump will succeed in any of this, though much is being made of his attack on American democracy itself, and the lasting damage he can do by further (!) debasing the Republican Party and poisoning public trust in the electoral system.

Many people, particularly among the most vulnerable, may feel a sense of relief that the open authoritarian drift of the presidency seems to have been halted by a Biden win. But the spectacle of thousands of people worldwide dancing in the streets over Biden's victory was sobering. Does Joe Biden—Joe Biden!—herald the poetry of the future? A key lesson of the 2020 election is how, structurally speaking, neoliberal centrism currently plays the erstwhile role of fascism in the management of capitalist crisis.

As we have insisted throughout, crisis indexes the normal functioning of capitalism rather than being an aberration. Historically, fascism steps in as a contender when the crisis becomes acute. In this sense, fascism is birthed by capitalism. Though much is made of its "populist" roots, the backbone of fascism is arguably a mass of small and middle business owners who demand a version of capitalism without capitalism. This is to say that while ostensibly supporting free competition and bootstrapping, they default to authoritarianism to avoid being crushed between organized labor and monopoly capital. To be clear, fascism "manages" the crisis in a way that must be loudly repudiated and fought to the death. But in its own way, it is embraced by segments of the population as a stabilizer.

Are we to conclude that Trump and his administration, displaying obvious fascist tendencies, played this historical role? Not at all. Trump, rather, wielded right-wing chaos in a way that permitted neoliberal centrism to play the stabilizing role. To hit once more upon our usual refrain—that none of this is really new—consider how in 2002, the fascist Jean-Marie Le Pen advanced to the second round of the French presidential election, thus provoking panic and an overwhelming 82% vote in favor of the widely mistrusted neoliberal Jacques Chirac. Similarly, a vote for Biden was ostensibly a vote against violence, hatred, and plague—but framed in these terms, how could you lose to violence, hatred, and plague? This was hardly more than political blackmail.

The question many have posed is whether there can be any credible alternative to neoliberalism within the Democratic Party. Here the mainstream media has muddied the waters, having steadily drubbed us with lazy and dishonest analyses of "populism," full of false equivalencies, for several years. As per Laclau, populism is the name of a political strategy wherein "the people" is defined and played off against an enemy.[1] Whether populism is "left" or "right" all depends on how the enemy is defined. To hear liberals tell it, it is the naming of an enemy, and the struggle against that enemy, that is dangerous in itself. But despite the media and the DNC's massive efforts to block him and paint him as such, Bernie Sanders is simply not some left-wing version of Trump. True, the strategy is formally similar, but it is in laughable bad faith to pretend that Bernie's demonizing of "the one percent" is morally equivalent to Trump's racism, ableism, misogyny, and contempt for the very lives of the masses. The liberal discourse around populism reveals itself for what it is: an invitation to abandon the very notion of the enemy. But this amounts to abandoning politics itself, in favor of submission to neoliberal management.

While figures like Bernie, the Squad, and Cornel West therefore offer a semblance of opposition via the populist strategy, there is also a credible discourse around their role in "sheepdogging"—i.e., bringing disaffected voters back into the fold of electoral politics. But we have seen with Bernie in the Democratic primaries how in the end the system enforces neoliberal consensus within that fold. The wolf of "Trumpism," slavering in the outer dark, helps to ensure this. The moment requires much more than this.

It requires us to push against neoliberalism *itself*—against necrocapitalism. This means having the courage to be the *communist*, the genuinely *antifascist* wolf.

NOTES TO CHAPTER 26

1. See Laclau's *On Populist Reason* (2018).

CHAPTER TWENTY-SEVEN

SCIENCE AND
SOCIAL WELFARE OPPORTUNISM

TRUMP DID NOT SUCCUMB TO THE CORONAVIRUS, despite hundreds of thousands of people in the US being not so lucky. The bourgeois electoral circus of 2020 concluded and neoliberal Joe Biden emerged as the new figurehead for American Imperialism. Of course, Trump and the majority of the Republican Party continued to push conspiracy theories about the election, having squandered countless resources promoting them, but the collective attention of American pundits and commentators generally shifted focus to the Biden administration. Biden and the Democrats wasted no time making it clear that "Trumpism" was generally inseperable from the neoliberalism of the contemporary imperialist order.

In December 2020 the Biden transition team announced a who's who of architects and ideologues of imperialist war, policy, and institutions that would make up part of Biden's presidential cabinet. Tony Blinken and Jake Sullivan respectively filled the positions of Secretary of State and National Security Advisor. These are classic American warmongers, instrumental in promoting Biden's vote for the invasion of Iraq and Hillary Clinton's support for war in Syria and Libya. Avril Hanes, ex–Deputy CIA Director under Obama, filled the role of National

Intelligence Director, bringing to bear against the world's people her experience in designing Obama's drone program for illegal political killings and her support for Trump's CIA Director pick, Gina Haspel—famous for implementing American black-site torture facilities and destroying videotape evidence of CIA torture. Alejandro Mayorkas was Biden's pick to serve as Secretary of Homeland Security. The imperialist media made much ado about Mayorkas being the "first Latino" to hold this dystopian office, but we must remember that he served as deputy secretary of the Department of Homeland Security under Obama and helped him earn the title "Deporter-in-Chief" by expanding deportations and family detentions. Mayorkas is so reactionary that the former head of the Florida GOP and of the American Conservative Union was prompted to tweet "hallelujah" upon learning of his selection.[1] Biden also selected Neera Tanden for the position of Office of Management & Budget Director, a selection that reaffirmed Biden's promise to wealthy campaign donors that "nothing would fundamentally change" with his election to the presidency. Tanden is famous for comments she made via a leaked email echoing the Trump administration's suggestion that the United States consider further military intervention in Libya solely to exploit Libya's oil resources. Tanden said "We have a giant deficit. They have a lot of oil ... having oil rich countries partially pay us back doesn't seem crazy to me."[2] Continued war for oil is the name of the game with this Biden pick, along with rabid anti-communism: in a now-deleted tweet, Neera Tanden blamed Hitler's rise to power on the communists' principled refusal to align with centrist elements in Germany and suggested that the death of communists at the hands of the Nazis was well deserved.[3]

Far from drawing a sharp line between the supposed oddity of far-right "Trumpism" and the neoliberal administrations of empire, the Biden cabinet picks go to the core of what America is today, oddities and all, and that is a decaying settler-colonial empire overstuffed with contradictions displayed in high-necrocapitalist relief.

While status quo liberals celebrate and pretend this cabinet of butchers is a counter to the state of affairs under Trump, Democrat and Speaker of the House of Representatives Nancy Pelosi is poised to accept a COVID-19 relief package for Americans that fails to include cash relief payments and offers a smaller purse of unemployment benefits than what was proposed prior to the election. Pelosi refused to accept a much better deal for poor people in America because she and the Democrats didn't want Trump and the Republicans to claim the COVID-19 relief package as a victory. When challenged about this ghoulish bit of electioneering, Pelosi ignored the issue of relief for the poor who have endured 10 months of the pandemic, soaring unemployment, and homelessness, saying that what matters is that there's a new president "who recognizes we need to depend on science," as well as the development of several new vaccines.[4] But vaccines for ordinary citizens in the United States would not be available until late spring in 2021, while the pandemic restrictions resulting in unemployment and homelessness continued in spite of vaccination.

Pelosi's comment about science was bizarre as a defense for failing to provide even the mildest relief for neoliberal

austerity during the pandemic. Science was opportunistically dragged about during the 2020 US election cycle by
American imperialists, and Pelosi's comment was part of
that. During the 2020 presidential campaign, for example,
Trump claimed that Biden would put an end to the practice of fracking to instill fear in the hearts of oil profiteers
and turn them against Biden. Biden denied this but had to
reconcile this denial with a supposed progressive stance
on the crisis of climate change. Since American presidential elections don't challenge class power, the situation
for people like Biden and the people he represents was
opportunistically political: appear progressive to appease
the non-revolutionary "left"—Biden called for a limited
ban on fracking on Federal land— but say nothing about
fracking generally on private land and let the capitalists
destroying the planet continue with business as usual to
garner their support. Position it as a job creation/retention
issue and march on to Washington. This was exactly what
Biden did. Science is important for the world's people and
when it informs the decisions of leaders who rise above
the threshold of opportunism, it may be the only thing
that has a chance of averting species extinction on the
planet. But science is not what Pelosi or Biden care about.

For the imperialists, science is a ploy used to either
advance imperialism or to maintain it, and it is no different with the politics of COVID-19 relief packages. In their
introduction to the recently republished *A New Outlook
on Health*, the Redspark Collective notes that "fighting
and containing pandemics requires both a conceptual
understanding of the 'public' by the masses and a public
infrastructure driven by public welfare rather than profit

motive."[5] In the United States there is no public infrastructure for surviving a pandemic and the recognition of
the need for such a thing among imperialist politicians is
opportunistic—can a COVID-19 relief package be used to
outmaneuver political opponents in a way that maintains
the status quo of necrocapitalist planned inequity, depra-
vation, and injustice? If it can, you can bet the imperialists will find a way. And they did. Pelosi's *let-them-wait-
it-out-until-we-get-back-to-"normal"* attitude while resisting COVID-19 relief for the people enduring hardship
revealed the basic condition of capitalism regarding public
welfare: the wealthy are mildly inconvenienced and get by
with their hoarded wealth in a system designed for them
to continue to consume, everyone else fights for base survival, and figures like Pelosi and other administrators of
imperialism position it as tough work to get back to "normal." The Redspark Collective accurately writes of the
United States's "failure" during the pandemic that "it is
not a mistake or malfunction of the system; it is the consequence of the steady march of imperialism, largely im-
pervious to the public good (unless it intersects with its expansion)."[6] Nancy Pelosi and the Democrats did not make
a "mistake" in failing to secure a more robust COVID-19
relief package; they merely acted in accordance with the
predictable workings of necrocapitalism and sided once
again with death and deprivation.

   It is important at this time for those looking to imagine
and implement meaningful alternatives to science and
social welfare opportunism from the imperialist camp
to look to leadership that is oriented toward solving the
practical problems faced by the most oppressed people

and those people who don't benefit from returning to the "normal" of Nancy Pelosi and the Democratic Party. We need solutions to homelessness, unemployment, poverty, environmental destruction, disease, patriarchy, racialized national oppression, ableism, and war, and there is none of that forthcoming from Joe Biden and his team of imperialist running dogs. Returning to Biden's partial cabinet selection—leadership leaves no room for careerism. Under necrocapitalism today, the drive of the oppressed to use science and wield power to transform the world for the better and for all is whittled away to nothing within the legal channels for the expression of political will. The ruling classes set the rules for leadership and are packing their administrations with cronies and death merchants whose main skill is longevity in carrying out imperialism. We need to change this. When oppressed people set the height of the bar for leadership we arrive at Stalin and Mao levels of leadership and we move away from meaningless parliamentary elections between sectors of the ruling class posturing about science and the social good in order to keep necrocapitalism going.

NOTES TO CHAPTER 27

1. https://twitter.com/AlCardenasFL_DC/status/1330947535700193288?s=20

2. Ben Norton, "Donald Trump's Libya policy is strikingly similar to one of Hilary's top surrogates" (https://www.salon.com/2016/06/20/

trump_proposed_taking_libyas_oil_in_return_for_
bombing_it_just_like_clinton_ally_neera_tanden/).

3. Subir, "What is Neera Tanden thinking?" (https://
www.dailykos.com/stories/2018/7/7/1778727/-What-is-
Neera-Tanden-thinking).

4. Erin Corbett, "Nancy Pelosi Says she will compromise on COVID relief now that Biden's been elected"
(https://www.refinery29.com/en-us/2020/12/10210479/
nancy-pelosi-stimulus-package-covid-relief-proposal-
backlash).

5. *A New Outlook on Health*, 29.

6. Ibid., 35.

CHAPTER TWENTY-EIGHT

THE CONTENT OF INSURGENCY

HAVING SUBJECTED US TO THE SPECTACLE OF ITS electoral circus for most of the pandemic, it was too much to hope that the US would stop clogging the global news cycle with the performances and rituals of its bourgeoisie's political competition. The world is more than the US — even the imperialist camp is larger than the US — and the global deployment of the vaccine, according to the vicissitudes of world capitalism, is now happening while other events, also over-determined by the pandemic, unfold in every corner of the globe. But it is the prerogative of the most powerful imperialist country to center its narratives, particularly the stories of its dominant class, and to demand that its voice and its concerns drown out everything else. Such was the case with the British Empire when it was the preeminent imperialist nation; such will be the case if and when the US is replaced by another leading imperialist power. In the past, in the early days of capitalism, the world was predominantly the world of the British Empire, despite other European nations competing for the same perceived right of "civilizational" domination, because that imperialist power possessed the economic and political power to declare itself the owner of the world — a world it saw as its destiny, along with less powerful European nation-states, to master and plunder. Most news that was newsworthy then (although the speed of news was much slower than it is today) centerd the pre-eminence of the British Empire, until one of its genocidal slave-state colonies seceded and, upon secession, worked tirelessly to become the next pre-eminent imperialist power. Rule Britannia was eventually replaced by Manifest Destiny, and the time of American Exceptionalism—for every imperialist power, especially the most powerful, accords itself an exceptionalism—was born.

We keep coming back to events unfolding in the US in our discussion of the necrotic characteristics of contemporary capitalism because these characteristics are best represented by the leading capitalist nation-state and the imposition of its will upon the world. Every other imperialist power, along with the compradors in the global peripheries, are still dragged along by events within the US along with events the US is involved with globally. So it was that, right when the vaccines appeared and started to be distributed globally according to the dictates of imperialism, the world found itself again focused on the fallout of US "democratic" ritual, the paroxysms resulting from Donald Trump's refusal to admit defeat, which led to his loyalists storming Capitol Hill because of a supposed stolen election.

To be clear, this narrative of a "stolen election" and the democratic sanctity of Biden's election should not matter to any militant who cares about breaking from and transcending this capitalist order. As noted, so-called "Trumpism" (a possibly American Exceptionalist term that assumes its version of right populism is unique) could not be sharply demarcated from the neoliberalism of the Biden/Harris regime. The point, here, is that all the mea culpas about the potential death of US democracy due to MAGA loyalists storming a site of US power tell us more about the degeneration of the myth of US democracy than an actual existential threat to democracy in general. What we actually observed was committed settlers, the backbone of US settler-capitalist society, just doing what the US has always done in every space in the world it has involved itself. There was nothing truly outside of the pale in their so-called "insurrection"—and the fact that the police collaborated with them is evidence of this—because it was merely the white settler garrison manifesting as it has always manifested, since the settler-colonial beginnings of the US monstrosity. Media lionizing of the few pigs who did try to halt this white power mob—the crocodile tears shed for the "hero" cop who died in the process—should not hide the fact that these same police were part of the repressive state apparatus engaged in the ongoing domestic warfare that had both set off the Spring and Summer rebellions of 2020 and that were involved in putting them down. Indeed, the surreal restraint the police demonstrated towards the so-called "insurrectionists" was nowhere evident in their responses to the spring and summer demonstrators. This difference in response revealed again "a rigorous analytic narrative of police violence as systemic, institutionalized, juridically condoned."[1]

The fact that the class composition of this supposed "insurrection" was by-and-large "upper middle class" should demonstrate that this is less of a heinous act and more of the US settler-colonial nature haunting itself.[2] That is, it was a point of social cannibalism. The US is eating itself and its own claims to democracy. Its pro-Confederate past is showing up in its hallowed sites, but it cannot condemn this past because, in the interest of "unity," it preserved this past against Black Reconstruction, through Jim Crow, and right up to its current anti-Black and pro-colonial carceral logic. Thus, when US Democrats complain about an attack on democracy, we should not care since we are merely observing the racist basis of this so-called "democracy" working itself out in real time, as a war between settler siblings.

But American Exceptionalism is such that other imperialist nation-states are forced to play along. Condemnations of Trump's claims about the US elections have been delivered by the other imperialist nations, and all of these condemnations have also been determined by the pandemic and the worry that so-called "Trumpism" will get in the way of the rollout of vaccines. A rollout, let us be honest, that will function according to the rules of imperialism no matter what happens in that exceptionalist realm of US blood and soil. None of these nations really cared about the content of Trump's politics when he was in power; liberal democracy is such that it can tolerate reactionaries as long as they play by the rules of electoral ritual. What it cannot tolerate are these rules being broken—which is why it could not tolerate the violence of the rebellions in the spring and summer while also tolerating the necrotic aspects of capitalism that were laid bare over the course of the pandemic. Hence, despite Trump's baseless claims about a stolen election in November and December, fascists such as Modi congratulated Biden for his victory. And following the January 6 events in the Capitol Building, a reactionary like Boris Johnson could join the chorus of other imperialist states condemning Trump for allowing the transgression of the hallowed conventions of bourgeois democracy.

This transgression has been cast in moralizing terms by liberal critics. We must cast aside these moralizing terms. A revolutionary, anticapitalist struggle must contend with the conquest of political power and must also contend with its enemies' attempts at conquest. The Capitol putsch was a disorganized and naive attempt to commandeer a symbol of American power, one revealing the equivocal relationship between American imperialism, the far right, and liberalism. Liberals hand-wring about the violence, about the violation of "democratic" conventions, and blather on about sedition and treason. But they did the same with the rebellions in the spring and summer and, as noted, subjected the populations involved in these rebellions to more state violence than what fascists who stormed the Capitol were subjected to. Fascists who were in fact enabled by the repressive state apparatus of the dictatorship of the bourgeoisie—the pigs participated, letting the Trump supporters inside—and have faced far less retribution. The dictatorship of the bourgeoisie can tolerate fascism to a certain extent because it is part of its political continuum, especially in a settler-capitalist formation. As long as fascists follow the rules of liberal decorum, other factions of the bourgeoisie are happy to enable them by giving their ideologues many of the platforms they desire. Biden could thus speak about "unity" amongst white supremacists and other US citizens once the embarrassment of the Capitol storming was overcome. Republicans who were once fine with Trump could entertain the notion of voting for impeachment (even though they largely voted *not* to impeach) because he broke the decorum generated by the myth of US democratic exceptionalism.

Multiple adages about the singular greatness of US democracy and how it was violated by the events of January 6 should make us laugh. The white supremacy that is foundational to that "great democracy" simply manifested; it was not in contradiction with the content of US politics, only with its form. "The racist in a culture with racism is therefore normal," writes Fanon: "He has achieved a perfect harmony of economic relations and ideology."[3] And Devin Zane Shaw has charted the ways in which system loyalty and system opposition function within white supremacist factions of settler-capitalist formations.[4]

All of this is to say that if the Capitol building was stormed by revolutionaries who desired to overthrow settler-capitalism there would in fact be nothing to condemn. The problem for us is the political content, not insurgency, whereas for liberals the problem is insurgency and they could give two shits about the politics involved: actually, they would be more likely to condemn communists, anarchists, and "Antifa" before condemning actual fascists. For our side, and against the return to neoliberal "normalcy," we want to remind ourselves and those we organize with that insurgency is correct, that the conventions of bourgeois democracy should be torn down, but that it is the political line that matters. We are now being exhorted to return to a neoliberal normalcy and to act as if the recent delirium of the most powerful imperialist nation was an aberration, when in fact we should be rejecting this violent and necrotic system altogether. As the war between siblings of the dictatorship of the bourgeoisie intensifies, and thus exposes more of the intrinsic violence of the system, we should be rejecting both the fascist and liberal wings of this bourgeois dictatorship. Capitalist normalcy must die if humanity is to live.

NOTES TO CHAPTER 28

1. Rodríguez, *White Reconstruction*, 149.

2. Katie McDonough, "Die laughing at the Capitol" (https://newrepublic.com/article/160846/die-laughing-capitol).

3. Fanon, *Toward the African Revolution*, 40.

4. Devin Zane Shaw, "Between system-loyal vigilantism and system-oppositional violence" (http://threewayfight.blogspot.com/2020/10/between-system-loyal-vigilantism-and.html).

F: NORMALIZATION

February 12 2021—May 8 2021

CHAPTER TWENTY-NINE

TWO ERRORS OF NORMALIZATION

IF THIS PROJECT BEGAN IN THE MIDST OF AN INDETER-
minate *miasmatic* temporality, the beginning of vaccinations—regardless of their success—draws us back into
periodization and demarcations. From the dichotomy of
"before times" and the pandemic, back to past, present,
and future. Political leaders touted not the end, but the
"beginning of the end" of the pandemic; though, given that
vaccination will follow distribution patterns and logistics
shaped by necrocapitalism, we can anticipate a long interregnum of an uneven geography of (potentially) post-
pandemic life. The return to "normalcy" will constitute
a regression toward the capitalist system that enabled the
pandemic to reach the scope that it has—and which continues to enable successive environmental crises.

The guiding hypothesis of this project has been that,
to quote Lenin, all crises "make manifest what has been
hidden; they cast aside all that is relative, superficial, and
trivial; they sweep away the political litter." Our explicit
goal has been to relate what is unprecedented to consti-
tutive features of capitalism. Thus, we began very early
on by challenging the hyperbolic assertions of several
prominent philosophers. Giorgio Agamben's position
veered very quickly toward close proximity to COVID-
denialism—the coronavirus was merely a ploy to extend
the state of exception into everyday existence, stifling

the meaningful bonds of public life.[1] Ironically, it was the United States, which once stood as the contemporary paradigm of the state of exception, that then underwent an inversion into spontaneous Agambenian resistance. And for that, it has recorded a disproportionate amount of preventable harm and death (though again, it is marginalized and oppressed groups which have disproportionately suffered this already disproportionate harm). Slavoj Žižek, by contrast, grasped that the COVID-19 pandemic would occasion a capitalist crisis, but he hoped that capitalist states and non-governmental institutions would suddenly impose the communist social relations they've so brutally suppressed over the last century.

Again, the concept of necrocapitalism does not constitute a radical rupture with the supposedly normal, smooth functioning of capital. In our view, what the pandemic casts in relief is the fact that capital accumulation is premised on exposing and subjecting the poor, the oppressed, the dispossessed, and the wretched of the earth to environmental harm and premature death. Crisis focuses the intensity of this exposure and subjection.

If public health officials are correct and vaccination heralds the beginning of the end of the pandemic, then revolutionary and leftist theorists and organizers must move forward while avoiding two errors.

First, we must refuse the widespread appeals to a return to normalcy. In what follows we will draw examples from North America. The implementation of neoliberal policy in the United States and Canada resulted in drastic cuts and/or privatization in public health care and disease-control infrastructure. However, this criticism of government policy should be understood in the broad sense that includes policy changes over decades. Yet even if these policies were different, this would not modify the fact that, as Angela Mitropoulos points out, shortages or supply-chain breakdowns in supplies of personal protective equipment are due to the fact that PPE is a commodity.[2]

Furthermore, the normalcy to which public officials appeal rests on a system of transnational capitalism that is powered by fossil fuel. There's already an attempt on the part of wealthier nations to pin responsibility for carbon emissions on countries that produce commodities—for export to these wealthier nations—without acknowledging how the drive to extract surplus-value by following cheap labor costs *drives* increased carbon emissions. As Andreas Malm shows in *Fossil Capital*, "globally mobile capital will speed up the consumption of fossil energy *through* its perpetual drive to maximise surplus-value."[3] More recently, Malm has expanded the scope of his analysis to examine how, beyond the concern of carbon emissions, ecologically unequal exchange between the Global North and Global South, enabled by fossil capital, is a "deep driver of deforestation, hence of biodiversity loss, hence of zoonotic spillover"—meaning that the present system of producing products such as coffee, beef, tea, sugar, and palm oil exercises more and more pressure on biodiverse ecosystems.[4] As Malm notes, according to a 2012 study:

> the top seven importers of biodiversity threats were ... the United States, Japan, Germany, France, UK, Italy, and Spain ... . Measured per capita, the variations in consumptive claims on

biodiversity are even more skewed, with rich but sparsely populated countries like Canada and Finland shooting up to the top ... The forces reaching out to forests and pulling out pathogens are nowhere as strong as in the central nodes of capital.[5]

Once we consider—to take a local example for some of us—that the Canadian economy remains tied to bitumen extraction, normalcy portends more environmental degradation, the continued expansion of fossil capital, the intensified threat to biodiversity, and pathogenic zoonotic spillover. In short, normalcy involves returning back to the material conditions which have enabled climate emergency and the present pandemic despite however many so-called moral lessons we exchange in our edifying post-pandemic discourses.

Second, we must not confuse the deployment of equitable, or perhaps more accurately, aspirationally-equitable, patterns of vaccination with underlying transformations of social, political, or economic relations. The electoral left tends to organize for forms of economic and political reform and mitigation rather than revolution, and thus social democratic parties and organizations will push for half-measures of so-called new deals, despite the fact that reformism lacks the scope to confront global, systemic capitalist crises. They will focus on instituting equitable patterns of distribution, but these leave inequalities in relations of production untouched.

In other words, *even if a given government institutes equitable patterns of vaccination, these equitable patterns do not constitute a rupture with underlying exploitative relations of economic production and social reproduction.* And the deployment of these patterns of distribution must be examined from the totality of social relations. For example, the federal government and at least some provincial governments in Canada have prioritized vaccination for Indigenous peoples. For some analysts, this signals a shift toward fulfilling the Canadian government's self-proclaimed mandate of nation-to-nation reconciliation between First Nations, Métis, and Inuit nations and the Crown. However, much of the government's policy remains the same. In October of 2020, the Trudeau government announced that the pandemic will interfere with a prior pledge to end long-term boil-water advisories—which must mean that COVID-19 has been in Canada for years, since the promise was made in 2015! Nor should we exclude the fact that Indigenous communities are especially vulnerable to the pandemic due to various ongoing structural manifestations of racism: the lack of services available to remote communities, biases affecting how health care is administered (or denied), and the stigmatization of Indigenous communities as supposed carriers of COVID-19—and that none of these factors has been mitigated. In fact, if we consider that Indigenous struggles, from the Wet'suwet'en solidarity blockades of February 2020 to the Mi'kmaq assertion of fishing rights, were met with escalating reactionary settler vigilante violence, and what amounts to tacit consent of the RCMP in these situations for vigilantism, it is plausible that Indigenous political struggle faces more antagonism than it did at the beginning of the pandemic. And if we consider that the government policies have enriched the bourgeoisie at the expense of the working classes, increased social inequalities, left many unemployed (with women—especially racialized women and women with disabilities—significantly impacted by job losses in the US), and exposed marginalized and oppressed communities to the deepening environmental injustices of adverse health-care outcomes through the pandemic, only a sliver of society has the means to return to "normal." In short, when public officials herald the beginning of the end of the pandemic, we must organize so that the return to so-called normalcy is merely a condition of the beginning of a renewed struggle against the conditions that make necro-capitalism possible.

NOTES TO CHAPTER 29

1. As it turns out, in a recent essay Giorgio Agamben has claimed that techniques for proving vaccination make those who refuse this system "bearers of a virtual yellow star."

The far-right anti-vaxxer movement has made repeated reference to their treatment, under current or proposed pandemic policies, as being similar to wearing the yellow star. Here Agamben, who we cannot believe is unfamiliar with this discourse, gives this trope an academic veneer. It must be firmly maintained that these references to wearing the yellow star are antisemitic, for (at least) two reasons.

First, in the assertion of a parallel between the treatment of anti-vaxxers and Germany's genocidal policies against Jewish peoples, this claim involves a form of genocide denialism by minimizing the persecution of Jews.

And second, given that the far-right anti-vaxxer movement has participants who trade in antisemitic and Holocaust-denying conspiracy theories (among others), the reference to the yellow star in this context is deeply problematic. Given the discourses that circulate within these groups, their attempt to draw a parallel between the conditions of present society and those of historical injustice and oppression is not as it appears—that is, an acknowledgement of these prior injustices. Recall that far-right groups regard human inequality as natural and desirable as long as their in-group is at the top of this hierarchy. In white supremacist ideology, Jewish peoples are the natural inferiors of "Aryans." For the white supremacist and antisemitic elements of anti-vaxxer groups, when they evoke the yellow star, they mean that what they take to be natural hierarchies have been overturned, and there the injustice occurs.

There are legitimate problems that arise with requiring people to produce immunization records, given that access to vaccinations follows patterns established by existing social inequalities. It is likely that "showing your papers" would rebound against already marginalized communities, and even more likely that if producing papers gets tied at all to police and security apparatuses, that force will be brought to bear disproportionally against racialized peoples, undocumented migrants, the homeless, and others who already "wear" how social inequality leaves them vulnerable to repressive violence and premature death. We don't need to evoke a "virtual yellow star" to make this oppression visible and legible. When Agamben alludes to far-right anti-vaxxer tropes, then, he merely raises, and legitimates, reactionary grievances.

The translation is provided here: Martin Paul Eve, "It's time we dropped Agamben," (https://eve.gd/2021/07/23/its-time-we-dropped-agamben/).

2. Mitropoulos, *Pandemonium*, 96ff.

3. Malm, *Fossil Capital*, 339.

4. Malm, *Corona, Climate, Chronic Emergency*, 54.

5. Ibid., 53–55.

CHAPTER THIRTY

TIME THEFT IN THE NEW NORMAL

We have so far cautioned against the ideological trap of a "return to normalcy." Since what is unprecedented in the pandemic indexes only the functioning of the inner logic of capitalism under specific historical conditions rather than any radical rupture, the return to normalcy is a concession to the very crisis-ridden system that we should rather be aiming to overcome.

On the other hand, we are everywhere enjoined to embrace a "new normal." It's worth reflecting further on this because here again the theme of novelty, the unprecedented, is perniciously mobilized, while the old logic of capitalism churns on. Irrationalities in vaccine rollouts and the proliferation of coronavirus variants are certainly emerging faces of crisis (not to mention parallel and compounding crises like the deadly climate-driven cold shock in Texas at the time of writing). But we must never forget that capitalism *runs* on crisis. Because it does, the contradiction between the "return to normalcy" and the "new normal" is only apparent.

What we are witnessing is capital seizing the moment, not simply to keep its grip on us, but also to *tighten* it. In a very basic way, pandemic-related unemployment swells the reserve army of labor and therefore puts pressure on those who are still working. But there are more specific ways the grip tightens as well. To take one example, many of us work in the education sector, and have had to shift to telework and online learning. The writing is on the wall that the current investment in this shift—made materially in large part by workers themselves, to be sure—is here to stay. Doubtless, we can point to emerging coronavirus variants or even to the next pandemic as reasons why a robust online infrastructure and workforce capacity are vital. But such work also offloads infrastructure costs onto workers, and potentially increases the pace and volume of their labor through the modification of spatial and temporal limits to teaching, grading, research, administrative tasks, and meetings. Let's not miss the implication: the more capitalism manifests openly as *necro*capitalism—that is, the more it mows people down by exposing frontline workers to infection for economic reasons—the better it can sell fixes that help it to extract even more surplus value from workers. More simply still: the more it kills us, the more capitalism can steal from us. This sounds perverse, but that's precisely the point: talk of "the new normal" masks capital's core perversion. It does this by conflating "normal" in the sense of usual or typical, with "normal" in the sense of normative. For this reason, we reserve the use of the term "normal" to simply mean the functioning of capitalism according to its core logic—which, of course, can manifest in various ways according to capital's needs of the moment.

Two of David Harvey's concepts are helpful here.[1] First, he often refers to "accumulation by dispossession," basically Marx's "primitive accumulation" but more forthright in name and further differentiated beyond the baseline examples of colonialism and plunder. In a word, accumulation by dispossession is the phase of capitalism in which "startup capital" is acquired through theft, force, or coercion. Harvey's terminology is preferable to Marx's because "primitive" has the ring to it of "historically prior" whereas this is not at all what Marx meant. "Primitive" accumulation—basically stealing, therefore "accumulation by dispossession"—can occur in any historical period and is likely to happen during crises of capital, when the market as such can no longer maintain the farce that it is capable of ironing out capitalist contradictions.

Second, Harvey often references the "free gifts of nature" that human beings give capitalism. Take reproduction and childrearing, which we've discussed at some length in previous chapters. It is costly to raise children, which is odd when you realize that by doing so you are equipping new workers for entry into the market. Basically, parents subsidize capital when they care for their children. And in other ways, such as through our creativity and our capacity for mutual aid, we likewise furnish capital with much it can put to its own uses and sell back to us at an inflated cost.

Let's put these concepts together. What we are suggesting is that we are living through a new round of accumulation by dispossession. But to speak solely of teleworkers, what is being demanded and taken also falls increasingly in the category of erstwhile free gifts of nature: unless we are deemed essential and put in harm's way as a matter of course, our working lives are shifted increasingly into our home or intimate lives, where care relations have to keep the whole damned thing going. The reduction of "junk time" through telework is double-edged, for in the very instant that it opens up free time, it also recasts us as beings who are *available for work*. This is, of course, what the poorest workers have always been to capital, but there is a palpable sense in the pandemic of digital proletarianization, and this is precisely one facet of what is peddled as a "new normal."

Finally, this bears on what we previously termed the "indeterminate *miasmatic* temporality" of the pandemic's opening. Arguably, over a year into the pandemic, this temporality continues into the calls for normalcy, but it now does so with a twist. We are told to wait; specifically, that we must wait for capital and its neoliberal political bunglers to outrun the rapidly mutating coronavirus through vaccination rollouts and therapeutics. But, simultaneously, we are also told that we can no longer wait; however grudgingly, we must accept the new normal, which is after all a return to the old normal but now with more of an employment blackmail hanging over us and more of our free "gifts" demanded as tribute to capital. Our call here is therefore simple: we must fight the imposed miasmatic temporality of waiting while working, of being made more and more available for work, with an active temporality of resistance and organizing. At a minimum, if telework imposes a broader span of time where we are available for work, then our watchword must be to practice so-called "time theft" whenever and as often as we can. But beyond this minimum, we must also form links in an organized chain of workers capable of constituting a genuine rupture, a break beyond the wildest dreams of capital's impoverished, stagnant, and utterly "normal" imagination.

NOTES TO CHAPTER 30

1. See Harvey's *Marx, Capital, and the Madness of Economic Reason* (2019).

CHAPTER THIRTY-ONE

RAMPAGE AND ROLLOUT

NECROCAPITALISM IS ON A RAMPAGE. BUT IF ALL YOU did was listen to the official media organs and figureheads you would think that capitalist society was making progress toward justice and that things are getting better. But they are not. Necrocapitalism is on a rampage.

On April 21 of 2021, one of George Floyd's killers, the pig Derek Chauvin, was found guilty of second-degree murder, third-degree murder, and second-degree manslaughter. That same day, figurehead for the US empire, President Joe Biden, said in a statement that the verdict was "a step forward," while claiming that "systemic racism is a stain on our nation's soul."[1] *Systemic racism,* a term in long currency among oppressed people critical of the United States, its "justice" system, and all the structures of capitalist oppression, is today a talking point for people like Joe Biden who are responsible for legitimizing and carrying out that oppression. Minnesota Attorney General Keith Ellison, a person who has made it his life's work to uphold systemic racism as part of America's "justice" system, also said "I would not call today's verdict justice, however, because justice implies true restoration. But it is accountability, which is the first step toward justice."[2] Ellison's comment, drawing a distinction between justice and accountability, resembles something that oppressed people fighting for the abolition of capitalism and its police have also long emphasized: that the repressive institutions of capitalism, the prisons, the courts, and the police, are not vehicles for justice.

We have emphasized in previous chapters that the revolutionary left must refuse the call to "return to the normalcy" of capitalism. And that we must also refuse to be conned into believing that the rolling out of vaccination in the imperialist countries is guided by anything more benevolent or "equitable" than the distribution patterns and logistics of necrocapitalism. We raise the same warning flag about the use of revolutionary sounding language by the representatives of capitalism.

After the conviction of the pig Derek Chauvin, will Joe Biden and Keith Ellison and all the other politicians making claims about justice and "first steps" towards it become committed fighters against the systems and institutions that brought about the murder of George Floyd? No. What Biden and Ellison and so many other figureheads of imperialism are committed to is the continuation of the normalcy in the "return to normalcy"—which, as we've noted time and again, is founded on the material conditions that produce all of the nightmarish features of necrocapitalism, including the current pandemic and the continued mass incarceration and murder of oppressed people at the hands of the police and the "justice" systems of capitalism. In the very same statement quoted above, Ellison went whole hog as an agent of capitalist repression and demanded that the oppressed carry out any further expressions of rage against injustice "calmly, legally, and peacefully"—a scornful reference to the year-long, global, mass actions of oppressed people who took to the streets to protest the police murder of George Floyd, which was indispensable for pressuring the capitalist justice system to bring charges against and convict Chauvin.

Meanwhile, it is business as usual: on the same day that the pig Derek Chauvin was found guilty of mur-der—indeed, only a few minutes after the verdict was announced, Makiyah Bryant, a Black girl who called the police because she was being jumped, was shot dead by the pigs in Columbus, Ohio. Bystanders at the scene after Makiyah Bryant's murder began shouting "No racist police!" and "Enough is enough!" The pigs on site began yelling the racist slogan "blue lives matter" at the crowd.[3]

Capitalism is not only incapable of producing justice for Black people and the oppressed; it is not only incapable of stopping the death of Black people and the oppressed at the hands of the police, it is also a state of affairs where even the possibility of stopping the mass death of the oppressed due to COVID-19 is controversial.

Take, for instance, the global deployment of COVID-19 vaccines. According to Abby Maxman of Oxfam America, "one in four citizens of rich countries have been vaccin-ated, and just one in 500 in poorer countries have done so." This is stemming from the fact that the United States, the UK and other WTO countries oppose a waiver on international bourgeois patent rights for COVID-19 vac-cines that would allow poor countries to manufacture the medicines. The consequence of this profits-before-people approach that is the status quo of capitalism is the increased spread of the COVID-19 virus, new variations of the virus, and the countless deaths of people from poor countries.

The imperialist class and the ruling classes in the imperialist countries are vehemently opposed to this waiver. Bill Gates, poster boy for "philanthropic" capitalism and a parasite who thrives solely because of the existence of bourgeois intellectual property rights, recently said that rich countries should not share vaccine recipes with poor countries. His "argument," which he gave no support for other than chauvinism against the poor, is that only by maintaining this inequitable status quo can the quality of vaccines be guaranteed.[4] Of course, we can ask "who cares about the opinions of a billionaire completely removed from global health concerns?" and move on, but there are other interests involved in the inequitable distribution of vaccines that also oppose patent rights wavers. Lobbyists for vaccine manufacturers have instructed the United States that patent rights waivers for COVID-19 vaccines could have the unthinkable, catastrophic result of other countries developing not only vaccines for COVID-19, but also cancer and heart disease, and as such should be opposed.[5]

The position of the pharmaceutical industry reminds us of what Lenin described as the "parasitism and decay of capitalism" in its imperialist stage.[6] The decay of capitalism refers to the tendency of advanced capitalism to halt technical progress and innovation by limiting production to what can produce monopoly profits. Lenin notes that it is the same in imperialism's relationship to the neo-colonies.[7] In the case of the manufacture of COVID-19 vaccines, pharmaceutical companies have little interest in producing lifesaving vaccines if they are unable to profit from them. So they pressure their lackeys in the imperialist governments to secure their monopoly on vaccine manufacture, no matter how many people die in the poor countries.

While keeping Lenin in mind, we recall that in *The State and Revolution* Lenin tells us that the exploiting classes need political rule to maintain exploitation.[8] What we see happening right now is the rich imperialist countries condemning poor people all over the world to death while squeezing neo-colonial governments for profit. Joe Biden and the representatives of imperialism provide that political rule. On the one hand, Biden talks about taking steps to achieve justice after the Derek Chauvin verdict, but on the other, his government colludes with the pharmaceutical companies to carry out injustice on a global scale, resulting in mass death. This situation is endemic to necrocapitalism and is a powerful reminder that there is no "return to normalcy" that does not carry a death toll for the poor and exploited. No matter what the figureheads of imperialism say about justice, and no matter how many times they project a faux optimism about things getting better, only the political rule of the proletariat can stop the rampage of necrocapitalism.

NOTES TO CHAPTER 31

1. Dartunorro Clark and Shannon Pettypiece, "Biden calls guilty verdict in Derek Chauvin trial 'a step forward'" (https://www.nbcnews.com/politics/joe-biden/president-joe-biden-calls-guilty-verdict-chauvin-trial-step-forward-n1264696).

2. Keith Ellison, "Today's verdict isn't justice. But accountability is a first step to justice" (https://www.the-guardian.com/commentisfree/2021/apr/20/keith-ellison-george-floyd-speech-minnesota-attorney-general).

3. Akshita Jain, "Ma'Khia Bryant: Ohio police tell bystanders 'blue lives matter' after girl shot dead as Chauvin verdict delivered" (https://www.independent.co.uk/news/world/americas/crime/ohio-police-blue-lives-matter-b1834897.html).

4. John Queally, "Bill Gates says no to sharing vaccine formulas with global poor to end pandemic" (https://www.salon.com/2021/04/26/bill-gates-says-no-to-sharing-vaccine-formulas-with-global-poor-to-end-pandemic_partner/).

5. Hannah Kuchler and Aime William, "Vaccine makers say IP waiver could hand technology to China and Russia" (https://www.ft.com/content/fa1e0d22-71f2-401f-9971-fa27313570ab).

6. Lenin, *Imperialism, the Highest Stage of Capitalism*, 119.

7. Ibid.

8. Lenin, *The State and Revolution*, 20.

CHAPTER THIRTY-TWO

"DISEASE POETICS"

As the vaccine rollout continues, unevenly and according to capitalist and imperialist logics, it is worth briefly returning our attention to the logics of family and the private sphere, and their connection to politics and economics—what Angela Mitropoulos has called the *oikos* and the connection between this space and the state and economy *oikonomia*.[1] We know very well the ways in which capitalism maintains an ideological fiction about the private and public divide, pretending that the state is restrained from the household when in fact it intervenes upon the households of the most marginalized and when the normative households promulgate dominant ideology—sometimes the most reactionary—as part of their foundational oikos. Domestic labor, domestic abuse, and the family as a state apparatus function smoothly as part of the familial "private." These patterns complement the public state, the latter interfering in domiciles it finds threatening: the Black households in the US, the Indigenous reserve homesteads in every settler-colonial formation, the migrant households where "illegals" are hidden.

But the appeal to the exceptional realm of the domicile, the oikos, has taken on an interesting characteristic during the pandemic, particularly during its latter half. As new variants of the plague spread, as the vaccine rollout is poorly managed, invectives regarding household and individual responsibility are being circulated. During an early 2021 lockdown, the Ontario government circulated an advertisement where the spreading of the plague was blamed solely on individuals who didn't follow safety procedures. Meanwhile, while this advertisement was circulating, the same government was talking about opening up the economy again—opening up the very spaces that all medical experts indicated caused viral contact.

By March, with case numbers still climbing, the Ontario government again trotted out this nonsense about individual responsibility and private gatherings and declared a more draconian lockdown.[2] A stay-at-home order was issued, police were mandated to stop and question pedestrians and drivers. Despite the fact that the medical experts had informed the government that the ICUs were filled with workers and that the problem was that workplaces, even those deemed "essential," were not providing the proper safety measures or paid sick leave, as usual the government responded in its typical manner: policing rather than care, which is the normative necrocapitalist response. The problem, according to the government, was private responsibility: the decisions of families, the decisions of individuals. Personal choice and not the governmental choice to restrain itself from interfering with the economy.

The household and the individuals within the household are, of course, the units upon which the capitalist state depends. "The oikonomic nexus of family, nation and race delivers up the gift of free labor in its most forceful senses through the interrelated boundaries of the wage contract and those of citizenship (that is, the social contract)," writes Mitropoulos. "It does so in the forms of unpaid domestic labour; migrant labour that, by way of visa stipulations or outright criminalisation, is compelled to work for as little as possible; the geographic organisation of cheap and below-subsistence labour; to mention the most notable."[3] Despite this fact, these "private" spaces are treated as the capitalist state's exceptions, its scapegoats, as if they are outside of the economy even though they are part of this economy's totality.

The oikos is the realm of reproductive labor; the liberal fiction of the private/public divide is in fact maintained and legislated by the state, intersecting with and paralleling the fictive division between the "free market" and the state:

> The oikonomics of present-day organisations of the economy … deliver a labour that has affective purchase, circulating as an extension of (rather than refusal of or indifference toward) care-giving domestic labour that significantly must appear as if it is not work at all, but freely and naturally given. Far from being marginal to the extraction of surplus labour, this expectation of a labour freely given has always been central to capitalist re/production.[4]

Just as deregulation is a misnomer since the capitalist state has consistently enforced such deregulation by setting up multiple institutions to make the market into a Friedmanesque fever dream, the private sphere is equally regulated. It remains conveniently beyond the state in instances of domestic violence and the promulgation of reactionary ideology (that's the private business of

families!), as well as in instances of poverty and desperation (it's the business of families to work out their home
economy!). At the same time, it is conveniently open
to state interference—or, more accurately, what Dylan
Rodríguez in *White Reconstruction* has rightly character-
ized as "domestic warfare"—if these families are from colonized or migrant backgrounds: let us not forget how, in
the opening months of the pandemic, Regis Korchinski-
Paquet was thrown from her balcony by Toronto pigs.

Moreover, the household is potentially an ideological
state apparatus, in that it is a space where reproductive
labor might intersect with the reproduction of dominant
social norms—where children are taught the ruling ideas
of the ruling class by their parents and the media their parents allow them to consume. We say *potentially* and *might*,
here, because not all homesteads are loyal—especially
those that are exposed to domestic warfare—which is why
the state interferes with those homes that do not conform
to a proper oikonomia. Look at the snitch phone lines set
up by various governments during the pandemic, encouraging proper households to call the police on neighbors
who appeared to be violating the rules of lockdown. Never
mind the fact that poor immigrant households often contain more than ten people, due to the fact that they need
to care for their elders and cousins; suddenly these households brimming with "foreigners" become suspect and
primed for state intervention.

Writing a few years before the pandemic, Mitropoulos
noted that "contagion seems to be as much a hermeneut-
ics of everything as it is a biological model of generation,
transmission and course of various diseases. Politics has

become epidemiological."⁵ In *Epidemic Empire*, Anjuli Fatima Raza Kolb echoes Mitropoulos:

> The infectious spaces of the Global South—hot, dirty, and teeming with illiterate and unhygienic bodies—have been represented by many health experts, policy makers, and popular science writers as out of sync with the supposed hypersmooth, sanitary space of the Western metropolis.⁶

Within the imperialist metropoles, these spaces are represented as the homesteads of the migrant and racialized poor; within those imperialist metropoles that are also settler-capitalist formations, these homesteads are also those that are located in the reserves—indeed every reserve, as a whole, is treated as a collection of infectious domiciles. Raza Kolb's point was that these tropes of infection, epidemic, and contagion have been common ways in which imperialism has conceived of its other—her historiography traces these tropes from the early 19th century to the present—and so even before a pandemic these spaces were already conceptualized, and overrepresented, according to the language of contagion. As *a priori* "infections" of the imperial body politic, then, it is only logical that they would be conceived as the most frightening vectors of contagion during an actual pandemic. The general population has learned to suspect those households that represent these "infectious spaces" and to suspect that they are the ones responsible for spreading the virus rather than, as is actually the case, those economic spaces reopened during the pandemic (since the capitalist economy must go on!), where many more bodies are in contact with each other in restaurants, shopping malls, and big box stores. Again, the fault is the "individual" and their households—not the economic re-openings or the failure to safeguard workers in "essential" workplaces—and especially those individuals and households that are deemed by racist ideology to be, in Fanon's words, "insensible to ethics."[7]

There is an irony here that requires attention. While it is indeed the case that the greatest spread of COVID has always occurred when the economy is reopened—when restaurants, malls, and multiple stores open their doors to customers—thus making the notion of "waves" an artificial conception,[8] it is also the case that the most socially marginalized populations have experienced greater rates of infection than their non-marginalized counterparts. This fact, at first glance, appears to justify the racist assumption that these "other" spaces, and these suspect families, require surveillance and state intervention. But this perspective fails to grasp that marginalized populations possess less social assets than non-marginalized populations and are thus "expose[d] to death"[9] and disease at a greater rate than those who can work from home, largely avoid disease transmission, and have better access to health care. The reality is that those populations who are *a priori* conceptualized as being an "infection" to the body politic have been made vulnerable and thus are always exposed to actual disease; they are made into the very vectors they were already conceptualized as being. They are overwhelmingly the ones working in the factories and other labor spaces that remain open during every lockdown;

they are the ones who are not given paid sick leave and so are forced to hide whatever symptom they might experience so as to feed themselves and their families.

This irony, that those vulnerable populations conceived of as a "disease" are simultaneously those who are made most vulnerable to actual disease, affects the practice of inoculation. As the vaccines are being produced and those states that have access to them attempt to think how to best inoculate their general population, it becomes a general health concern to figure out which populations are most vulnerable to COVID-19 and to inoculate these populations first, so as to prevent further spread and stress upon state health systems. It was thus basic risk management when the Canadian state, for example, chose to distribute the first round of vaccines to at-risk Indigenous communities. This distribution was not an act of kindness, or even "benevolent" colonial paternalism (though it occasionally depicted itself as such), because settler-capitalism is far from benevolent. Rather, it was simple cost-benefit logistics: if you inoculate those most likely to contract the virus due to their social vulnerability, you end up saving money in the long run by preventing these populations from overburdening intensive care units. But when the CBC reported on this phase of the vaccine rollout,[10] the video on its YouTube channel was flooded with thousands of comments by settlers upset about "Indigenous privilege."[11]

Settler ideology is such, after all, that any prioritization of Indigenous populations over the "proper" Canadian citizen—no matter how logistically sound—will be seen as privilege and even the contamination of the normative rights of the (white settler) citizen. The colonized domicile ought to be exposed to death and disease, according to "empire's disease poetics,"[12] because the colonized (along with other racially marginalized populations) contaminate the stability of the settler-capitalist state. The notion that settler families and individuals are more deserving of state assets than their colonized counterparts is a well-worn trope that cuts against basic cost-benefit logistics. The settler domicile—the garrison building block of every settler-colonialist society—must always be prioritized, lest the body politic be contaminated! And those settler families who possess the economic means will defy the pandemic logistics of their own state if and when they can. Echoing the settler couple who travelled to a remote Indigenous community to escape COVID in the first months of the pandemic, the wealthy Baker family travelled to the Yukon and posed as members of the community so as to receive early inoculation.[13] Despite the fact that the Bakers were publicly castigated as "selfish" by a general population that has no tolerance for millionaires jumping the queue,[14] the truth is that many settler families and individuals would jump this queue if they possessed the resources. The antipathy towards the Bakers was less acrimonious than the antipathy towards these Indigenous populations. The hatred of the former was more to do with the fact that they used resources that the majority of settlers did not possess. The hatred of the latter concerned their very right, as humans, to receive anything from the settler state.

Besides, let us be clear, this simple cost-benefit analysis was always paltry. While some marginalized communities were able to be inoculated first, others were ignored if

and when it directly interfered with the economic sphere.
Aside from the instance cited above, vaccine rollout has
largely benefitted the bourgeois and petty-bourgeois who
have the time to book an appointment and the training
to navigate the labyrinth of state bureaucracy. The households containing individuals who work from home, possess negotiable work schedules, might even hire domestic
labor to look after their kids, and are acclimatized citizens,
are the households whose members are better able to get
their shots.

Hence, the ways in which even the vaccine rollout is
understood are determined by an oikonomic reasoning
that brushes up against the state's logistics. And every time
state representatives emphasize the responsibility of the
private household or individual, they valorize this already
politicized space (because, as discussed, it is an ideological
state apparatus) so that an idea of proper social contract
mediates inoculation logistics. Presuming that safety in the
pandemic is primarily the business of the private sphere,
individuals and private households also exist under the
assumption that inoculation is also primarily their business. Such an assumption not only pits individual against
individual and private home against private home in a bid
to get vaccinated first—like selfish, serialized teenagers
jostling for a place at the front of a bus or movie queue—
it also functions according to those dominant ideologies
that are transmitted within these oikonomic spaces. This
is why the multiple "biopolitical" analyses are incomplete.

After all, it makes perfect "biopolitical" sense to
manage populations according to the aforementioned
logistical analysis—to manage health and hygiene during a

biological emergency in a way that protects state resources. There is nothing intrinsically nefarious in such management, despite the Agambens telling us otherwise, because the actual problem is pre-existing: the capitalist, imperialist, and settlerist ideology that precedes and determines "biopolitical" (and "necropolitical") pandemic management. What Mitropoulos calls the oikos—that private sphere that among other things is also an ideological state apparatus—is indeed one space that predetermines so-called biopolitical management. "Whereas epidemics and pandemics, by definition, presume an extrinsic risk," Mitropoulos writes, "the contagion that appears from outside the body (politic), the endemic posits uncertain oikonomic arrangements as an instrinsic pathology of, simultaneously, territory and population."[15]

Hence, biopolitical management is mediated by preexisting ideology that takes root within the ideological state apparatus of the family and blossoms out from this "private" sphere into the schools and other state institutions/structures. Perhaps one of the reasons why Foucault's understanding of race/racism was so impoverished was because he located it on the level of biopolitical management rather than a pre-existing ideological affect that, having developed through colonial warfare and the plantation system, sunk itself within the dominant oikos of the capitalist-imperialist states that it also generated. As noted above, the logistical management of the pandemic—which is paradigmatically what has been called "biopolitical"—was overdetermined by pre-existing racist ideology.

Indeed, the violence of colonial conquest marked modernity and thus the rise of the tropes that would be

designated as "biopolitical." This violence is the inheritance of capitalism and has affected all of actually existing capitalism's characteristics and mechanisms, whether
we call them biopolitical, necropolitical, oikonomical, or
whatever other label is useful to describe the day-to-day
functioning of global capitalism. Again: capitalism comes
into existence "dripping from head to foot, from every
pore, with blood and dirt."[16] While a pandemic, with its
management and its tropes, is taken by some to be evidence of a foundational biopolitical logic, this logic is in
fact epiphenomenal. Born out in the capitalist oikos that
was generated by the period of mercantilism and so-called
"primitive" accumulation:

> the conceptualization and epistemological fram-
> ing first of world health and later of global health
> emerge from the immunological crisis of col-
> onial contact. The management of global and
> potentially global epidemics is not just a figure
> for competing immunities, a metaphor for the
> struggle over the robustness and survival of state
> forms; it is as central to the praxis of colonialism
> as is the extraction of raw materials, the conscrip-
> tion of labor in various forms, the annexation of
> markets, and cultural hegemony.[17]

Hence, both the biopolitical management of pandemic
and the oikonomics of contagion are secondary to the
brutal material reality of capitalism coming into being
through modern colonialism. All of the tropes and language existed ahead of time, derived from what capitalism

actually was at its "rosy dawn"—despite early bourgeois ideologues' vision of a utopian anti-aristocratic society, despite the republican dreams of the Jacobins—that is, a horrendously genocidal reality. In a word: *necrocapitalism*, the permanent characteristic of capitalism.

As a final point in this chapter, we would be remiss not to mention that the ideological conception of othered households and colonial populations as figures of contagion is, in a very important sense, capitalist projection. Centuries before "the conceptualization and epistemological framing" of the "immunological crisis of colonial contact," colonial conquest generated epidemics as biological warfare. The intentional spread of smallpox in South America that decimated the Mexica was echoed in the spread of smallpox blankets in North America by the colonial formations that would become the US and Canada. Hence, imagining that the colonized and their rebellions were akin to contagion was an actual inversion of the contagions intentionally spread by the colonizers. Today's conspiracy theory imaginary that COVID-19 was created and spread by a Chinese military facility is thus a white supremacist projection of what European colonial powers actually did from the 16th century onwards. Moreover, this colonial use of contagion has been naturalized so that there is, in Raza Kolb's terms, a "depoliticization of conflict."[18] That is, despite the fact that there is much empirical evidence that the colonizers intentionally created these epidemics as biological warfare, there is also the ideological narrative that it was non-intentional, that disease just happened to appear, and that the colonized necessarily succumbed to the forces of nature, which nobody could predict. The memory of these intentional contagions, which dominant ideology refuses to recognize as biological warfare, are thus projected onto an actual pandemic—and this projection comes from a history of projecting contagion upon the global peripheries.

With this final point in mind, it is worth noting that the analogy and metaphor of pandemic does not have to be colonialist or imperialist. Although this "disease poetics" has a long history of imperialist deployment, in *Epidemic Empire* Raza Kolb also notes how it has been requisitioned by revolutionary movements to conceptualize the ill-health generated by colonial occupation.[19] While it is indeed the case that imperialism has used the figure of contagion in a violent manner, it is also the case that modern colonialism has literally generated contagion. More importantly, in response to the actual contagions generated by capitalism and imperialism, revolutionary movements capable of setting up dual power have drawn on the "function of [their] proto-state as a giver of care" and have thus launched themselves "into the realm of believable governance, an organized authority that can replace [the oppressive] state."[20]

As this pandemic has made clear, capitalism is incapable of caring for people in a meaningful manner; thoroughly necrotic, it ultimately exposes them to disease and death.

Revolutionary movements that grasp the fact that the actual virus is capitalism, that might even employ a counter "disease poetics"—one which is more accurate about who is responsible for creating and spreading and refusing to prevent epidemic—will generate a better understanding of health and care. "In the struggle to take care of our bodies in a new, more human way," a collective led by James Boggs wrote in 1975, "we can discover a new humanity in ourselves—a humanity which will manifest itself not only in the good health of the individual but in healthier relations among all of us in the communities where we live and the places where we work."[21]

NOTES TO CHAPTER 32

1. Mitropoulos, *Contract and Contagion*, 49–75.

2. Sean Davidson, "Ontario extends stay-at-home order" (https://toronto.ctvnews.ca/ontario-extends-stay-at-home-order-restricts-interprovincial-travel-as-province-loses-battle-against-covid-19-1.5390016).

3. Mitropoulos, *Contract and Contagion*, 163–164.

4. Ibid., 164.

5. Ibid., 205.

6. Raza Kolb, *Epidemic Empire*, 6.

7. Fanon, *The Wretched of the Earth*, 41.

8. Each "wave" of higher infection rates always corresponds to the reopening of the economy. It is not as if COVID-19 is a thinking creature that decides to go away with every successive lockdown, only to come back stronger when it chooses. The fact is that the possibility of infection and its exponential growth remained

constant pre-vaccination; it blossoms when the contact between individuals is increased because it spreads through increased contact. The "waves" always correspond with social phenomena that place people in greater contact with other people. Despite claims by government officials that this is the fault of individuals and households holding large social events (and again, we should ask which individuals and households are being blamed), and despite the fact that failure to abide by the suggestions of proper health during Christmas and New Year's probably did contribute to the spread of infection, the multiple re-openings of the economy have been what have actually correlated with these "waves."

9. Mbembe, *Necropolitics*, 66.

10. Angela Sterritt, "More than 24,000 Indigenous people in 113 BC communities have received COVID-19 vaccine as Phase 2 begins" (https://www.cbc.ca/news/canada/british-columbia/24000-indigenous-people-receive-covid-19-vaccine-1.5933803).

11. See https://www.youtube.com/watch?v=TwJi-MWPWFM

12. Raza Kolb, *Epidemic Empire*, 17.

13. "Canada couple charged after taking COVID jab meant for Indigenous" (https://www.aljazeera.com/news/2021/1/26/rich-couple-took-covid-vaccine-meant-for-indigenous-charges).

14. Leyland Cecco, "Backlash grows for 'selfish millionaire' who got vaccine meant for Indigenous people"

(https://www.theguardian.com/world/2021/jan/27/rodney-baker-canada-vaccine-indigenous-first-nations-scandal).

15. Mitropoulos, *Contract and Contagion*, 132–133.

16. Marx, *Capital*, vol. 1, 712.

17. Raza Kolb, *Epidemic Empire*, 36–37.

18. Ibid., 47.

19. Ibid., 183.

20. Ibid.

21. *A New Outlook on Health*, 90.

EPILOGUE

At the end of May 2021, when the imperialist countries were proclaiming the beginning of the end of pandemic (for them at least) and a return to business as usual, a mass grave was discovered at the site of a former Indian Residential School in Kamloops — one of Canada's largest residential schools, which closed in 1978. This grave held the remains of 215 Indigenous children, some as young as three years old, victims of the Canadian colonial system.[1] Similar sites at other former residential schools would eventually be excavated. Predictably, the ruling class parties and their ideologues publicly lamented this grisly discovery. The truth, however, is that survivors of the residential school system had long claimed the existence of such graves, and the official Truth and Reconciliation Report had asked that these claims be investigated. Such claims were derided by the government, the claimants dismissed as delusional, and the architects of the residential school system were conceived as well-intentioned but misguided individuals. In this context, the public displays of sadness on the part of Justin Trudeau, the Canadian Prime Minister at the time, or Erin O'Toole, the leader of the Conservative opposition, were particularly gross. Trudeau's government had once denied funding to the Truth and Reconciliation Committee to investigate the claims of mass graves. Erin O'Toole and his party had long celebrated the architects of the residential school system, angrily denouncing the "cancel culture" of those who demanded the statues built to these individuals be removed.

All of the official political parties of the Canadian bourgeoisie were recently united in building the pipeline that dispossessed Indigenous people, and they saw no reason to apologize for, let alone reverse, the same colonial mechanisms responsible for a mass grave filled with the corpses of colonized children. (As one of us wrote elsewhere during the early stages of the pandemic, it is likely that "the Canadian settler-state will intensify resource extraction [and thus Indigenous dispossession] under the pretense of funding economic 'recovery' and 'paying back' the cost of concessions won during the pandemic.")[2] Then the performatively mournful statement of the RCMP, Canada's FBI, whose official Twitter account lamented this horror, partially acknowledged its role in this monstrosity (it was, after all, instrumental in the maintenance of the residential school system, arresting runaways as truant and returning them to these violent sites of colonial capture) but acted as if there was a great chasm between its present activities and the past. The same RCMP has not only been active in violently policing every moment of Indigenous resistance up into the present, it has also and quite recently been revealed—in an independent inquest—to have intentionally mishandled the death of Colton Boushie by siding with Boushie's settler murderer: harassing Boushie's mother, allowing the crime scene to be contaminated, destroying records, and doing everything possible to prevent any form of justice in a situation where Gerald Stanley, a white settler farmer in Manitoba, had executed Colton Boushie simply for being an Indigenous teenager.[3]

The necrotic aspect of capitalism is such that another of its mass graves can be unearthed and the system's ideologues can react with horror while failing to recognize that this is simply business as usual. This is a business it has carried out since its emergence and right into the present. A business emphasized by the deployment of violence throughout a pandemic that, though starkly illustrating how capitalist states will always place profit and imperialist power above life itself, will persist into the unevenly vaccinated new normal. While the living memory of the intergenerationally traumatized attests to the "hatred" and "spirit of sacrifice … nourished by the image of enslaved ancestors,"[4] the capitalist imaginary responds by demanding we see this as an aberration and ignore that, despite all its talk of human dignity and civilization, it is in fact engaged in murdering people "everywhere they find them, at every one of their own streets, in all the corners of the globe."[5] The liberal ideologues of this imaginary manifest every time there is a revelation of capitalism's intrinsic horror, to reassure those who are still captivated by this imaginary that these horrors are just an aberration, that they too are appalled, while continuing to pursue and justify present and future horrors.

Just weeks before this discovery in Kamloops, Israel's ongoing ethnic cleansing of Palestine erupted yet again. Following a pogrom in Jerusalem, and the Hamas response to this pogrom, Israel unleashed a wave of violence upon its open-air prison. All of this during a pandemic where Israel had been upheld as an exemplar of

vaccination—an exemplar that refused to extend vaccination protocols to its colonized population. Rather, it chose
to bomb them into submission. Such violence was not
treated as exceptional or strange: again, this was business
as usual. The very same ideologues who would express
their mournfulness about the mass grave in Kamloops
would defend identical ethnic cleansing in Palestine. But it
would not be long before settler ideologies aligned: within
a couple of weeks the mainstream news networks were
running opinion editorials disparaging the notion of using
the term genocide in regards to the mass grave, ideologues
and outraged settlers would call in to talkshows and complain that the destruction of Egerton Ryerson's statue was
an example of "racism" against white people.[6] When four
members of a Muslim family were murdered by a white
nationalist in London, Ontario, politicians and the press
would elide how the miasma of anti-Palestianian and
Islamophobic discourse feeds and prods far-right reaction.
"This isn't us" is the liberal equivalent of the conservative's
"thoughts and prayers."

In other words, necrocapitalism continues unabated.

A few concluding remarks are in order. From a revolutionary perspective, we must remember that state intervention in capitalist countries during the pandemic is not,
and does not herald, socialism. It affects distribution, but
it does not transform relations of production. This error
was made by critics such as Slavoj Žižek (as pointed out

in Chapter Two), it has been made by other "leftist" critics, and it will continue to be made by opportunists touting a socialism of half-measures. We must, as the third chapter noted, dive beneath the surface froth. As we have argued, these are interventions that have sought to shore up political hegemony in the face of crisis, which is hardly a conversion to socialism. These state interventions are more accurately described, in Torkil Lauesen's apt turn of phrase, as "pandemic Keynesianism."[7]

We must situate this pandemic Keynesianism within the parameters of the present challenges to political hegemony in its neoliberal forms. Neoliberal policy as generally understood—*policy* being our preferred term here—involves deregulation of business, the privatization of social welfare services, shifting tax burdens from rich to poor, accumulation by dispossession (see Chapter Thirty), and the greater integration of transnational capital. Drawing on the work of Ruth Wilson Gilmore (in Chapter Fourteen), we also observed that the rise of the political hegemony of law and order and the implementation of neoliberal policy in the late 1960s and 1970s were concurrent developments, whose legacy is the "prison fix," the use of carceral systems to absorb surpluses of finance capital, land, and state spending capacity while managing surplus populations of the reserve army of labor and the lumpenproletariat. We have chosen to call it "policy" because it is one *implementation* of capital accumulation, not an altogether new *form* of capitalism. Also, following Harney and Moten's deployment of the term, we have chosen this terminology to highlight the practical ramifications of fighting neoliberalism: it is not enough to reform *policy* when the revolutionary goal is to overthrow *capitalism*. And we cannot peremptorily declare the end of neoliberal policy without viewing its historical development in its totality. The antipolice uprising of 2020, then, marked a profound attack on the very pillars of contemporary settler-state hegemony in the US, but it did not complete the task.

Between its ascendency, its predominance, and its potential senescence, neoliberalism has shaped the last five decades of policy to different degrees. There are two points, anticipated throughout our discussion, where we want to challenge the conventional view of neoliberalism. The first we have already indicated: the rise of the carceral state cannot be separated from neoliberal policy, and as such it shows that state spending capacity did not merely evaporate, but was rather redirected toward carceral ends. And then, second, we reject the common notion that neoliberalism diminished the sovereignty of the nation-state and borders. Here, we follow Angela Mitropoulous:

> Against the conventional view of neoliberalism, not only did borders proliferate, but they did so largely without challenging the assumption that they are a means of protection against the ravages of capitalist exploitation rather than the arbitrage which makes exploitation possible.[8]

While neoliberal policy has facilitated the movement of transnational capital and expanded international circuits of resource extraction, commodity production, and exchange, borders have become more impenetrable than ever before for the proletarian and subaltern classes. As highlighted in Chapter Eighteen, the economies of the Global North rely on the exploitation of undocumented or temporary migrant labor, which lacks (if not de jure, then de facto) the protections of legal and permanent work, leaves workers underpaid relative to prevailing legal standards of expropriation (that is, minimum wage) and, especially in the case of the feminized labor of live-in-caregivers or domestic workers (such as nannies), vulnerable to other forms of exploitation (long hours or expectations of round-the-clock availability, sexualized and patriarchal violence, harassment, and abuse). These are concerns *before* we even address the threat COVID-19 poses to migrant workers who don't have access to vaccination regimes in the Global North, *before* we consider the plight of migrant workers and families caught in the dragnets of the Global North's deportation apparatuses (see, for example, Chapter Sixteen). We might be witnessing, against the orthodoxies of neoliberal policy, a return to social welfare supports, but this return must be gauged against the ongoing techniques of border control. There is a danger that the quarantine logic of border closures (the use of borders to quarantine between states) becomes naturalized and depoliticized, and permanently entrenched. In which case, the return to "the state of social peace" of welfare capitalism will be justified, through a post-pandemic apparatus, by imperialist chauvinism.⁹ Social welfare, in this case, deepens the divisions between those within the ambit of citizenry and the migrant proletariat upon which they depend. In other words, political reforms that mitigate features of neoliberal policy without challenging its border regimes furnish the grounds for more racism and xenophobia, which obviously and already animate far-right reactionaries, but which could easily push the contemporary parliamentarian left further towards an explicitly normalized imperial-nationalist, democratic chauvinism. Such a "left" chauvinism existed before the pandemic, of course, and has arguably been the implicit undercurrent of social democracy within the imperialist metropoles, but now it might become normative and explicit.[10]

We must never forget that capitalism will murder, torture, incarcerate, and devour anything and everyone. Throughout its entire history—from its settler-colonial and plantation initiation to its contemporary imperialist promulgation—this system has been so insatiable in its brutal appetite for profit that it has continuously sacrificed entire populations to sate its hunger. Throughout this vile history, its ideologues have worked overtime to convince everyone, especially those living in its heartlands, that it is the best and only system for all of humanity. For some absurd reason it was able to maintain this lie, even when it subjected entire populations within these heartlands to domestic warfare and incarceration. Indeed, capitalism used the lie that it was promoting the best way of life—a life where everyone could flourish as long as they were good citizens—to justify its violence. And yet, in the midst of pandemic, it proved itself incapable of even providing the minimal standards of such a promise:

ignoring the advice of medical experts, the leaders of the most powerful capitalist states were happy to expose their populations to disease and death if and when they could reopen the economy. Some pretended to care, proclaimed we were all in this together, and sadly declared the necessity of reopening the economy while refusing to subject corporations to health regulations because of a "way of life" that needed to be protected over life in and of itself. Some encouraged pandemic denial while secretly dumping stocks and reinvesting in other stocks so as to profit from disease. Others callously argued that the virus should be allowed to tear through society, killing off the "weak" and making the "strong" stronger, as if this eugenicist fantasy was the best path to herd immunity.

For a brief moment, despite the unevenness of health measures, the notion that "we are all in this together" *did* flicker across the consciousness of the general population. And many even began to realize that this "we" was compromised, as it always has been, due to the disparate treatment and care different populations received.

For at the same time, the grossest continuation of imperialism persisted: the War on Terror was not interrupted; vaccine apartheid was brutally enforced, despite the shock of variants in India; the pro-imperialist government of Colombia violently suppressed workers demanding economic and health security; Bolsonaro's fascist government in Brazil hunted down the League of Poor Peasants; Israel unleashed another wave of genocidal violence upon the Palestinians, with every imperialist nation and their ideologues cheering it on; transnational capital plunged deeper into natural habitats for resource extraction ... we could go on and on. The point is that capitalism is essentially incapable of responding to human needs because, by its very nature, it is parasitic upon these needs. The pandemic ought to have revealed this nature to global capitalism's most house-broken citizens, but many were domesticated further as marginalized and recalcitrant populations were brutalized. By the time the vaccines were being produced and disseminated, it was clear that there was no universal "we" that mattered. Loyal citizens in imperialist countries opposed the very idea of donating vaccines to India and other nations hit hard by the pandemic. Regardless of the medical evidence indicating that it would be better for everyone if the pandemic were treated globally since, by definition, it was a global problem, those living within the imperial strongholds demanded that they be treated first and, in some cases, exclusively. Even within these strongholds, vaccination centers designed to treat the most at-risk populations—again, because it would be good for everyone and not because the capitalist governments had suddenly developed a conscience—were descended upon by "vultures" from wealthy neighborhoods demanding that they get their second shot before these beleaguered communities even received their first.[11]

Within the imperialist metropoles where we live, work, and organize, rage against this death world did manifest, especially during the spring and summer of 2020. Although the pandemic made it extremely difficult for long-term organizing, and in fact stalled innumerable organizing ventures beyond mutual aid, protests did break out. Protests against racist police violence, protests against brutal incarceration and the spread of the virus in these spaces, protests against structural violence, protests against imperialism and settler-colonialism, and even protests against liberal institutions that sanctify this overall violence (e.g., StrikeMoMA).

We need to examine, though, how much of this protest energy was sapped by the electoral process that brought Biden into power (both in the US and in those imperialist states that still look to the US as the leader of their camp), so that the energy of radical planning—of the possibility of organizing against capitalism with all the hatred of the general antagonism—was sapped by official state policy. We also need to examine how the reactionary wing of capitalism has been organizing during the pandemic: there have been fascist insurgencies (the march on the Michigan Capitol in April 2020, the march on the United States Capitol in January 2021), there have been anti-vaxxer demonstrations, and there is also the current weaponization of a discourse around "cancel culture" and "critical race theory," designed to denigrate all attempts to challenge white supremacy and settler-capitalism. Such an overall examination immediately reveals a weakness in our movements, here in the imperialist metropoles, which is largely due to their location and history: disunification and impoverishment from decades of anti-communism and a labor aristocracy built upon the living corpse of settler-capitalism—there is no unified movement, historical memory has been obliterated, and the search for multiple panaceas abounds.

The lack of a unified and comprehensive revolutionary movement capable of responding to this violence and the ideological justification of this violence means the lack of a historical counter-memory where "the oppressed class" can become "the depository of historical knowledge."[12] Without such a movement and the depository it can become, every visceral reminder of capitalism's necrotic nature will be either ephemeral or fragmented, and "every image of the past that is not recognized by the present as one of its own concerns threatens to disappear irretrievably."[13] When such a movement is absent, as it is in the imperialist metropoles, multiple theoretical diagnostics that are largely epiphenomenal will circulate. Indeed, biopolitical diagnostics circulated at the beginning of the pandemic because, on the level of metaphor, they seemed quite apt: there was a medical state of emergency and so a theoretical constellation embedded in medicalized topoi appeared appropriate; its theorists were absorbed by the very metaphor they sought to critique—society as a body, the biopolitical theorist as the doctor performing a proper diagnosis. But when the execution of George Floyd yet again exposed the deeper material facts of life—specifically Black life, specifically the heritage of settler-capitalism—within the imperialist belly of the beast, the primacy of biopolitical analyses was replaced by the primacy of abolitionist analyses. For the pandemic itself was epiphenomenal, and if we are to remember the politics it revealed then we need much more than these cosmetic diagnostics.

This project's analysis is not enough, which is why it has not pretended to be a replacement for these fragmentary diagnostics but, instead, a reminder of the living theory of struggle. A reminder of what capitalism has always been; a recovery of counter-hegemonic memory in the face of wholesale denial and the appeal to chic academic theorizations. An appeal to a communist alternative and an attempt to place our theoretical interventions in the service of organizational possibilities pursuing this alternative. A refusal to obliterate the memory of past interventions, based on the hatred of capitalism and imperialism, which cannot be silenced. An injunction that this is not about playing theory as a game or hobby; it's about understanding the ongoing civil war in the hope of victory. Such an understanding demands comprehensive revolutionary movements, and it is our hope that, here in the imperialist metropoles, such movements will be built.

We concluded this project around the time that the vaccine rollouts were in full force. We recognize that the implications of our thought can only be realized through future revolutionary organization. It has often been noted that our collective senses of time, temporality, and memory have been undermined during the pandemic. This radical plague journal, though we hadn't exactly planned it this way, incrementally charts the course of global capitalist management during a pandemic and demarcates its limits, restoring a sense of chronology to the overwhelming miasma. By integrating these moments of a quickly receding past into a coherent whole, we hope that it is able to serve as a partial record for future struggles. We hope that such an offering will contribute to revolution, to the transgression of the necrotic limits of capitalist business as usual.

NOTES TO EPILOGUE

1. Jana G. Pruden, "Discovery of children's remains at Kamloops residential school 'stark example of violence' inflicted upon Indigenous children" (https://www.theglobeandmail.com/canada/article-bodies-found-at-kamloops-residential-school-site-in-bc/).

2. Devin Zane Shaw, *The Politics of the Blockade*, 2.

3. Stephanie Taylor, "Colton Boushie's family to respond to watchdog report that found discrimination" (https://toronto.citynews.ca/2021/03/22/colten-boushies-family-to-respond-to-watchdog-report-that-found-discrimination/).

4. Benjamin, *Illuminations*, 260.

5. Fanon, *The Wretched of the Earth*, 311.

6. Egerton Ryerson was one of the architects of the residential school system in Canada, a key institution in the ongoing genocide of Indigenous peoples. Toronto's Ryerson University was named after this individual and, in light of the revelations of mass graves, his statue on the university campus was defaced and then demolished. The statue's head later turned up at 1492 Landback Lane, where members of the Six Nations of the Grand River are resisting further Indigenous dispossession.

7. Lauesen, *The Principal Contradiction*, 119.

8. Mitropoulos, *Pandemonium*, 4.

9. Moufawad-Paul, *Austerity Apparatus*, 46.

10. See, for example, Sam Gindin's "Building a Mass Socialist Party" published by *Jacobin* (https://www. jacobinmag.com/2016/12/socialist-party-bernie-sanders-labor-capitalism/) where the author argues that leftists need to drop demands for open borders in order to connect with the white working class. Far from being an anachronistic thinker or an outlier, Gindin was heavily involved, along with the late Leo Panitch, in attempting to organize a social democratic movement in Canada based on these principles.

11. Jon Woodward, "Stop 'vaccine vultures' from swooping in on COVID-19 clinics looking for second dose" (https://www.iheartradio.ca/funny/funny-1060/local-news/stop-vaccine-vultures-from-swooping-in-on-covid-19-clinics-looking-for-second-dose-volunteers-1.15321544).

12. Benjamin, *Illuminations*, 260.

13. Ibid., 255.

WORKS CITED

Althusser, Louis. *Lenin and Philosophy and Other Essays.* New York: Monthly Review, 1971.

A New Outlook on Health. Paris: Foreign Languages Press, 2020.

Baptist, Edward E. *The Half Has Never Been Told: Slavery and the Making of American Capitalism.* New York: Basic Books, 2016.

Beauvoir, Simone de. *The Second Sex.* New York: Vintage Books, 1989.

Benatar, David, *Better Never to Have Been: The Harm of Coming into Existence.* Oxford: Oxford University Press, 2006.

Benjamin, Walter. *Illuminations.* New York: Schocken Books, 1988.

Brown, Wendy. *Undoing the Demos: Neoliberalism's Stealth Revolution.* New York: Zone Books, 2015.

Burley, Shane. *Why We Fight: Essays on Fascism, Resistance, and Surviving the Apocalypse* (Chico: AK Press, 2021).

Butler, Judith. *Undoing Gender.* New York: Routledge, 2009.

Byrd, Jodi A. *The Transit of Empire: Indigenous Critiques of Colonialism.* Minneapolis: University of Minnesota Press, 2011.

Chávez, K. "Pushing Boundaries: Queer Intercultural Communication," *Journal of International and Intercultural Communication*, 6, no. 2 (2013): 83–95.

Comay, Rebecca and Frank Ruda. *The Dash*. Cambridge: MIT Press, 2018.

Cooper, Melinda. *Family Values: Between Neoliberalism and the New Social Conservatism*. New York: Zone Books, 2019.

Davis, Angela Y. *Abolition Democracy: Beyond Empire, Prisons, and Torture*. New York: Seven Stories, 2005.

Du Bois, W.E.B. *Black Reconstruction in America*. Oxford: Oxford University Press, 2007.

Dunbar-Ortiz, Roxanne. *An Indigenous Peoples' History of the United States*. Boston: Beacon Press, 2014.

Dunn, Timothy J. *The Militarization of the U.S.-Mexico Border: Low Intensity Conflict Doctrine Comes Home*. Austin: Center for Mexican American Studies, University of Texas at Austin, 1996.

Edelman, Lee. *No Future: Queer Theory and the Death Drive*. Durham: Duke University Press, 2004.

Fanon, Frantz. *The Wretched of the Earth*. New York: Grove Press, 1963.

Fanon, Frantz. *Towards the African Revolution*. New York: Grove Press, 1964.

Featherstone, L. *False Choices: The Faux Feminism of Hillary Rodham Clinton* [Kindle Cloud Reader version]. London/New York: Verso, 2016.

Federici, Silvia. *Caliban and the Witch: Women, the Body and Primitive Accumulation*. New York: Autonomedia, 2004.

Fisher, Mark. *Capitalist Realism*. Winchester: Zero Books, 2009.

Foucault, Michel. *The History of Sexuality*, vol. 1. New York: Vintage Books, 1990.

Ghandy, Anuradha. *Philosophical Trends in the Feminist Movement*. Utrecht: Foreign Languages Press, 2018.

Ghandy, Anuradha. *Scripting the Change: Selected Writings of Anuradha Ghandy*. Edited by Anand Teltumbde and Shoma Sen. Delhi: Daanish Books, 2011.

Gilmore, Ruth Wilson. *Golden Gulag: Prisons, Surplus, Crisis, and Opposition in Globalizing California*. Berkeley: University of California Press, 2007.

Harney, Stefano and Fred Moten. *The Undercommons*. Brooklyn: Minor Compositions, 2013.

Hartman, Saidiya V. *Scenes of Subjection: Terror, Slavery, and Self-making in Nineteenth-Century America*. Oxford: Oxford University Press, 1997.

Harvey, David. *Marx, Capital, and the Madness of Economic Reason*. Oxford: Oxford University Press, 2019.

Horne, Gerald. *Apocalypse of Settler Colonialism: The Roots of Slavery, White Supremacy, and Capitalism in Seventeenth-Century North America and the Caribbean*. New York: Monthly Review Press, 2018.

Irigaray, Luce. *Speculum of the Other Woman*. Ithaca: Cornell University Press, 1985.

Kling, Jennifer and Megan Mitchell. "Bottles and Bricks: Rethinking the Prohibition against Violent Political Protest." *Radical Philosophy Review*. 22, no. 2 (2019): 209–237.

Kruks, Sonia. "Beauvoir and the Marxism Question." In *A Companion to Simone de Beauvoir*. Edited by Laura Hengehold and Nancy Bauer, 236–248. New Jersey: John Wiley & Sons, 2017.

Laclau, Ernesto. *On Populist Reason*. London: Verso, 2018.

Lauesen, Torkil. *The Principal Contradiction*. Montreal: Kersplebedeb, 2020.

Lem, Stanislaw. *Memoirs Found In A Bathtub*. San Diego: Harcourt Brace Jovanovich, 1973.

Lenin. V.I. *Collected Works*. Moscow: Progress Publishers, 1960–1970. Abbreviated as *CW*.

Lenin, V.I. *Imperialism the Highest Stage of Capitalism*. New York: International Publishers, 1939.

Lenin, V.I. "Lessons of the Crisis." In *Selected Works*, vol. 2. Moscow: Foreign Languages Publishing House, 1960, 87–90.

Lenin, V.I. *The State and Revolution*. Paris: Foreign Languages Press, 2020.

Liebknecht, Karl. *Militarism*. Toronto: William Briggs, 1917.

Ligotti, Thomas. *The Conspiracy Against The Human Race*. New York: Penguin Books, 2018.

London, Jack. *The Iron Heel*. Edinburgh: Rebel Inc. Classics, 1999.

Malm, Andreas. *Corona, Climate, Chronic Emergency: War Communism in the Twenty-First Century*. London: Verso, 2020.

Malm, Andreas. *Fossil Capital: The Rise of Steam Power and the Roots of Global Warming*. London: Verso, 2016.

Manne, Kate. *Down Girl: The Logic of Misogyny* [Kindle Cloud Reader version]. New York: Oxford University Press, 2018.

Mao Zedong. *On Contradiction (Study Companion by Redspark Collective)*. Paris: Foreign Languages Press, 2019.

Margalit, Avishai. *On Compromise and Rotten Compromises*. Princeton: Princeton University Press, 2013.

Márquez, Gabriel Garcia. *One Hundred Years of Solitude*. New York: Avon Books, 1970.

Marx, Karl. *Capital*, vol. 1. London: Lawrence & Wishart, 2003.

Marx, Karl. *The Civil War in France*. In *The First International and After*. Political Writings, vol. 3, edited by David Fernbach, 187–236. Middlesex: Penguin, 1974.

Marx, "Critical Notes on 'The King of Prussia and Social Reform." In *Writings of the Young Marx on Philosophy and Society*, edited by Loyd D. Easton and Kurt H. Guddat, 338–358. Garden City: Double Day and Co., 1967.

Marx, Karl. *Grundrisse*. London: Penguin Books, 1993.

Marx, Karl and Friedrich Engels. *Collected Works*. New York: International Publishers, 1975–2004. Abbreviated as *MECW*.

Mbembe, Achille. *Necropolitics*. Durham: Duke University Press, 2019.

Meillassoux, Quentin. *After Finitude: An Essay on the Necessity of Contingency*. London: Bloomsbury, 2008.

Mitropoulos, Angela. *Contract and Contagion: from Biopolitics to Oikonomia*. Williamsburg: Minor Compositions, 2012.

Mitropoulos, Angela. *Pandemonium: Proliferating Borders of Capital and the Pandemic Swerve*. London: Pluto Press, 2020.

Moufawad-Paul, J. *Austerity Apparatus*. Montreal: Kersplebedeb, 2016.

Moufawad-Paul. J. *Critique of Maoist Reason*. Paris: Foreign Languages Press, 2020.

Nair, Yasmin. "Marry the State, Jail the People: Hillary Clinton and the Rise of Carceral Feminism" in *False Choices: The Faux Feminism of Hillary Rodham Clinton*, edited by Liza Featherstone, 101–110. [Kindle Cloud Reader version]. London/New York: Verso, 2016.

Neocleous, Mark. "War as Peace, Peace as Pacification," *Radical Philosophy* 159 (January/February 2010): 8–17.

Puar, Jasbir. *The Right To Maim*. Durham: Duke University Press, 2017.

Raza Kolb, Anjuli Fatima. *Epidemic Empire: Colonialism, Contagion, and Terror 1817–2020*. Chicago: University of Chicago Press, 2021.

Red Spark Collective. "Introduction" in *A New Outlook on Public Health* (James Boggs). Paris: Foreign Languages Press, 2020.

Rockhill, Gabriel. *Counter-History of the Present.* Durham: Duke University Press, 2017.

Rodríguez, Dylan. *White Reconstruction: Domestic Warfare and the Logics of Genocide.* New York: Fordham University Press, 2021.

Sakai, J. *Settlers: The Mythology of the White Proletariat.* Morningstar Press, 1989.

Sartre, Jean-Paul. "Elections: A Trap for Fools." In *Life/Situations.* Trans. Paul Auster and Lydia Davis. New York, Pantheon Books, 1977, 198–210.

Sharpe, Christina. *In The Wake: On Blackness and Being.* Durham: Duke University Press, 2016.

Shaw, Devin Zane. *Philosophy of Antifascism: Punching Nazis and Fighting White Supremacy.* London: Rowman and Littlefield International, 2020.

Shaw, Devin Zane. *The Politics of the Blockade.* Montreal: Kersplebedeb, 2020.

Steven, Mark. *Splatter Capital.* London: Repeater Books, 2017.

Valencia, Sayak. *Gore Capitalism.* South Pasadena: semiotext(e), 2018.

Veracini, Lorenzo. 2010. *Settler Colonialism: A Theoretical Overview.* New York: Palgrave Macmillan, 2010.

Wright, Gavin. *The Political Economy of the Cotton South: Households, Markets, and Wealth in the Nineteenth Century.* New York: W.W. Norton & Co. Inc., 1978.

Žižek, Slavoj. *Pandemic! Covid-19 Shakes the World.* O/R Books, 2020.

Žižek, Slavoj. *Revolution at the Gates: Selected Writings of Lenin from 1917.* London: Verso, 2002.

ACKNOWLEDGEMENTS

ALL WRITING IS A COLLECTIVE PROCESS AND THUS there are always many people to thank, more so when the writer is itself a collective. Everyone involved has comrades, family, and friends to thank—doubtless the list would be long—hence we will limit ourselves to a general set of acknowledgements directly pertaining to the project. Thanks to Mree Henry for providing the idea of the name of the project's "writer" just before the prologue was originally posted. Thanks to Breht at Revolutionary Left Radio for his willingness to interview one of us in the early days of the project, thus promoting it widely. Thanks to Jasbir, Anjuli, and Dylan for taking the time to read a finalized draft and provide gracious blurbs. Finally, thanks to both Karl and Casey at Kersplebedeb: Karl, for his willingness to publish the completed version and doing all the hard work of layout and final edits; Casey for the promotional work.

ABOUT THE AUTHORS

Mateo Andante is an LA-based Maoist philosopher, logician, revolutionary activist, and ex-academic. He is the founder of the Bourgeois Philosophy Project, a blog, study-group series, and book project investigating the connection between academic philosophy and imperialism. His work has been featured on the Revolutionary Voices Podcast and on Philosophy Tube.

Johannah May Black is an educator, activist, and ex-academic. She is passionate about proletarian feminism and cats.

Alyson Escalante is a co-host on the Red Menace podcast. Her work focuses on presenting accessible introductions to revolutionary theory that emphasizing the relevance of revolutionary classics to our current moment of crisis.

D.W. Fairlane is a jazz musician and former food services worker, moonlighting as a platformist intellectual.

J. Moufawad-Paul lives in Toronto and works as casualized contract faculty at York University where he received his PhD in philosophy. He is the author of several books, including *Continuity and Rupture: Philosophy in the Maoist Terrain* (2016), *Crtitique of Maoist Reason* (2020), and, published by Kersplebedeb, *Austerity Apparatus* (2017) and *The Communist Necessity* (2014).

Devin Zane Shaw is the author of numerous books, including *Philosophy of Antifascism: Punching Nazis and Fighting White Supremacy* (2020) and *Egalitarian Moments: From Descartes to Rancière* (2016). He is co-editor of the book series Living Existentialism, published by Rowman and Littlefield. He teaches philosophy at a community college in so-called British Columbia.

ALL POWER TO THE PEOPLE
ALBERT "NUH" WASHINGTON • 1894820215 • 111 PP. • $10.00

A collection of writings by the late Albert Nuh Washington, a former member of the Black Panther Party and Black Liberation Army. One of the "New York 3," Washington was imprisoned in 1971 as a result of the U.S. government's war against the Black Liberation Movement; he died in prison almost thirty years later, on April 28, 2000, from cancer. (2002)

AMAZON NATION OR ARYAN NATION:
WHITE WOMEN AND THE COMING OF BLACK GENOCIDE
BOTTOMFISH BLUES • 9781894946551 • 160 PP. • $12.95

The massive New Afrikan uprisings of the 1960s were answered by the white ruling class with the destruction of New Afrikan communities coast to coast, the decimation of the New Afrikan working class, the rise of the prison state and an explosion of violence between oppressed people. Taken on their own, in isolation, these blights may seem to be just more "social issues" for NGOs to get grants for, but taken together and in the context of amerikkkan history, they constitute genocide. (2014)

A SOLDIER'S STORY: REVOLUTIONARY WRITINGS
BY A NEW AFRIKAN ANARCHIST, 3RD EDITION
KUWASI BALAGOON • 9781629633770 • 272 PP. • $19.95

Kuwasi Balagoon was a participant in the Black Liberation struggle from the 1960s until his death in prison in 1986. A member of the Black Panther Party and defendant in the infamous Panther 21 case, Balagoon went underground with the Black Liberation Army (BLA). Captured and convicted of various crimes against the State, he spent much of the 1970s in prison, escaping twice. After each escape, he went underground and resumed BLA activity. This is the most complete collection of his writings, poetry, and court statements ever collected, along with recollections from those who knew him, and who have been inspired by him since his passing. (2019)

BASIC POLITICS OF MOVEMENT SECURITY
J. SAKAI & MANDY HISCOCKS • 9781894946520 • 68 PP. • $7.00

Introducing the issues of movement security, and the political ramifications thereof. A transcript of a talk Sakai gave at the Montreal Anarchist Bookfair in 2013, and an interview with Hiscocks about how her political scene and groups she worked with were infiltrated by undercover agents a year before the 2010 G20 summit in Toronto. (2014)

BEGINNER'S KATA:
UNCENSORED STRAY THOUGHTS ON REVOLUTIONARY ORGANIZATION
J. SAKAI • NO ISBN • 15 PP. • $3.00

Plain talk with J. Sakai about what we do and don't know about revolutionary organization, and, indeed, about being revolutionaries. (2018)

KERSPLEBEDEB, CP 63560, CCCP VAN HORNE, MONTREAL, QUEBEC, CANADA H3W 3H8

CATEGORIES OF REVOLUTIONARY MILITARY POLICY
T. DERBENT • 9781894946438 • 52 PP. • $5.00

An educational survey of the concepts of military doctrine, strategy, tactics, operational art, bases of support, guerilla zones, liberated territories, and more. A study of what has been tried in the past, where different strategies worked, and where they failed, all from a perspective concerned with making revolution. (2013)

CHICAN@ POWER AND THE STRUGGLE FOR AZTLAN
CIPACTLI & EHECATL • 9781894946742 • 320 PP. • $22.95

From the Amerikan invasion and theft of Mexican lands, to present-day migrants risking their lives to cross the U.$. border, the Chican@ nation has developed in a cauldron of national oppression and liberation struggles. This book by a MIM(Prisons) Study Group presents the history of the Chican@ movement, exploring the colonialism and semi-colonialism that frames the Chican@ national identity. It also sheds new light on the modern repression and temptation that threaten liberation struggles by simultaneously pushing for submission and assimilation into Amerika. (2015)

THE COMMUNIST NECESSITY, 2ND EDITION
J. MOUFAWAD-PAUL • PREFACE BY DAO-YUAN CHOU • 9781989701003
168 PP. • $13.00

A polemical interrogation of the practice of "social movementism" that has enjoyed a normative status at the centers of capitalism. Aware of his past affinity with social movementism, and with some apprehension of the problem of communist orthodoxy, the author argues that the recognition of communism's necessity "requires a new return to the revolutionary communist theories and experiences won from history." (2020)

CONFRONTING FASCISM: DISCUSSION DOCUMENTS FOR A MILITANT MOVEMENT, 2ND EDITION
XTN, D. HAMERQUIST, J.SAKAI, M. SALOTTE • 9781894946872 • 219 PP. • $14.95

Essays grappling with the class appeal of fascism, its continuities and breaks with the "regular" far right and also even with the Left. First published in 2002, written from the perspective of revolutionaries active in the struggle against the far right. (2017)

THE DANGEROUS CLASS AND REVOLUTIONARY THEORY: THOUGHTS ON THE MAKING OF THE LUMPEN/PROLETARIAT
J. SAKAI • 9781894946902 • 308 PP. • $24.95

This book starts with the paper of that name, on the birth of the modern lumpen/ proletariat in the 18th and 19th centuries and the storm cloud of revolutionary theory that has always surrounded them. Going back and piecing together both the actual social reality and the analyses primarily of Marx but also Bakunin and Engels, the paper shows how Marx's class theory wasn't something static. His views learned in quick jumps, and then all but reversed themselves in several significant aspects. While at first dismissing them in the Communist Manifesto

KERSPLEBEDEB, CP 63560, CCCP VAN HORNE, MONTREAL, QUEBEC, CANADA H3W 3H8

as "that passively rotting mass" at the obscure lower depths, Marx soon realized that the lumpen could be players at the very center of events in revolutionary civil war. Even at the center in the startling rise of new regimes. This is followed by the detailed paper "Mao Z's Revolutionary Laboratory and the Role of the Lumpen/Proletariat." As Sakai points out, the left's euro-centrism here prevented it from realizing the obvious: that the basic theory from European radicalism about the lumpen/proletariat was first fully tested not there or here but in the Chinese Revolution of 1921–1949. Under severely clashing political lines in the left, the class analysis finally used by Mao Z was shaken out of the shipping crate from Europe and then modified to map the organizing of millions over a prolonged generational revolutionary war. One could hardly wish for a larger test tube, and the many lessons to be learned from this mass political experience are finally put on the table. (2017)

DARING TO STRUGGLE, FAILING TO WIN:
THE RED ARMY FACTION'S 1977 CAMPAIGN OF DESPERATION
ANDRÉ MONCOURT & J. SMITH • 9781604860283 • 43 PP. • $4.00
Emerging from the West German New Left in the early 1970s, the Red Army Faction was to become the most well-known urban guerilla group in Europe, remaining active into the 1990s. This pamphlet looks at the RAF's activities in the seventies, and how their struggle to free their prisoners culminated in a campaign of assassinations and kidnappings in 1977. (2008)

DEFYING THE TOMB: SELECTED PRISON WRITINGS AND ART OF
KEVIN "RASHID" JOHNSON FEATURING EXCHANGES WITH AN OUTLAW
KEVIN "RASHID" JOHNSON • 9781894946391 • 386 PP. • $20.00
In a series of smuggled prison letters and early essays, follow the author's odyssey from lumpen drug dealer to prisoner, to revolutionary New Afrikan, a teacher and mentor, one of a new generation rising of prison intellectuals. (2010)

DIVIDED WORLD DIVIDED CLASS: GLOBAL POLITICAL ECONOMY AND
THE STRATIFICATION OF LABOUR UNDER CAPITALISM, 2ND ED.
ZAK COPE • 9781894946681 • 460 PP. • $24.95
The history of the "labour aristocracy" in the capitalist world system, from its roots in colonialism to its birth and eventual maturation into a full-fledged middle class in the age of imperialism. Pervasive national, racial, and cultural chauvinism in the core capitalist countries is not primarily attributable to "false class consciousness" or ignorance as much left and liberal thinking assumes. Rather, these and related forms of bigotry are concentrated expressions of the major social strata of the core capitalist nations' shared economic interest in the exploitation and repression of dependent nations. (2012)

EUROCENTRISM AND THE COMMUNIST MOVEMENT

ROBERT BIEL • 9781894946711 • 215 PP. • $17.95

A work of intellectual history, exploring the relationship between Eurocentrism, alienation, and racism, while tracing the different ideas about imperialism, colonialism, "progress," and non-European peoples as they were grappled with by revolutionaries in both the colonized and colonizing nations. Teasing out racist errors and anti-racist insights within this history, Biel reveals a century-long struggle to assert the centrality of the most exploited within the struggle against capitalism. The roles of key figures in the Marxist-Leninist canon—Marx, Engels, Lenin, Stalin, Mao—are explored, as are those of others whose work may be less familiar to some readers, such as Sultan Galiev, Lamine Senghor, Lin Biao, R. P. Dutt, Samir Amin, and others. (2015)

EXODUS AND RECONSTRUCTION:
WORKING-CLASS WOMEN AT THE HEART OF GLOBALIZATION

BROMMA • 9781894946421 • 37 PP. • $3.00

The position of women at the heart of a transformed global proletariat: "Family-based rural patriarchy was so deeply imbedded within capitalism for so long that abandoning it was nearly unthinkable. A change of such magnitude would require the development of much more advanced global transportation and commodity markets and a tremendous reorganization of labor. It would require a major overhaul of political systems everywhere. It would be a sea-change in capitalism. That sea-change is what's happening now." (2013)

FALSE NATIONALSM FALSE INTERNATIONALISM:
CLASS CONTRADICTIONS IN THE ARMED STRUGGLE

E. TANI AND KAÉ SERA • 9781989701089 • 327 PP. • $26.95

A critical history of revisionism, opportunism, and parasitical relationships between white and Black revolutionary organizations in the United States. Chapters address important aspects of the Russian and Chinese revolutions; different forms of solidarity with the antifascist resistance in Spain and Ethiopia; the racist settlerist machinations of the CPUSA; relationships between revolutionaries in the New Left, including the Weather Underground and the Black Panther Party; and, finally, the tragic experiences of the Revolutionary Armed Task Force. This book first appeared in 1985 as an attempt to evaluate the rise in radical armed activity in the U.S. during the 1960s and 1970s from an activist perspective. (2021)

FULL BODY SCAN: IMPERIALISM TODAY

GABRIEL KUHN & BROMMA • 9781894946957 • 36 PP. • $4.00

Gabriel Kuhn's "Oppressor and Oppressed Nations: Sketching a Taxonomy of Imperialism," with a response from Bromma, debating the nature of nations, nation-states, and countries, and the distribution of privilege and potential in the world today. (2018)

KERSPLEBEDEB, CP 63560, CCCP VAN HORNE, MONTREAL, QUEBEC, CANADA H3W 3H8

THE GLOBAL PERSPECTIVE:
REFLECTIONS ON IMPERIALISM AND RESISTANCE
TORKIL LAUESEN • 9781894946933 • 544 PP. • $24.95

Bridging the gap between Third Worldist theory and the question of "What Is To Be Done?" in a First World context, The Global Perspective is an important contribution towards developing an effective political practice based on the realities of the global situation, avoiding the pitfalls of sugarcoating the situation with the First World populations, or of falling into pessimistic quietism. As Lauesen says, "It is a book written by an activist, for activists. Global capitalism is heading into a deep structural crisis in the coming decades, so the objective conditions for radical change will be present, for better or for worse. The outcome will depend on us, the subjective forces." (2018)

THE GREEN NAZI: AN INVESTIGATION INTO FASCIST ECOLOGY
J. SAKAI • 0968950396 • 34 PP. • $3.00

A critical look at the relationship between social and natural purity, the green movement and the far right, settlerism and genocide. The text jumps off from a review of Blood and Soil, a book by academic Anna Bramwell, disputing her flattering portrayal of Third Reich Imperial Peasant Leader Walther Darre. (2002)

THE HISTORICAL FAILURE OF ANARCHISM:
IMPLICATIONS FOR THE FUTURE OF THE REVOLUTIONARY PROJECT
CHRISTOPHER DAY • 9781894946452 • 26 PP. • $4.00

An exposition of the failure of anarchism to successfully carry out or defend revolution in the 20th century, raising questions for the future. (2009)

INSURGENT SUPREMACISTS:
THE U.S. FAR RIGHT'S CHALLENGE TO STATE AND EMPIRE
MATTHEW LYONS • 9781629635118 • 384 PP. • $24.95

A major study of movements that strive to overthrow the U.S. government, that often claim to be anti-imperialist and sometimes even anti-capitalist yet also consciously promote inequality, hierarchy, and domination, generally along explicitly racist, sexist, and homophobic lines. Revolutionaries of the far right: insurgent supremacists. Intervening directly in debates within left and anti-fascist movements, Lyons examines both the widespread use and abuse of the term "fascism" and the relationship between federal security forces and the paramilitary right. His final chapter offers a preliminary analysis of the Trump Administration's relationship with far-right politics and the organized far right's shifting responses to it. (2018)

IS CHINA AN IMPERIALIST COUNTRY?
N.B. TURNER ET AL. • 9781894946759 • 173 PP. • $17.00

Whether or not China is now a capitalist-imperialist country is an issue on which there is some considerable disagreement, even within the revolutionary left. This book brings together theoretical, definitional and logical considerations, as well as the extensive empirical evidence that is now available, to demonstrate that China has indeed definitely become a capitalist-imperialist country. (2015)

KERSPLEBEDEB, CP 63560, CCCP VAN HORNE, MONTREAL, QUEBEC, CANADA H3W 3H8

JAILBREAK OUT OF HISTORY:
THE RE-BIOGRAPHY OF HARRIET TUBMAN, 2ND EDITION
BUTCH LEE • 9781894946704 • 169 PP. • $14.95

Anticolonial struggles of New Afrikan/Black women were central to the unfolding of 19th-century amerika, both during and "after" slavery. "The Re-Biography of Harriet Tubman" recounts the life and politics of Harriet Tubman, who waged and eventually led the war against the capitalist slave system. "The Evil of Female Loaferism" details New Afrikan women's attempts to withdraw from and evade capitalist colonialism, an unofficial but massive labor strike which threw the capitalists North and South into a panic. The ruling class response consisted of the "Black Codes," Jim Crow, re-enslavement through prison labor, mass violence, and ... the establishment of a neocolonial Black patriarchy, whose task was to make New Afrikan women subordinate to New Afrikan men just as New Afrika was supposed to be subordinate to white amerika. (2015)

KARL MARX AND FRIEDRICH ENGELS:
ON COLONIES, INDUSTRIAL MONOPOLY AND THE WORKING CLASS
MOVEMENT
INTRODUCTION BY ZAK COPE & TORKIL LAUESEN
9781894946797 • 160 PP. • $10.00

Selections from Marx and Engels, showing the evolution of their ideas on the nascent labor aristocracy and the complicating factors of colonialism and chauvinism, with a focus on the British Empire of their time. In their introduction, Cope and Lauesen show how Marx and Engels' initial belief that capitalism would extend seamlessly around the globe in the same form was proven wrong by events, as instead worldwide imperialism spread capitalism as a polarizing process, not only between the bourgeoisie and the working class, but also as a division between an imperialist center and an exploited periphery. (2016)

LEARNING FROM AN UNIMPORTANT MINORITY
J. SAKAI • 9781894946605 • 118 PP. • $10.00

Race is all around us, as one of the main structures of capitalist society. Yet, how we talk about it and even how we think about it is tightly policed. Everything about race is artificially distorted as a white/Black paradigm. Instead, we need to understand the imposed racial reality from many different angles of radical vision. In this talk given at the 2014 Montreal Anarchist Bookfair, J. Sakai shares experiences from his own life as a revolutionary in the united states, exploring what it means to belong to an "unimportant minority." (2015)

LOOKING AT THE U.S. WHITE WORKING CLASS HISTORICALLY
DAVID GILBERT • 9781894946919 • 97 PP. • $10.00

On the one hand, "white working class" includes a class designation that should imply, along with all other workers of the world, a fundamental role in the overthrow of capitalism. On the other hand, there is the identification of being part of a ("white") oppressor nation. Political prisoner David Gilbert seeks to understand the origins of this contradiction, its historical development, as well as possibilities to weaken and ultimately transform the situation. (2017)

KERSPLEBEDEB, CP 63560, CCCP VAN HORNE, MONTREAL, QUEBEC, CANADA H3W 3H8

LUMPEN: THE AUTOBIOGRAPHY OF ED MEAD

ED MEAD • 9781894946780 • 360 PP. • $20.00

When a thirteen-year-old Ed Mead ends up in the Utah State Industrial School, a prison for boys, it is the first step in a story of oppression and revolt that will ultimately lead to the foundation of the George Jackson Brigade, a Seattle-based urban guerrilla group, and to Mead's re-incarceration as a fully engaged revolutionary, well-placed and prepared to take on both his captors and the predators amongst his fellow prisoners. This is his story, and there is truly nothing like it. (2015)

MEDITATIONS ON FRANTZ FANON'S WRETCHED OF THE EARTH: NEW AFRIKAN REVOLUTIONARY WRITINGS

JAMES YAKI SAYLES • 9781894946322 • 399 PP. • $20.00

One of those who eagerly picked up Fanon in the 60s, who carried out armed expropriations and violence against white settlers, Sayles reveals how behind the image of Fanon as race thinker there is an underlying reality of antiracist communist thought. From the book: "This exercise is about more than our desire to read and understand Wretched (as if it were about some abstract world, and not our own); it's about more than our need to understand (the failures of) the anti-colonial struggles on the African continent. This exercise is also about us, and about some of the things that We need to understand and to change in ourselves and our world." (2010)

THE MILITARY STRATEGY OF WOMEN AND CHILDREN

BUTCH LEE • 0973143231 • 116 PP. • $12.00

Lays out the need for an autonomous and independent women's revolutionary movement, a revolutionary women's culture that involves not only separating oneself from patriarchal imperialism, but also in confronting, opposing, and waging war against it by all means necessary. (2003)

MY ENEMY'S ENEMY: ESSAYS ON GLOBALIZATION, FASCISM AND THE STRUGGLE AGAINST CAPITALISM

ANTI-FASCIST FORUM • 0973143231 • 116 PP. • $10.00

Articles by anti-fascist researchers and political activists from Europe and North America, examining racist and pro-capitalist tendencies within the movement against globalization. (2003)

NIGHT-VISION: ILLUMINATING WAR AND CLASS ON THE NEO-COLONIAL TERRAIN, 2ND EDITION

BUTCH LEE AND RED ROVER • 9781894946889 • 264 PP. • $17.00

A foundational analysis of post-modern capitalism, the decline of u.s. hegemony, and the need for a revolutionary movement of the oppressed to overthrow it all. From Night-Vision: "The transformation to a neo-colonial world has only begun, but it promises to be as drastic, as disorienting a change as was the original european colonial conquest of the human race. Capitalism is again ripping apart & restructuring the world, and nothing will be the same. Not race, not nation, not gender, and certainly not whatever culture you used to have. Now you have

KERSPLEBEDEB, CP 63560, CCCP VAN HORNE, MONTREAL, QUEBEC, CANADA H3W 3H8

outcast groups as diverse as the Aryan Nation and the Queer Nation and the Hip Hop Nation publicly rejecting the right of the u.s. government to rule them. All the building blocks of human culture—race, gender, nation, and especially class—are being transformed under great pressure to embody the spirit of this neo-colonial age." (2009)

1978: A NEW STAGE IN THE CLASS WAR?
SELECTED DOCUMENTS ON THE SPRING CAMPAIGN OF THE RED BRIGADES
ED. JOSHUA DEPAOLIS • 9781894946995 • 218 PP. • $19.95

For the first time in English, a selection of the key documents on the strategic logic and conjunctural analysis behind the 1978 offensive of the Red Brigades, the kidnapping and execution of Italy's President Aldo Moro, which brought the BR's strategy of "attack on the heart of the state" to a climax and induced a national political crisis. The book includes: the February 1978 "Resolution of the Strategic Leadership," the nine communiqués issued by the group during Moro's captivity, the editorial "Achtung Banditi" from the June 1978 issue of the Marxist-Leninist journal Corrispondenza Internazionale, and the March 1979 document "The Spring Campaign: Capture, Trial and Execution of the President of the DC, Aldo Moro." (2019)

NOTES TOWARD AN UNDERSTANDING OF CAPITALIST CRISIS & THEORY
J. SAKAI • 1894946316 • 25 PP. • $2.00

An examination of Marx's theories of capitalist crisis, in light of the current economic crisis, asking some tentative questions about what it all might mean in terms of strategy, and things to come. (2009)

ON THE VANGUARD ONCE AGAIN...
KEVIN "RASHID" JOHNSON • 9781894946445 • 23 PP. • $4.00

A response to anarchist criticisms of Marxism-Leninism, defending the concepts of the vanguard party and democratic centralism, from the perspective of the New Afrikan Black Panther Party Prison Chapter. (2013)

OUR COMMITMENT IS TO OUR COMMUNITIES:
MASS INCARCERATION, POLITICAL PRISONERS,
AND BUILDING A MOVEMENT FOR COMMUNITY-BASED JUSTICE
DAVID GILBERT • 9781894946650 • 34 PP. • $5.00

In this pamphlet, interviewed by Bob Feldman, political prisoner David Gilbert discusses the ongoing catastrophe that is mass incarceration, connecting it to the continued imprisonment of political prisoners and the challenges that face our movements today. (2014)

KERSPLEBEDEB, CP 63560, CCCP VAN HORNE, MONTREAL, QUEBEC, CANADA H3W 3H8

**PANTHER VISION: ESSENTIAL PARTY WRITINGS AND ART OF
KEVIN "RASHID" JOHNSON, MINISTER OF DEFENSE,
NEW AFRIKAN BLACK PANTHER PARTY-PRISON CHAPTER**

KEVIN "RASHID" JOHNSON • 9781894946766 • 496 PP. • $24.95

Subjects addressed include the differences between anarchism and Marxism-Leninism, the legacy of the Black Panther Party, the timeliness of Huey P. Newton's concept of revolutionary intercommunalism, the science of dialectical and historical materialism, the practice of democratic centralism, as well as current events ranging from u.s. imperialist designs in Africa to national oppression of New Afrikans within u.s. borders. And much more. (2015)

THE PRINCIPAL CONTRADICTION

TORKIL LAUESEN • 9781989701034 • 157 pp. • $14.95

An introduction the philosophy of dialectical materialism as a tool for changing the world. Dialectical materialism allows us to understand the dynamics of world history, the concept of contradiction building a bridge between theory and practice, with the principal contradiction telling us where to start. Identifying the principal contradiction is indispensable for developing a global perspective on capitalism. This methodology is not just a valuable tool with which to analyze complex relationships: it also tells us how to intervene. (2020)

PRISON ROUND TRIP

KLAUS VIEHMANN • PREFACE BY BILL DUNNE • 9781604860825 • 25 PP. • $3.00

First published in German in 2003 as "Einmal Knast und zurück." The essay's author, Klaus Viehmann, had been released from prison ten years earlier, after completing a 15-year sentence for his involvement in urban guerilla activities in Germany in the 1970s. Here he reflects on how to keep one's sanity and political integrity within the hostile and oppressive prison environment; "survival strategies" are its central theme. (2009)

**THE RED ARMY FACTION, A DOCUMENTARY HISTORY
VOLUME 1: PROJECTILES FOR THE PEOPLE**

ANDRE MONCOURT & J. SMITH EDS. • 9781604860290 • 736 PP. • $34.95

For the first time ever in English, this volume presents all of the manifestos and communiqués issued by the RAF between 1970 and 1977. Providing the background information that readers will require to understand the context in which these events occurred, separate thematic sections deal with the 1976 murder of Ulrike Meinhof in prison, the 1977 Stammheim murders, the extensive use of psychological operations and false-flag attacks to discredit the guerilla, the state's use of sensory deprivation torture and isolation wings, and the prisoners' resistance to this, through which they inspired their own supporters and others on the left to take the plunge into revolutionary action. With introductions by Russell Maroon Shoatz and Bill Dunne. (2009)

KERSPLEBEDEB, CP 63560, CCCP VAN HORNE, MONTREAL, QUEBEC, CANADA H3W 3H8

**THE RED ARMY FACTION, A DOCUMENTARY HISTORY
VOLUME 2: DANCING WITH IMPERIALISM**
ANDRE MONCOURT & J. SMITH EDS. • 9781604860306 • 480 PP. • $26.95

This work includes the details of the Red Army Faction's operations, and its communiqués and texts, from 1978 up until its 1984 offensive. This was a period of regrouping and reorientation for the RAF, with its previous focus on freeing its prisoners replaced by an anti-NATO orientation. Subjects examined include: the possibilities and perils of an armed underground organization relating to the broader movement, the contrasting experiences of the Revolutionary Cells and 2nd of June Movement, the emergence of the Autonomen, accusations of the RAF's relationship to the East German Stasi, and the abortive attempt by West Germany's liberal intelligentsia to defuse the armed struggle during Gerhard Baum's tenure as Minister of the Interior. With an introduction by Ward Churchill. (2013)

REMEMBERING THE ARMED STRUGGLE: LIFE WITH THE RED ARMY FACTION
MARGRIT SCHILLER • 9781629638737 • 239 PP. • $19.95

Former Red Army Faction political prisoner Margrit Schiller recounts the process through which she joined her generation's revolt in the 1960s, going from work with drug users to joining the antipsychiatry political organization the Socialist Patients' Collective and then the RAF. She tells of how she met and worked alongside the group's founding members, Ulrike Meinhof, Andreas Baader, Jan-Carl Raspe, Irmgard Möller, and Holger Meins; how she learned the details of the May Offensive and other actions while in her prison cell; about the struggles to defend human dignity in the most degraded of environments, and the relationships she forged with other women in prison. (2021)

**RIDING THE WAVE: SWEDEN'S INTEGRATION INTO THE
IMPERIALIST WORLD SYSTEM**
TORKIL LAUESEN • 9781989701126 • 249 PP. • $20.00

Examining how Sweden rides on the wave of colonialism and imperialism, how it was integrated as a core-state in global capitalism, and how the Swedish "people's home" has been paid for by value transfer from global production chains stretching throughout the Global South. This is also the story of Social Democracy and how the struggle in the Second International between two lines—one reformist, nationalist, and pro-imperialist, the other internationalist and anti-imperialist—remains relevant to this day.. (2021)

**SETTLERS: THE MYTHOLOGY OF THE WHITE PROLETARIAT
FROM MAYFLOWER TO MODERN**
J. SAKAI • 9781629630373 • 456 PP. • $20.00

America's white citizenry have never supported themselves but have always resorted to exploitation and theft, culminating in acts of genocide to maintain their culture and way of life. As recounted in painful detail by Sakai, the United States has been built on the theft of Indigenous lands and of Afrikan labor, on the robbery of the northern third of Mexico, the colonization of Puerto Rico, and the expropriation of the Asian working class, with each of these crimes being accompanied by violence. This new edition includes "Cash & Genocide: The True Story of Japanese-American Reparations" and an interview with author J. Sakai by Ernesto Aguilar. (2014)

STAND UP STRUGGLE FORWARD: NEW AFRIKAN REVOLUTIONARY WRITINGS ON NATION, CLASS AND PATRIARCHY

SANYIKA SHAKUR • 9781894946469 • 208 PP. • $13.95

Firmly rooted in the New Afrikan Communist tradition, laying bare the deeper connections between racism, sexism, and homophobia and how these mental diseases relate to the ongoing capitalist (neo-)colonial catastrophe we remain trapped within. (2013)

STRIKE ONE TO EDUCATE ONE HUNDRED:
THE RISE OF THE RED BRIGADES 1960S-1970S

CHRIS ARONSON BECK, REGGIE EMILIANA, LEE MORRIS,
AND OLLIE PATTERSON • 9781894946988 • 296 PP. • $24.95

Today there are many books and countless papers and articles about the Red Brigades' history, but most are from a police and state point of view. Strike One is a unique and practically useful work, because it tells the other side, of innovative anti-capitalism. It details how the spectre of urban guerrilla warfare grew at last out of the industrial centers of modern Italy, showing how this was a political project of a young working class layer that was fed up with reformism's lies. The authors, who were varied supporters who chose to remain anonymous due to Italy and NATO's draconian "anti-terrorist" laws, tell much of this story in the militants' own words: in translations of key political documents, news reports, and communiqués. Indispensable. (2019)

THE STRUGGLE WITHIN: PRISONS, POLITICAL PRISONERS,
AND MASS MOVEMENTS IN THE UNITED STATES

DAN BERGER • 9781604869552 • 128 PP. • $12.95

An accessible, wide-ranging historical primer about how mass imprisonment has been a tool of repression deployed against diverse left-wing social movements over the last fifty years. Berger examines some of the most dynamic social movements across half a century: Black liberation, Puerto Rican independence, Native American sovereignty, Chicano radicalism, white antiracist and working-class mobilizations, pacifist and antinuclear campaigns, and earth liberation and animal rights. (2014)

TURNING MONEY INTO REBELLION: THE UNLIKELY STORY OF DENMARK'S REVOLUTIONARY BANK ROBBERS

ED. GABRIEL KUHN • 9781604863161 • 224 PP. • $20.00

One of the most captivating chapters from the European anti-imperialist milieu of the 1970s and '80s; the Blekingegade Group had emerged from a communist organization whose analysis of the metropolitan labor aristocracy led them to develop an illegal Third Worldist practice, sending millions of dollars acquired in spectacular heists to Third World liberation movements. (2014)

KERSPLEBEDEB, CP 63560, CCCP VAN HORNE, MONTREAL, QUEBEC, CANADA H3W 3H8

V.I. LENIN ON IMPERIALISM & OPPORTUNISM

V.I. LENIN • INTRODUCTION BY TORKIL LAUESEN

ISBN 9781894946940 • 191 PAGES • $13.00

The connection that Lenin posits between imperialism and opportunism—that is, the sacrifice of long-term socialist goals for short-term or sectional gains—is more pronounced than ever. Imperialism may, in many respects, have changed its economic mechanisms and its political form, but its content is fundamentally the same, namely, a transfer of value from the Global South to the Global North. (2019)

WHEN RACE BURNS CLASS: SETTLERS REVISITED

J. SAKAI • 9781894820264 • 32 PP. • $4.00

An interview with author J. Sakai about his groundbreaking work Settlers: Mythology of the White Proletariat, accompanied by Kuwasi Balagoon's essay "The Continuing Appeal of Imperialism." Sakai discusses how he came to write Settlers, the relationship of settlerism to racism and between race and class, the prospects for organizing within the white working class, and the rise of the far right. (2011)

THE WORKER ELITE: NOTES ON THE "LABOR ARISTOCRACY"

BROMMA • 9781894946575 • 88 PP. • $10.00

Revolutionaries often say that the working class holds the key to overthrowing capitalism. But "working class" is a very broad category—so broad that it can be used to justify a whole range of political agendas. Bromma breaks it all down, criticizing opportunists who minimize the role of privilege within the working class, while also challenging simplistic Third Worldist analyses. (2014)

KERSPLEBEDEB, CP 63560, CCCP VAN HORNE, MONTREAL, QUEBEC, CANADA H3W 3H8

KER SPL EBE DEB

Since 1998 Kersplebedeb has been an important source of radical literature and agit prop materials.

The project has a non-exclusive focus on anti-patriarchal and anti-imperialist politics, framed within an anticapitalist perspective. A special priority is given to writings regarding armed struggle in the metropole, the continuing struggles of political prisoners and prisoners of war, and the political economy of imperialism.

The Kersplebedeb website presents historical and contemporary writings by revolutionary thinkers from the anarchist and communist traditions.

Kersplebedeb can be contacted at:

Kersplebedeb
CP 63560
CCCP Van Horne
Montreal, Quebec
Canada
H3W 3H8

email: info@kersplebedeb.com
web: www.kersplebedeb.com
www.leftwingbooks.net

Kersplebedeb

Printed in the USA
CPSIA information can be obtained
at www.ICGtesting.com
LVHW021048091123
763499LV00025B/290